Madness in the Multitude
Human Security and World Disorder

Fen Osler Hampson

with

Jean Daudelin, John B. Hay,

Holly Reid, and Todd Martin

D0112258

OXFORD
UNIVERSITY PRESS

OXFORD
UNIVERSITY PRESS

70 Wynford Drive, Don Mills, Ontario M3C 1J9
www.oup/ca

Oxford University Press is a department of the University of Oxford.
It furthers the University's objective of excellence in research, scholarship,
and education by publishing worldwide in

Oxford New York

Athens Auckland Bangkok Bogotá Buenos Aires Cape Town
Chennai Dar es Salaam Delhi Florence Hong Kong Istanbul Karachi
Kolkata Kuala Lumpur Madrid Melbourne Mexico City Mumbai Nairobi
Paris São Paulo Shanghai Singapore Taipei Tokyo Toronto Warsaw

with associated companies in Berlin Ibadan

Oxford is a trade mark of Oxford University Press
in the UK and in certain other countries

Published in Canada
by Oxford University Press

Copyright © Oxford University Press Canada 2002

National Library of Canada Cataloguing in Publication Data

Hampson, Fen Osler
Madness in the multitude: human security and world disorder

Includes bibliographical references and index.
ISBN 0–19-541524-8

1. Security, International. I. Daudelin, Jean, 1960- II. Title

JZ5588.H34 2001   327.1'72   C2001-901439-2

1 2 3 4 - 05 04 03 02

Cover Design: Brett J. Miller
Cover Image: CP Photo (Andre Forget)

This book is printed on permanent (acid-free) paper ∞ .
Printed in Canada

CONTENTS

Contributors   iv

Preface   v

Chapter 1   Introduction: Madness in the Multitude   1

Chapter 2   The Many Meanings of Human Security   14

Chapter 3   Human Security as a Global Public Good   38

Chapter 4   Promoting Human Rights and the Rule of Law:
            The International Criminal Court   62

Chapter 5   Promoting the Safety of Peoples:
            Banning Anti-Personnel Landmines   80

Chapter 6   Promoting the Safety of Peoples:
            Controlling Small Arms   98

Chapter 7   Hard Power and Human Security:
            Eastern Zaire and Kosovo   125

Chapter 8   Human Security and the
            Global Development Agenda   150

Chapter 9   Portfolio Diversification and Human Security   170

            Bibliography   186

            Index   210

Contributors

Jean Daudelin is a senior associate with the North-South Institute, Ottawa, Canada.

John B. Hay is a consultant in international affairs and a former journalist.

Todd Martin is a recent graduate of The Norman Paterson School of International Affairs, Carleton University, and was an intern with the Arias Foundation in Costa Rica.

Holly Reid is a recent graduate of the joint MA-LLB program of The Norman Paterson School of International Affairs, Carleton University, and the Faculty of Law, University of Ottawa. She now practises law in Toronto.

Preface

The 1994 *Human Development Report* of the United Nations Development Program popularized the concept of human security, as did such international initiatives as the 1997 Convention on Anti-Personnel Mines and the international campaign that preceded it. Canadian Foreign Minister Lloyd Axworthy championed the concept, as has UN Secretary-General Kofi Annan. International leaders, such as Britain's Foreign Minister Robin Cook and Czech President Václav Havel, also invoked the concept in defence of military intervention in support of humanitarian objectives. Although 'human security' has entered the lexicon of international politics, the concept nonetheless remains highly controversial. Not only is the definition of 'human security' contested, but many do not accept its suppositions about international order and how states should conduct their foreign policy.

This book is an attempt to explain the historical origins or antecedents of the contemporary concept of human security and to explore its implications for how we think about international politics and international order. It argues that many of the assumptions that underlie the concept are not new but grounded in traditional liberal democratic theory and precepts. However, the human security paradigm does offer a new way of looking at international relations, not only in its understanding of what constitute the main threats to international peace and security, but also of how best to secure and maintain international order. In exploring this paradigm at a conceptual level and through a series of case studies, this book explores the strengths and weaknesses of human security as an organizing principle for the conduct of international relations.

The idea for this book developed a number of years ago when Foreign Minister Lloyd Axworthy began to promote some of his ideas about human security through his statements and speeches. A spirited debate—one of the liveliest in recent years—about the direction in which Canadian diplomacy was moving soon followed. Even so, there was no real attempt to situate human security concepts within a broader historical or theoretical context or to probe their deeper implications for international diplomacy.

When I began to write this book, I was fortunate to be able to enlist three of my former students and Jean Daudelin, a colleague at the North–South Institute with whom I had previously written about human security, in adding a number of case studies of specific human security initiatives. It is both a pleasure and privilege to include them as co-authors in this collaborative venture. Holly Reid wrote about the International Criminal Court, Todd Martin about small arms, John Hay about Zaire and Kosovo, and Jean Daudelin about international development assistance.

I would like to thank Laura Macleod, Len Husband, and Phyllis Wilson at Oxford University Press for their unwavering support for this project from its inception through to its completion and Richard Tallman for his careful editing of the text. Special thanks also go to Brenda Sutherland, who cheerfully typed the manuscript under a tight deadline. In addition, I wish to thank the two anonymous reviewers of the initial project proposal for their extraordinarily useful and constructive advice on how to frame the problem and develop the contents. The two anonymous reviewers of the completed manuscript also provided many useful suggestions and detailed commentary, which have helped to strengthen the book. Pamela Aall, Karen Abousaid, Chester Crocker, Vivian Cummins, Philip Hampson, Stanley Hoffman, David Long, Edward Luck, Maureen Molot, Joseph Nye, Dane Rowlands, and Janice Gross Stein also deserve special thanks for reading portions or all of the manuscript and for providing much constructive criticism.

Fen Osler Hampson
Chelsea, Québec

Chapter 1

Introduction:
Madness in the Multitude

Though the effect of folly, in them that are possessed of an opinion of being inspired, be not visible alwayes in one man, by any very extravagant action, that proceedeth from such Passion; yet when many of them conspire together, the Rage of the whole multitude is visible enough. For what argument of Madnesse can there be greater, than to clamour, strike, and throw stones at our best friends? Yet this is somewhat lesse than such a multitude will do. For they will clamour, fight against, and destroy those, by whom all their life-time before, they have been protected, and secured from injury. And if this be Madnesse in the multitude, it is the same in every particular man. For as in the middest of the sea, though a man perceive no sound of that part of the water next to him; yet he is well assured, that part contributes as much, to the Roaring of the Sea, as any other part, of the same quantity; so also, though wee perceive no great uniquietnesse, in one, or two men; yet we may be well assured, that their singular Passions, are parts of the Seditious Roaring of a troubled Nation.

Thomas Hobbes, Leviathan, Part I, Chapter 8

We continue to relive to the present day the horror and shock that Thomas Hobbes experienced in trying to explain why Englishmen would turn against each other to fight a civil war, as they did in the seventeenth century when Oliver Cromwell's 'Roundheads' rose in revolt against King Charles I. From the killing fields of Cambodia, to the blood-soaked volcanic slopes of Rwanda, to the scorched towns and villages of Bosnia, Kosovo, Sierra Leone, and East Timor, neighbours have pillaged each other's homes and murdered each other with a degree of vengeance and ferocity that is barely imaginable. Such 'madnesse in the multitude', as Thomas Hobbes called it, is as much a feature of the present day as it was of previous eras. But civil violence aided and abetted by modern technology is seen on a truly unprecedented scale.

Do individuals living in other societies have any sort of moral obligation to stop this madness when civil conflict and violence erupt in another country? When Thomas Hobbes wrote his seminal treatise, *Leviathan*, on the subject of how societies could prevent civil wars from occurring, it was generally assumed that there was no such obligation. The problem of civic order was one that citizens of a country had to deal with on their own terms. Hobbes's answer to the problem was to construct a political order in which citizens would relinquish their own personal 'sovereignty' to the state 'Leviathan'—in exchange for a steadfast guarantee that their own physical security and right to go about their peaceful business would not be violated. However, the bargain was always a conditional one. Individuals reserved the right to take back their sovereignty from Leviathan if their physical security was threatened or could not be guaranteed. Hence, the individual's 'right to revolution' was retained, and with it the risk of civil war.

Other liberal theorists, such as John Locke, were of the view that civic order could only be secured under democratic systems of governance and accountability where individual rights also would be guaranteed (Locke, 1952). The only way to avoid social and political anarchy was through the franchise, elections, and legal 'due process'. But again, like Hobbes, these theorists construed the problem of how to secure political order and stability when the safety and security of individuals were concerned largely in domestic terms. Much of the debate about political order among liberal democratic theorists centred on the appropriateness of different systems of governance and the advantages of different kinds of institutional arrangements that could serve as a check on the power of the executive branch of government.

This is not to say that political theorists did not worry about the problem of how best to maintain international order. But the problems of international order were seen primarily in terms of how best to manage *interstate* relations because state sovereignty was largely taken for granted. Thus, concepts such as the balance of power or collective security were based on co-ordinating and organizing principles directed at state actors. Immanuel Kant was the first democratic theorist to argue that there is a link between the domestic constitution (or order) of states and international order (Kant, 1992). Kant believed that the most peaceful kind of international arrangement would be based on a confederation of democratic states because democracies are less inclined to go to war than authoritarian or despotic regimes. But Kant himself sidestepped the question of whether democracies have an obligation to export or promote democracy outside their borders or to defend human rights and basic political liberties when they are challenged elsewhere. Democracies could demonstrate the advantages of their system of government by their example, but that was about as far as Kant was prepared to go in making the case for 'intervention' into the internal affairs of another state.

Some liberal theorists, such as John Stuart Mill, believed that there was a case to be made for intervention in instances where national self-determination was denied to a people. A liberal regime, therefore, had to govern with the consent of the people; where national minorities were oppressed and their right to self-deter-mination denied, genuine democracy could not exist (Mill, 1939: 949–1041; also see Thompson, 1976). But as Stanley Hoffmann (1998: 72) notes:

> The international side of liberalism offered a vision but not really a program, and the issue of intervention for liberalism turned out to be deeply divisive. Kant's scheme was resolutely noninterventionist—among liberal states. Mill saw a fundamental difference between interventions for self-government (which he rejected) and inter-ventions for self-determination (which he endorsed). The gamut ranged from what we today would call isolationism on the one side to moral crusades on other.

In the late nineteenth and early twentieth centuries the idea that citizens living in a democracy have a moral obligation to help secure for others the rights and privileges that they enjoy gained currency in the foreign policies of democratic states. In the traditional Westphalian system, the sovereignty of states was considered to be a prohibition against foreign intervention, although, as we see in the next chapter, sovereignty was always conditional and not absolute. Historically, though, an attempt by one country to intervene in the internal affairs of another state when human rights were threatened was considered to be in violation of the basic precepts of international law. President Woodrow Wilson challenged this principle with his famous 14 points, which recognized the right of national self-determination of the peoples of Central and Eastern Europe following World War I and the collapse of the Austro-Hungarian Empire. Further refinements and qualifications to the principle of sovereignty came with the Nuremberg trials of Nazi war criminals following World War II and the UN Declaration of Human Rights. But although the Cold War saw frequent interventions by the two superpowers into the internal affairs of other states, these interventions were typically undertaken in the defence of democracy or communism and not of individual human or communal rights per se.

With the end of the Cold War a growing number of democratic states have come to share the view that state sovereignty is conditional and that when egregious violations of human rights occur within the borders of a sovereign state, outsiders have an obligation to intervene to defend those rights. Genocide and 'ethnic cleansing', therefore, cannot be tolerated by the international community, nor can other systematic violations of individual rights involving torture, inhuman punishment and detention, and the denial of basic liberties (see Gilbert, 1999). As Václav Havel, President of the Czech Republic, argued before the Canadian Parliament, the war in Kosovo was not being fought on the basis of national or NATO alliance interests. Rather:

> If it is possible to say about the war that it is ethical, or that it is fought for ethical reasons, it is true of this war. Kosovo has no oil fields, whose output might perhaps attract somebody's interest. No member country of the Alliance has any territorial claims there, and Milosevic is not threatening either the territorial integrity or any other integrity of any NATO member. Nevertheless, the Alliance is fighting. It is fighting in the name of human interest for the fate of other human beings. It is fighting because decent people cannot sit back and watch systematic, state directed massacres of other people. Decent people simply cannot tolerate this and cannot fail to come to the rescue if a rescue action is within their power. (Havel, 1999)

However, the normative principle that threats and violations of basic individual liberties cannot be allowed to go unchallenged and that the international community has an obligation to intervene to prevent them from occurring is one that is not fully accepted and that has been applied extremely unevenly. In Rwanda, the international community sat on the sidelines as the Hutus embarked on a brutal campaign to exterminate the local Tutsi population. In Bosnia the story repeated itself until the slaughter at Srebrenica caught the media's attention and NATO air strikes and US mediation pressure forced the parties to the bargaining table and averted further tragedy. In Kosovo, NATO air strikes eventually halted Milosevic's campaign of ethnic cleansing, but not before hundreds of thousands of refugees were forced to flee to neighbouring Albania and Macedonia. Some even argued that air power worsened the problem by accelerating the flight of Kosovars from their homes. In East Timor, UN pressure forced the Indonesian government to hold a referendum on Timorese independence. In spite of dire predictions that in the absence of an international military presence the Indonesian military would go on a killing spree to seek revenge, the international community waited until the slaughter had begun before deploying an international peacekeeping force under UN authority.

Definition of Human Security

Notwithstanding these varying international responses to genocide and human rights atrocities, an important normative change in international relations is evidenced in a considerable and growing body of international law and international conventions and treaties on human rights; in various international campaigns to ban anti-personnel landmines, light arms, and nuclear weapons; in moves to establish international criminal tribunals, and an International Criminal Court that would prosecute those accused of war crimes and other massive human rights violations; in initiatives to protect civilians and especially vulnerable groups, like women and children, in armed conflict; and in efforts to pay greater attention to social and economic reconstruction efforts once the fighting has stopped.

Underlying these various initiatives is a shared desire to advance and promote human rights and to ensure that individuals, especially those in the greatest danger of having their physical security and well-being trampled, are placed out of harm's way. Although the individual's physical security and protection of basic liberties lie at the core of this evolving conception of human security, it is also recognized that these are minimal conditions for human welfare and survival. If individuals are to prosper and develop, their economic needs and interests also will have to be met and therefore attention also has to be paid to the broader social and economic environment—domestic and international—and how it impacts on the welfare and livelihood of the individual.

In a fundamental sense, the concept of 'security' can be defined as the absence of threat to these core human values, including the most basic human value, the physical safety of the individual. Because large numbers of human values go beyond the safety of the individual, this security concept can lead to an enormous number of types of security. It is useful, therefore, to aggregate some of these values under the term 'human security', recognizing that the problems or threats to human security are diverse and that the instruments to relieve them likely will be quite varied.

Three different conceptions of human security inform current debates and thinking about the subject. The first is what might be termed the 'natural rights/rule of law' conception of human security, which is anchored in the fundamental liberal assumption that individuals have a basic right to 'life, liberty, and the pursuit of happiness' and that the international community has an obligation to protect and promote these rights. A second view of human security as humanitarian is one that, for example, informs international efforts to deepen and strengthen international law, particularly regarding genocide and war crimes, and to abolish weapons of warfare that are especially harmful to civilians and non-combatants. The humanitarian view also lies at the heart of interventions directed at improving the basic living conditions of refugees and those who have been uprooted from their homes and communities as a result of war. On those rare occasions when military force has been used ostensibly to avert genocide and ethnic cleansing, it usually has been justified also on rather narrow humanitarian grounds, such as the need to restore basic human rights and dignity.

These two views of human security, which relate to basic human rights and their privation, stand in sharp contrast to a view that suggests human security should be broadly constructed to include economic, environmental, social, and other forms of privation that adversely affect the overall livelihood and well-being of individuals. A strong social justice component resides in the broader conception of human security, as well as a wider consideration of the array of threats in the international environment that may adversely affect the survival and health of individuals (or have the potential to do so). According to this third view, which is arguably the most controversial of the three conceptions of human security, the state of the global economy, the forces of 'globalization', and the health of the environment, including the world's atmosphere and oceans, all are legitimate subjects of concern in terms of how they impact on the 'security' of the individual.

In reality, many human security initiatives, such as the current international campaign to ban light weapons, tend to fall somewhere between the narrower and the broader definitions of human security. But there is a lively debate among scholars and practitioners as to what legitimately should be the scope of efforts to promote and advance human security at the international level and whether we should define human security in more restrictive or broader terms. This debate is discussed at greater length in Chapter 2.

Human Security and International Order

These various perspectives share a common understanding that human security is critical to international security and that international order cannot rest solely on the sovereignty and viability of states—it depends, as well, on individuals and their own sense of security. This clearly is a departure from traditional liberal internationalism, which sees international order as resting on institutional arrangements that, in varying degrees, help secure the viability and integrity of the liberal democratic state by attenuating threats in the state's external environment. To the extent that individual interests are served, they are of secondary importance to those of the liberal democratic state itself. In the human security 'paradigm' this order of priority is reversed: individuals and communities of individuals rather than governments or 'states' are the primary point of reference. Using the individual as the key point of reference, the human security paradigm also assumes that the safety of the individual is the key to global security; by implication, when the safety of individuals is threatened so, too, in a fundamental sense, is international security.

Although the logic of this argument is spelled out in greater depth in subsequent chapters, some observers will undoubtedly dismiss or at the very least question the proposition that when individuals are threatened so, too, is international security. Some might argue, for example, that if the murder rate in New York City rises, individuals are less safe there but that has very little effect on international security. This is obviously true. But New York is a very different place from Rwanda or East Timor, where there is nothing to prevent violence from occurring and where systematic and gross abuses of human rights have assumed massive and even genocidal proportions, and where the forced displacement of persons has reverberated across national borders. Clearly, there is a matter of scale in the extent to which individual lives are threatened and fundamental human rights violated from one society to another. But it is also readily apparent that in some societies there are well-entrenched instruments and institutions to curb violence and to arrest, detain, and prosecute the perpetrators of violence, whereas in others there are not. In those latter societies, furthermore, the risk that violence and bloodshed will infect neighbours or drag other parties into the conflict is a matter of deep concern not just to a country's immediate neighbours but to the wider international community.

If the safety and security of individuals is one of the keys to international security, accordingly, the key criterion for assessing policies is their impact on people as opposed to, for example, the national interest or various conceptions of national security. Under the human security paradigm, global challenges have to be assessed in terms of how they affect the safety of peoples and not just states. Proponents of the enlarged or maximalist conception of human security also argue that these threats arise not merely from military sources, but also from non-military ones, such as worsening environmental conditions and economic inequalities that can, in some instances, exacerbate conflict processes.

The Role of the State and Civil Society

Although human security takes precedent over 'national' security in the human security paradigm, the state is still viewed as one of the principal instruments for securing the rights and physical security of the individual. Due process of law, for example, depends on a judicial system that is both accountable and transparent. When individuals are physically threatened, the state is supposed to come to their defence because it enjoys a monopoly on violence and the instruments of coercion. A liberal democratic state in which due process and political accountability are guaranteed is ultimately the best defence against threats to the life, liberty, and property of the individual.

The other key to human security, however, is a healthy and vibrant civil society. Much of the recent work by political scientists and students of democracy underscores the proposition that a healthy and vibrant democracy depends, in turn, on a vibrant and politically active civil society through which citizens are able to participate in the political process outside of elections. Democracy is not simply about casting votes in a formal election, it is also about participating in the day-to-day decision-making process of government at all levels from the local to the national. In a fundamental sense, democracy depends on what Gabriel Almond and Sidney Verba (1963) almost 40 years ago called a 'civic culture'. As Robert Putnam (1993) argues, among the key indicators of a healthy civic culture is a society in which individuals have affiliations and memberships in a wide variety of voluntary organizations ranging from the community bowling league to the local branch of a political party. These organizations not only help to inform and engage the populace, but they serve as key instruments of interest articulation and aggregation, conveying and transmitting the needs and interests of constituents to their political leaders. In societies where such organizations are lacking or where membership is limited or weak, democracy tends to suffer because citizens are not engaged in the decisions of government and political accountability is weakened.

In the human security paradigm, civil society has a critical role to play not just in strengthening and promoting democracy within the nation-state, but also in the various tasks associated with social and economic reconstruction in war-torn societies. Because war-torn societies often lack viable state institutions and administrative structures, many of the traditional functions of the state, including the provision of basic services, have to be carried out by other actors such as non-governmental organizations or various community groups and associations. These actors and institutions effectively serve as substitutes or surrogates for national or local governmental authorities that normally carry out these various functions. Their sources of funding and financial support also typically come from outside the state, i.e., from external donors and international relief agencies. As international efforts shift from emergency assistance and short-term humanitarian relief to the tasks of long-term social and economic reconstruction, NGOs and civil society actors tend to play a central role not only in providing services and functions vital to social and economic development, but also in projecting human security values and ensuring that a civic culture takes root.

Why the Focus on Human Security Now?

We argue here that although the concept of human security is not new, a number of factors help to explain the growing salience of human security concerns in international politics.

First, an international regime of legal norms, principles, and precedents that aims to bolster and strengthen the protection of human rights across a wide spectrum ranging from the most basic rights to wider social, economic, and political rights has developed and been strengthened by recent initiatives such as the successful conclusion of negotiations to establish an International Criminal Court. This emerging human rights regime has developed at two levels: the global and the regional. Although the regime is stronger in some corners of the globe than in others, there is some evidence of a growing convergence in the basic norms, principles, and values that inform different human rights regimes not only at the global level but also across different regions.

Second, it is unquestionably true that the end of the Cold War has seen the widespread growth of democracy as the preferred system of government in the world. Not only has the absolute number of democracies in the world increased markedly with the collapse of the Soviet Union and its empire in Eastern Europe, but the democratic model has been transplanted to societies where the international community has been actively involved in implementing negotiated peace agreements, which ended violent conflict such as that in El Salvador, Guatemala, Namibia, Mozambique, and Cambodia. Although the overall success of these efforts at broad-scale social and political engineering is a matter of continuing debate, there can be no question that these efforts to promote democracy have been paralleled by growing efforts to promote human rights and to strengthen judicial and legal systems in countries where human rights have traditionally been flaunted. Human security concerns are at the forefront of these attempts to consolidate democracy because it is generally recognized that democracy depends on the protection of human rights and the advancement of the rule of law.

A third factor is the growing impact of non-governmental organizations, particularly those working in the humanitarian and development fields, which have raised the profile of human security concerns by stressing the need to address the plight of refugees and particularly vulnerable groups, such as women and children, who are often the most seriously affected victims of armed conflict. Transnational social and political movements have also developed in support of new arms control initiatives directed at mitigating the adverse impact of weapons of warfare that indiscriminately kill civilians and threaten the prospects of economic development once the fighting has stopped. The most notable of these in recent years has been the international campaign to ban anti-personnel landmines—a campaign that was ultimately successful in securing a new anti-personnel landmines treaty. Non-governmental organizations were at the forefront of this campaign, and similar campaigns have developed in support of efforts to control the supply and distribution of light arms and to ban weapons of mass destruction.

A fourth factor is the media—what is sometimes dubbed the 'CNN effect'. Television brought the Vietnam War into living rooms around the globe. Since then, with the advent of 24-hour news channels, like CNN, and the spread of satellite and cable networks, the world has truly come to resemble a 'global village'— to quote Marshall McLuhan (for a contrary view, see Moisy, 1997). When conflict erupts in some far-off land, television has the capacity to create a sense of immediacy and urgency, especially when thousands of refugees are starving and dying and whose story is told night after night on the evening news (Strobel, 1997). But it is not just television that has created a moral affinity between the viewer and the victims of war and natural disasters; the spread of the Internet is helping to shape public perceptions as well. Citizens no longer depend on news organizations to filter the news by bringing pictures and stories of suffering and disaster into their living rooms—they can log on to the Internet and communicate with the victims directly. During the Kosovo crisis, for example, Albanian Kosovar teenagers were able to tell the story of their suffering to the world and with a much greater sense of immediacy and potency than any journalist could because they spoke in the first person.

A fifth factor is the changing nature of international politics and the emergence of a new tier of 'middle powers' committed to advancing the concept of human security and to strengthening the normative foundations of international institutions from a human security standpoint. History suggests that middle powers regularly made important contributions to international order, and international politics in the late twentieth century and the early twenty-first century is no exception. During the Cold War, middle powers tended to be frozen out of international politics because of the domination of the US-Soviet rivalry and its impact on world affairs. As the Cold War ended and the Soviet empire collapsed, the world was left with one superpower, the United States. However, the United States has found itself constrained by its own internal politics and long-standing historical ambivalence about playing a leadership role in world affairs. Middle powers, like the Lilliputians in Jonathan Swift's *Gulliver's Travels*, have tried to fill the leadership gap by working to erect a new global order attentive to the needs and concerns of the world's most vulnerable citizens. They have worked closely with non-governmental organizations to fashion this new order, but the enterprise is not without controversy, and, they, like the Lilliputians, recognize that they must somehow engage the world's Gulliver if they are to succeed.

Sixth, it must be recognized that the forces of economic globalization are transforming international politics and recasting relationships between states and peoples with important implications for human security. Globalization is not only intensifying trade and economic connections, but the pace or velocity at which economic and social change is occurring is also speeding up. Further, it is not just goods and capital that are being exchanged across borders, but also ideas, information, and people. In the ongoing debate about the causes and consequences of globalization, considerable concern has been expressed by some about the impact of globalization on the world's poor and needy. On the one hand, the enthusiasts of globalization argue that the breakdown of national barriers to trade and the spread of global financial and capital markets are helping to raise world incomes and contribute to the spread of wealth. Although there are clear winners and losers in the world economy, the old divisions between the advanced northern economies and peripheral southern economies are breaking down and being replaced by an increasingly complex architecture of economic power (Held et al., 1999: 4). On the other hand, critics of globalization argue that although some countries in the South have benefited from globalization, many have not, and inequalities of income between the world's richest and poorest countries are grow-ing. They suggest that trade and investment flows are intensifying between those countries that can compete in the global economy while leaving those that cannot behind. As income gaps and deep-rooted social and economic inequalities widen, so, too, do the prospects for violence and civil strife. According to the critics, glob-alization raises a new set of challenges for human security as patterns of world trade, production, and finance take on dimensions that, if left unregulated and uncontrolled, will further impoverish the world's poor with dire social and politi-cal consequences (for various views on this debate, see Keohane and Nye, 2000; Roderick, 1997).

A seventh factor is the changing nature of international conflict, coupled with a new understanding about the factors that can fuel conflict and lead to violence. During the Cold War, the superpower rivalry contributed to the progress and esca-lation of 'proxy wars', that is, wars fought between local belligerents with the direct support and aid of the United States, the Soviet Union, and sometimes China. Many of these conflicts had their origins in nationalism, intercommunal or ethnic strife, socio-economic factors, or disputes resulting from decolonization and the drawing/redrawing of state boundaries, but they tended to be cast in ideological terms as a result of the projection of superpower influence into the far corners of the world. As the Cold War ended and a new spirit of détente and co-operation set in, the superpowers worked together to disengage from these conflicts by cutting their dependents loose and forging political settlements.

However, in other regions new conflicts erupted that neither the superpowers nor regional actors seemed able or willing to control. Many of these conflicts were the result of state failure: in Asia, the Middle East, Africa, and Central and South America internally divided states (often lacking political legitimacy) found them-selves unable to provide basic services and security to their citizenry, let alone adhere to democratic principles and the rule of law. As these weak states fragmented, the potential for local conflict increased as different ethnic and social groups became involved in conflicts over resources and land. Some even fell prey to their more powerful neighbours seeking to expand their influence and power in the region. The growing importance of the politics of identity, along with the end of Commu-nist ideology and rule in such countries as the former Yugoslavia, also has weakened social and political cohesion and undermined the artificial unity of the old social order. Even so, some armed conflicts are propelled less by the politics of identity than by the efforts of different groups to control economic resources such as diamonds, drugs, timber concessions, oil, and even so-called renewable resources like water (on the politics of identity and secessionism, see Gurr, 2000).

Intervention, Human Security, and International Order

To many, the term 'intervention' implies the pursuit of national objectives. The changes, however, in the nature of international global conflict and a growing sense of moral urgency, partly driven by modern communications, have added humanitarian emergencies and protection of human rights as well as peacekeeping and enforcement missions to the list of objectives for which international military intervention is a distinct option.

Detractors of the concept of human security argue that most military interventions in the name of human security have either gone awry or proven counterproductive in terms of the goals they profess to advance or achieve (see, for example, Betts, 1996; Luttwak, 1999). These detractors do not argue that the concept of 'human security' itself is necessarily flawed; rather, they argue that human security principles are impossibly difficult to achieve in practice and that the foreign policy of a nation must of practical necessity adhere to a much narrower concept of the 'national interest', i.e., the preservation and security of the state. As we argue in this book, there is considerable merit to these claims. As an article of foreign policy (as opposed to an 'article of faith' or a matter of principle), the concept of human security is notoriously difficult to apply with any precision, consistency, or even moral certainty, especially when the use of force (threatened or actual) is involved. Foreign policy decision-makers confront tough choices requiring trade-offs between competing values and moral claims when taking actions in the name of (or in defence of) human security. Values involving the defence of basic human rights, including the safety of individuals and their protection under the rule of law, have to be squared with very real questions about resource availability and whether the leaders of democratic states are willing to put the lives of their own soldiers at risk in the process of trying to secure the safety of citizens in another state when there is no ostensible threat to their own 'national security'. Questions of the real (as opposed to theoretical) responsibilities and obligations of democratic states to help secure the lives and safety of citizens who do not enjoy the same levels of personal (i.e., physical) security and liberty, for example, are not easily answered even within the human security paradigm. Nor are such questions as how to address competing values—one's desire for international order versus the pursuit of other values such as 'justice' or 'equity'. In a world where actions (especially of the military variety) have unintended consequences as soon as intervention occurs, moral compasses tend to spin wildly in all directions. In lowering the barriers to intervention by devaluing the currency of 'sovereignty' in international relations, the human security paradigm still falls short by failing to offer policy-makers any sort of coherent guide or conceptual road map to making the tough value choices in foreign policy.

But the human security paradigm does have something useful to offer the policy community in its suggestion that intervention and engagement in pursuit of human security objectives can take many forms other than coercive action. By identifying a clear place for the exercise of 'soft power' in the form of diplomatic and 'unofficial' interventions, it points to a whole series of other avenues for preventing, managing, and resolving conflict, including pre-emptive actions, such as well-planned demobilization and disarmament efforts, mediation, private track-two activities, economic incentives, and development assistance. Although military power, i.e., 'hard power', is crucial to international order, its uses in pursuit of human security objectives are exceedingly problematic and we must recognize that there are other instruments and tools for advancing human security. To quote Kofi Annan, Secretary-General of the United Nations:

> 'intervention' should not be understood as referring only to the use of force. A tragic irony of many of the crises that go unnoticed or unchallenged in the world today is that they could have been dealt with by far less perilous acts of intervention than the one we saw this year in Yugoslavia. And, yet, the commitment of the world to peacekeeping, to humanitarian assistance, to rehabilitation and reconstruction varies greatly from region to region, from crisis to crisis. If the new commitment to humanitarian action is to retain the support of the world's peoples, it must be—and be seen to be—universal, irrespective of the region or nation. Humanity, after all, is indivisible. (Annan, 1999)

Later chapters in this book cover the debate about the utility of 'soft' versus 'hard' power in pursuit of human security objectives. This debate underscores both the importance of the human security paradigm to our understanding of the changing normative landscape of international politics, but also the difficulties of translating human security norms and principles into practice.

Structure of This Book

In order to shed light on how our conceptions of human security have evolved and how the human security approach differs from traditional realist, liberal, and socialist conceptions of international politics, this book is structured as follows. In the next chapter, we examine in greater detail the differing conceptions of human security. This chapter is followed by a discussion of the human security 'paradigm' in which we compare it to other conceptual approaches in international politics. In subsequent chapters we offer case studies of different human security initiatives to illustrate the complex mix of international actors behind a wide range of current efforts to promote and advance the human security agenda and the considerable difficulties associated with applying the human security template in international politics. The concluding chapter discusses the changing role of international institutions in the maintenance of international peace and security, how the human security agenda fits this changing role, and the policy and operational difficulties associated with the human security approach to international politics.

Our view is that human security is increasingly perceived as international public good in international relations, though this acceptance is by no means universal. Although definitions and conceptions of the key elements of this public good vary, they all share a common focus in elevating basic human social, economic, and political needs to a level that supersedes the status and importance of the nation-state. This has profound implications for our understanding of international politics, of which actors and institutions can and should provide this public good, and at what cost to themselves and to others. As we see in subsequent chapters there is lively debate about precisely which actors and institutions in international politics are (and should be) human security (or public goods) providers.

There is certainly not an international consensus that human security should replace 'traditional' values, such as sovereignty and non-intervention in the internal affairs of other states, and consequently the human security enterprise is, at best, problematic. As we see in the chapters that follow, some of this resistance comes from those states that clearly eschew democratic principles or honour them in the breach, but it also comes from democratic states (many of them in the developing world) who fear the implications of an interventionist philosophy that espouses minority rights and might give aid and comfort to secessionist movements within their own borders. But the human security enterprise has also met with resistance in some quarters in the world's most prosperous and powerful democracy, the United States, where there are deep reservations about the implications of new human security institutions for the conduct of national security and the projection of US power and influence abroad.

The human security enterprise and debate also raise serious questions about the future of international institutions, especially the United Nations. Although there is a concerted effort under way to adapt and mould international institutions so that they can better address the problems of human security, there is nonetheless considerable resistance to the idea of using these instruments for the purposes of advancing human security. There are those who argue that international institutions should be done away with or replaced because the current quest for human security does not sit well with the existing international institutional architecture. Some even suggest that the world's last remaining superpower—the United States—can promote human security on its own without the United Nations (Kaplan, 2000a, 2000b).

We argue that international organizations and institutions are needed more than ever if human security is to be advanced and promoted in international politics. Ad hoc improvisation, tinkering, and the occasional, bold, humanitarian gesture are no substitute for co-ordinated, international responses that take place within the normative framework and under the administrative and legal auspices of international institutions, particularly the United Nations. Even so, the continuing tension and conflict between competing international norms and continuing prohibitions against the use of force, except when international (i.e., interstate) order is threatened, suggest that the quest for a new international order based on evolving principles and concepts of human security will continue to be an uphill struggle that will continue to meet with strong resistance in many quarters.

Chapter 2

The Many Meanings of Human Security

Debates about the meaning and legitimacy of what constitutes 'security' in international politics are not new. During the Cold War, for example, there was a widespread—though by no means universal—consensus among international relations scholars that 'security' meant 'national security', i.e., the interests and survival of the state. Distinctions often were made between 'high' and 'low' politics in international relations. High politics was the realm of national security whereas low politics referred to the mundane world of international trade and finance and various forms of economic and social transactions that crossed international borders. With the oil shocks in the early 1970s and the crisis brought on by the Arab oil embargo in 1973 following the Middle East War, the distinction between high and low politics became increasingly difficult to sustain. Economics was clearly a matter of high politics if the economic health of the state was to be jeopardized by skyrocketing energy prices. If essential sources of supply were threatened because of war or the actions of oil-producing states, there was clearly little practical distinction between an 'economic' and a 'national security' crisis. As scholars and practitioners developed a better appreciation of how relations of economic interdependence affect the fundamental health and welfare of states, the purview of national security studies—and with it, the concept of security—expanded (see Buzan et al., 1998).

Although many were prepared to accept a definition of national security that included an economic component, others were resistant to the idea of expanding the concept further to include other kinds of non-military threats, such as those of the environmental, biological, and even human (e.g., refugee) variety (Walt, 1998). Proponents of environmental security argued that problems such as ozone depletion in the upper atmosphere or the prospect of global warming posed threats to human health and survival that were just as serious, if not more so, than the threat of war from hostile states (see Homer-Dixon, 1999). With the end of the Cold War, they argued that the risks and potential costs of these human-induced environmental threats were more serious than traditional military threats and that therefore they should receive more attention and correspondingly greater resources to address them. Defenders of the narrower conception of security based on traditional military threats to the state retorted that if the concept of security was expanded to include every conceivable threat to humanity, it would be so diluted as to mean nothing and would therefore be of little analytical or policy relevance. They also argued that although the threat of military confrontation between the two super-powers had diminished with the end of the Cold War, the prospect of intercommunal strife and regional conflict had grown and military power still had its uses.

Even so, some environmentalists believed that the language of national security was ill-equipped to address problems of the global commons that required co-operative, as opposed to independent, national solutions (see World Commission on Environment and Development, 1987: 290–307). They argued that the language of national security needlessly 'militarized' problems, and in a psychological way that was damaging to developing new cognitive frames of reference that would foster international co-operation. During the Cold War, there were also critics within the traditional security studies camp who believed that the existence of nuclear weapons had fundamentally changed the nature of warfare and international conflict such that the risks of escalation of conventional conflict to the nuclear level were unacceptable. These critics advocated a conception of 'co-operative' or 'common' security premised on the view that nation-states—especially those with nuclear weapons—had more to gain from co-operation when it came to reducing the risks of war and avoiding nuclear annihilation (Independent Commission on Disarmament and Security Issues, 1982). They questioned the premise that nuclear weapons were useful for deterrence because the risks of nuclear war were simply too great and the threat of nuclear use was simply not credible.

The newest turn in the debate about the meaning and content of security comes from champions of the concept of human security (see Commission on Global Governance, 1995; DFAIT, 1999; Lauren, 1998; Nef, 1995; Rothschild, 1995; UNDP, 1994; UN, 1995). Like earlier critics, advocates of human security share grave doubts about the utility of a concept of security anchored on the nation-state and abstract definitions of 'national interest'. They believe that although human beings may be divided by language, culture, ethnicity, religion, and political beliefs, they also share many things in common, including a desire for physical security, access to economic opportunities that go beyond mere economic survival, freedom of speech and of association, legal and political rights that include the right to association, the right to express and practise one's own religion, and fair and equitable treatment, including the right of due process, in a court of law. However, the concept of human security is not just an argument about securing basic human rights. It is a conception that goes much further in its understanding, both about the potential sources of threat (or privation) to these rights and about the conditions and kinds of institutions and governance arrangements (domestic as well as international) required to sustain human rights.

Some proponents of human security also have decidedly ambivalent feelings about the role of the nation-state in advancing and promoting human security (UNDP, 1994; Nef, 1995). Although they recognize that democracy is necessary for human security, they also believe that the state itself has a potentially limited role to play in securing many of the conditions necessary for human security and well-being. Certain aspects of the modern state are even considered to be obstacles or impediments to the advancement of human security. Opinions about the relationship and importance of the state to human security naturally differ: some human security advocates have a strong pro-statist orientation because they believe that a strong, democratic state is ultimately the best guarantee and instrument of human security (Kritz, 1995). Others, however, believe that given the changing nature and structure of the international system and the emergence of a wide range of transnational forces and actors, new kinds of governance arrangements that transcend the territoriality and traditional functions of the nation-state must be created in order to promote human security. They also believe that current international institutions are also not especially well-suited to addressing the new threats and challenges to human security because of the inherent bias towards the nation-state and principles of sovereignty in these institutions (UNDP, 1994; Commission on Global Governance, 1995).

Conceptions of Human Security

In discussing what is meant by the term 'human security' it is important to recognize that there are different schools of thought about the meaning and implications of the concept (see Figure 2.1). Just as there is an active debate about the meaning of 'security' so, too, is there a growing and lively debate about the definitional boundaries of 'human security' and how the concept relates to the wider meanings of security.

Figure 2.1 Three Dimensions of Human Security

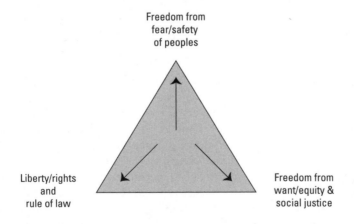

Although there is an obvious danger in drawing artificial distinctions in the current (and admittedly evolving) discourse about 'human security', three rather different understandings about how best to understand and promote human security have emerged in this ongoing debate. The first approach is what might be called a rights-based approach to human security centred on a fairly broad definition of human security (in the sense of entertaining a wide variety of different legal rights), but nonetheless anchored in the rule of law and treaty-based solutions to human security. The rights-based approach to human security seeks to strengthen normative legal frameworks at both the international and regional levels while also deepening and strengthening human rights law and legal and judicial systems at the national level, i.e., within the nation-state. According to the human rights/rule-of-law view of human security, international institutions are central to developing new human rights norms and for bringing about a convergence in different national standards and practices.

The second approach to human security is centred primarily, though not exclusively, on a humanitarian conception of human security where the 'safety of peoples' (sometimes described as 'freedom from fear') is the paramount objective behind international interventions. This conception of human security sees war as one of the principal threats to human security and draws an important moral distinction between combatants and non-combatants. Given the nature of modern warfare, non-combatants are increasingly being put in harm's way not only because of the way wars are being fought, but also by the kinds of weapons used to fight them. Since the founding of the International Committee of the Red Cross (ICRC) in the nineteenth century, the notion that people should be protected from violent threats and, when they are harmed or injured, that the international community has an obligation to assist them has gained widespread acceptance. Many humanitarian intergovernmental and non-governmental organizations have had their origins in wars.

The 'safety of peoples' approach to human security also sees a need to go beyond the provision of emergency and humanitarian relief in war-torn societies and conflict settings by addressing the *underlying* causes of conflict and violence. As the United Nations and the international community in general became involved in long-term political and economic reconstruction as a result of the conclusion of formal peace settlements, many of which were negotiated in the late 1980s and early 1990s, the importance was recognized of adopting 'an integrated approach to human security' that would, at the same time, address the deeper causes of conflict such as 'economic despair, social injustice, and political oppression' (Boutros-Ghali, 1992). Reflecting this change in thinking, the United Nations Security Council issued a declaration in 1992 formally recognizing that 'the non-military sources of instability in the economic, social, humanitarian, and ecological fields have become threats to peace and security' (quoted in UNHCR, 1994: 12). The goals of human security thus came to be linked to preventive and post-conflict peacebuilding and to a considerably enlarged understanding of the challenges the international community confronted in reducing the potential for armed conflict and civil violence around the globe.

The third and, in some respects, most expansive definition of human security is what might be termed the 'sustainable human development' view of human security. This conception is associated with the United Nations *Human Development Report* (1994), which offered a wide-ranging analysis and assessment of the different dimensions of human security. Human security was defined in terms of economic, food, health, environmental, personal, community, and political security. The *Report* argued that the end of the Cold War provided real opportunities to capture the 'peace dividend' and that the real threats to human security in the twentieth and twenty-first centuries were coming from diseases such as AIDS and from drug trafficking, terrorism, global poverty, and environmental problems. These problems were not local (or national) but global in scope, requiring new ways of thinking and new institutions and forms of global co-operation to deal with them. However, underlying many of these problems—though obviously not all—are fundamental problems of inequality and a lack of social justice in international relations (also referred to as the 'freedom from want' dimensions of human security).

Although these three different definitions or conceptions of human security have much in common insofar as their main focus of attention and concern is the individual rather than the state, they also have somewhat different understandings about what constitute the main threats to human security, what the appropriate responses and mechanisms are for dealing with these threats, and what kinds of international institutions and governance structures are required to address them. In the discussion that follows, we will elaborate on these three different conceptions of human security and consider the similarities and differences between them.

Rights and Rule of Law

The rights and rule-of-law conception of human security has its origins in liberal democratic theory and the foundations of the modern democratic state. It considers the main threat to human security to lie in the denial of fundamental human rights, including the right of national self-determination, and the absence of the rule of law (see Donnelly, 1986, 1993; Lauren, 1998). Of these rights, the issue of minority rights is the most problematic because minority rights may conflict not just with the 'will of the majority' but also with the rights of the individual. Although some argue that minority rights trump many other civil and political rights (e.g., in the area of language and cultural policy), others argue that minority rights are not unlimited and that the political and social space occupied by such group rights must not curtail or restrict the fundamental civic rights of the individual (see Kymlicka, 1996, 2000).

In international politics, the belief that respect for human rights is linked to international peace and security arguably goes back to the so-called Peace of Westphalia, enshrined in the Osnabrück and Munster Treaties of 1648, which not only ended the religious wars of Europe and formalized the principle of sovereignty,[1] but also sought to guarantee for religious minorities the right to practise their own religion with the understanding that all parties to the treaties would respect these rights in exchange for territorial (i.e., sovereign) control (Krasner, 1999). In the American and French revolutions the 'rights of man' were given political and legal effect, although there was no immediate universal acknowledgement of these rights. That would come after World War II in the UN Charter and Declaration of Human Rights. However, in the late nineteenth and early twentieth centuries, international recognition of minority rights grew. French forces intervened in Turkey in 1860 to protect the local Christian population in Lebanon from being massacred by the Druses, and Russia intervened in Bulgaria in the 1870s to halt the murder of Christians.

With the end of World War I, minority rights became equated with the concept of self-determination. Woodrow Wilson's '14 points' in his address to the US Congress on 8 January 1918 called for the return of Alsace-Lorraine to France, the readjustment of Italy's frontiers 'along clearly recognized lines of nationality', limited self-government for the people of Austria-Hungary, independence for the Balkan countries, independence for Poland, and 'an opportunity to develop self-government' for those nationalities 'under Turkish rule' (Moynihan, 1993: 78). Although Wilson tried to secure formal protection of minority rights in the Covenant of the new League of Nations, this approach was rejected in favour of a series of individual, minority treaties that legally obligated a number of countries in Central and Eastern Europe and the Balkans, though pointedly not the colonial powers, to respect the collective rights of minorities living within their borders. The mechanisms of protection included the right of minorities to petition the League if they felt their rights under the treaties were being violated, the establishment of special Minorities Committees in the League to oversee these disputes, and advisory jurisdiction of the Permanent Court of International Justice on issues pertaining to the interpretation or application of the treaties. The League of Nations was to ensure compliance with these treaties, but its record of protection after an auspicious start in the 1920s worsened in the 1930s because those countries bound by the treaties rejected the double standard that forced a distinction between them and the colonial powers.

The Versailles conference in 1919 also saw an attempt to secure rights to religious freedom and racial equality in the League's Covenant. However, Woodrow Wilson strongly opposed any mention of race in the Charter, so the proposal to include these rights was withdrawn. There was a second attempt in the 1930s, led by France and Poland, to develop an international agreement on human rights, but this, too, came to naught because of international opposition as well as for fear of antagonizing Nazi Germany.

The experience with fascism in the 1930s, coupled with Nazi and Japanese atrocities during World War II, underscored the need for the international community to pay much greater attention to human rights. Although the UN Charter does not define the content of human rights per se, it does suggest a linkage between human rights and international peace and security. This linkage is implied in the various affirmations in the Preamble and in Article 1, which spell out the purpose of the organization. The Preamble to the Charter 'reaffirm[s] faith in fundamental human rights, in the dignity and worth of the person, in the equal rights of men and women and of nations large and small.' Unlike the Covenant of the League of Nations, the United Nations Charter states that one of the main purposes of the organization is 'To develop friendly relations among nations based on respect for the principle of equal rights and self-determination of people' (Article 1, Section 2). In addition, the United Nations aims to encourage 'respect for human rights and for fundamental freedoms for all without distinction as to race, sex, language, and religion' (Article 1, Section 3). In Articles 55 and 56 all members of the organization pledge themselves to take 'joint and separate action in co-operation with the Organization' to promote the 'conditions of stability and well-being which are necessary for peaceful and friendly relations among nations based on respect for the principle of equal rights and self-determination of peoples' and, in addition, 'universal respect for and observance of, human rights and fundamental freedoms for all without distinction as to race, sex, language, or religion'.

International efforts to codify and specify the content of human rights began with the adoption of the Universal Declaration of Human Rights in 1948 by the General Assembly of the United Nations. The resolution was not binding, but it did identify some 30 human rights principles, which included the following clusters of rights (see Morsink, 1998):

- personal rights (e.g., right to life, recognition before law, protection against cruel or degrading forms of punishment, and protection against racial, ethnic, sexual, or religious discrimination);
- legal rights (e.g., access to legal remedies for violations of basic rights, right of due process, including fair and impartial public trials, protection against arbitrary arrest, detention, or exile, etc.);
- civil liberties (e.g., freedom of thought, conscience, and religion);
- subsistence rights (e.g., right to food and basic standards of health and well-being);
- economic rights (e.g., right to work, rest and leisure, social security); and
- political rights (e.g., right to take part in elections and participate in government, etc.).

Subsequent UN conventions and covenants have given additional content and meaning to these rights. They include the Convention on the Prevention and Punishment of the Crime of Genocide (1948); the Convention relating to the Status of Refugees (1951); the International Convention on the Elimination of All Forms of Racial Discrimination (1965); the International Covenant on Civil and Political Rights (1966); the International Covenant on Economic, Social, and Cultural Rights (1966); the Convention on the Elimination of All Forms of Discrimination against Women (1979); the Declaration on the Elimination of All Forms of Intolerance and of Discrimination Based on Religion or Belief (1981); the Convention against Torture and Other Cruel, Inhuman, or Degrading Treatment and Punishment (1984); and the Convention on the Rights of the Child (1989) (see Lauren, 1998; Alston, 1992).

Strategies and Instruments

The human rights/rule-of-law approach to human security has tended to rely on three different kinds of instruments to promote human security. These instruments typically have aimed at altering the political calculations of governments so as to deepen and entrench human rights norms and principles in national legislation and domestic law. Setting aside military force, which has been used in a growing number of humanitarian interventions under Chapter VII of the UN Charter, and which is discussed at greater length in subequent chapters of this book, following Moravcik (1995) the three instruments for promoting domestic protection of human rights are as follows: sanctioning, shaming, and co-optation. Sanctions seek to promote respect for human rights by denying domestic groups access to foreign goods, services, markets, and capital. When the instrument is effective, domestic élites will change policies in favour of greater protection of human rights. Relevant examples include UN sanctions against Rhodesia/Zimbabwe following the Unilateral Declaration of Independence by the Smith regime (1966–79); UN sanctions against South Africa during the apartheid era; UN sanctions against Iraq following Saddam Hussein's invasion of Kuwait (1989); and UN sanctions against Haiti following the overthrow of Bertrand Artistide's government by General Cedras and his cohorts, which were in effect in 1993–4 (Doxey, 1996).

In contrast, shaming works on public opinion by focusing the international spotlight on state policies and practices that are detrimental to human rights and at variance with established international norms, principles, and rules. This process can be instigated through the close monitoring of human rights by international bodies and through the dissemination of information and the publicity given to individuals and groups whose rights have been violated or denied. A well-mounted international campaign, over a period of time, may tip the domestic balance of power in favour of greater protection of human rights and force governments that are fearful of the impact of continuing negative publicity on their political reputations abroad to change their human rights policies and practices. Such pressure can also be generated by mobilized constituencies and groups within states, such as business associations or non-governmental organizations that are keen to see policies changed. Although intergovernmental organizations and bodies such as the UN Human Rights Commission and its various subcommissions, along with human rights commissions in regional organizations, are key instruments of shaming, it must also be recognized that non-governmental organizations, like Amnesty International, have had an equal if not greater impact in a large number of countries through their well-orchestrated and internationally publicized human rights campaigns.

The process of co-optation is more subtle and typically works through a combination of direct and indirect means. As noted by Moravcik (1995), co-optation methods involve the use of international or region-wide courts and commissions that seek to enforce human rights and promote democracy by promulgating legal norms and suggesting reforms of domestic juridical structures and legal systems. These bodies also work with various intergovernmental bodies and networks of organized pressure groups (transnational and non-governmental) to change domestic behaviours and law. The European Court of Justice, for example, has more or less successfully co-opted domestic courts that request and enforce its judgements. The process of co-optation is also evident in the various legal and juridical processes behind the incorporation of the European Convention on Human Rights into domestic jurisprudence and statutes.

Global and Regional Institutions

In addition to the various declarations and conventions noted above, the UN has established a complex array of committees and commissions to review states' compliance with existing treaties as well as other monitoring mechanisms that have relied largely on the instruments of shaming, co-optation, and, with increasing frequency, sanctions.

The UN Human Rights Commission, for example, reviews the reports of parties to the 1966 International Covenant on Civil and Political Rights. The Human Rights Commission has the power to investigate complaints involving alleged gross and systematic human rights abuses, but, in practice, its various subcommissions, such as that on Protection of Minorities, have been more active. The Human Rights Commission only began to deal with human rights violations in the 1960s and focused almost exclusively on South Africa, Chile, and Israel. Beginning in the early 1980s it began to deal with a wider range of cases and developed more intrusive monitoring procedures. In recent years, non-governmental organizations have played a key role in the work of the Commission and its subcommissions; as a result these bodies have come to play a more visible role in human rights (see Donnelly, 1986; Farer and Gaer, 1994).

Some of the UN's most important work has involved the administration of human rights in the course of implementation of internationally negotiated peace agreements. Human rights teams have been deployed in El Salvador, Cambodia, Haiti, and Mozambique (Kritz, 1995; Hampson, 1996). They have reviewed human rights cases and abuses and monitored violations by security forces of the state. In addition, the UN has helped support the establishment of truth commissions in countries such as El Salvador where there has been a desire to come to grips with the past and promote a process of reconciliation so that society can move forward.

For much of the past century, as noted by Donnelly, the UN human rights regime has acted as a promotional regime that tries to set international standards for human rights. Its activities have rarely gone beyond the exchange of information, and its implementation and compliance mechanisms have generally tended to be weak. According to Donnelly, the problem is that a stronger regime 'does not rest on any perceived material interest of a state or coalition willing and able to supply it. In the absence of a power capable of compelling compliance, states participate in or increase their commitment to international regimes more or less voluntarily' (Donnelly, 1986: 616).

In recent years, however, considerable effort has gone into the development of legal instruments that have broken new ground in trying to stop gross human rights violations such as genocide, political murder, and rape and to prosecute those charged with perpetrating these crimes. Two international war crimes tribunals were created by the UN Security Council, one for the former Yugoslavia and the other for Rwanda. The two tribunals have tried, convicted, and sentenced perpetrators of war crimes, crimes against humanity, and genocide, including former national leaders, some of whom have been given jail sentences for life. The newest of these institutions is the International Criminal Court (ICC). In 1998, the international community adopted a statute establishing the Court and once 60 countries have ratified the statute the Court will become operational. The ICC will be the first permanent international court in history and will have the power to prosecute individuals for genocide, war crimes, crimes against humanity, and, eventually, crimes of aggression (see Bass, 2000; Lee, 1999).

A discussion of regional human rights regimes is outside of the scope of this chapter, but such regimes exist in Europe, the Americas, and Africa. In the Middle East the Arab League adopted a Charter for Human Rights in 1994 but this is still very much in the early evolutionary stages. A regional human rights regime for the Asia-Pacific region has yet to emerge. For those regions where human rights regimes do exist, they have drawn much of their inspiration from the UN Charter and the Universal Declaration of Human Rights.

The Safety of Peoples

The humanitarian or 'safety of peoples' conception of human security has traditionally focused on securing the moral and legal rights of non-combatants in war or situations of violent conflict and on providing emergency assistance to those in dire need. This view of human security is somewhat more narrowly focused on the security needs and rights of individuals in times of war, recognizing that the instruments that may be required to protect human security in situations of violent, armed conflict may be different from those in times of peace.

The idea that the conduct of war should be subjected to moral and legal restraints is a relatively new one in international politics. The distinguished Dutch jurist of the seventeenth century, Hugo Grotius, believed that any and all violent means were justified in warfare, including the killing of women and children, provided that the war itself was being fought for a 'just' cause. Like many of his contemporaries, Grotius saw no moral distinction between combatants and non-combatants because anyone who inhabited enemy territory owed allegiance to the local ruler and was therefore a threat to the other side. With the rise of mercenary armies, the distinction between combatants and non-combatants became harder to sustain and war was increasingly seen as a contest between opposing armies and not civilian populations. As ethical and legal norms changed, not only was it considered immoral and illegal to go out of one's way to inflict injury and death on innocent civilians, but it also became increasingly accepted that one should carry out military operations in a such a way that the risk of harming civilians would be limited. The Hague Conventions with Respect to the Laws and Customs of War on Land of 1899 and 1907 and the Geneva Conventions of 1949 gave universal expression and legal sanction to these principles.

Other norms of warfare, which were eventually given expression in international treaties, included the principle that individuals who were sick, wounded, or made prisoners of war should not be harmed. The Geneva Conventions of 1864, 1906, 1929, and 1949 codified this principle and the legal obligations that fell on the parties to these conventions regarding the wounded and the sick. Along with the Hague Conventions of 1899 and 1907, the Geneva Conventions also laid down detailed provisions regarding the confinement and humane treatment of prisoners.

Humanitarian concerns for the life and suffering of human beings exposed to the ravages of war have led to various prohibitions on the production, use, and stockpiling of certain kinds of weapons that are indiscriminate or particularly injurious in terms of their ability to prolong the suffering of victims. The Declaration of St Petersburg of 1868, for example, prohibited the use of lightweight projectiles charged with explosives or inflammable substances. The Hague Declaration of 1899 prohibited the use of expanding or dumdum bullets. Over the years international conventions prohibiting the production, use, and stockpiling of chemical, gas, and bacteriological instruments of warfare have also been negotiated, as have a large number of treaties regulating the production and development of nuclear weapons. In addition to controlling the production and prohibiting the use of weapons of mass destruction, there is growing interest in controlling the production, sale, and use of conventional weapons that have the capacity to harm or maim civilians. The anti-personnel landmines treaty signed in Ottawa in 1997 is a leading example of these efforts.

The twentieth century also witnessed a changing attitude towards war itself along with a desire to avoid war. The Hague Peace Conferences of 1899 and 1907, the League of Nations of 1919, the Kellogg–Briand Pact of 1928 that outlawed 'aggressive war', and the United Nations itself all see the avoidance of war as their ultimate purpose and objective.

In addition to developing new norms for the conduct of warfare and the treatment of prisoners of war and civilians, the 'safety of peoples' approach to human security has also witnessed the strengthening of international institutional mechanisms to provide emergency assistance and humanitarian relief to peoples in conflict settings. In addition to the continuing activity of the International Committee of the Red Cross, which was founded in the nineteenth century, World War II saw the establishment of new intergovernmental mechanisms to help victims who were in distress. The first such agency was the United Nations Relief and Rehabilitation Administration, founded in 1943 to give aid to countries ravaged by war. Its European operations continued until 1947 and the organization was formally dissolved in 1949. However, other UN agencies began to play a variety of roles in the provision of humanitarian and emergency assistance. The Office of the High Commissioner for Refugees (UNHCR) was created by the General Assembly in 1950 and began formal operations in 1951. The agency has played a key role working closely alongside NGOs in co-ordinating and directing the provision of medical assistance and key goods and services to displaced persons. Under the 1951 Convention relating to the Status of Refugees, signatory states are legally obligated to protect refugees in accordance with the Convention and to co-operate with the UNHCR. The other main UN agencies involved in helping the victims of armed conflict include the World Health Organization (WHO), United Nations Relief and Works Agency (UNRWA), United Nations Children's Fund (UNICEF), and the United Nations Development Program (UNDP), although these agencies clearly have a much wider mandate than the provision of emergency assistance and humanitarian relief (see Moore, 1996).

Many non-governmental organizations that have sprung up in this century have also come to play a key role in advancing the human security needs and interests of victims of armed conflict. They include such groups as the Red Cross, Catholic Relief Services, Doctors Without Borders, World Vision, and CARE. As Mary Anderson notes, many of these organizations were 'formed during or immediately after war, explicitly to provide emergency relief to war victims. Others—such as the American Friends Service Committee, which was started by the Quakers in 1917—were formed to provide an alternative to military service for young men whose consciences would neither permit them to carry weapons nor to sit on the sidelines watching the suffering occur' (Anderson, 1996: 346). And even those NGOs, such as Oxfam, that were formed in the 1960s and 1970s to provide emergency disaster relief or development assistance, soon found themselves operating in conflict settings.

Humanitarian assistance and emergency relief to a large extent constitute the core activities in the humanitarian or 'safety of peoples' approach to human security. In the 1980s and early 1990s, however, there was growing awareness that this approach to human security was inadequate and that a different approach was required to address the needs and interests of victims of armed conflict. Critics, some of whom came from within the NGO community itself, argued that it was not enough simply to do 'good works' in situations of armed conflict. To quote Mary Anderson again, 'in the post-Cold War instrasocietal conflicts that mark a number of societies, NGO interventions—even when they are effective in humanitarian, development, or human terms—very often exacerbate the local tensions and suspicions that underlie the violence of the societies they seek to help' (ibid., 347). And within the UN itself there was a growing sense that a much better strategic approach was required to prevent those conflicts that had just ended (usually as the result of a negotiated peace settlement) from re-escalating after the international community withdrew its peacekeeping forces and stopped providing humanitarian relief and assistance. Many senior officials and academics, including the Secretary-General of the United Nations, argued for a broader conceptual approach as well as the creation of new strategies and tools to promote human security (Boutros-Ghali, 1992; Moore, 1996; UN, 1995, 1996; UNDP, 1997).

Strategies and Instruments

In the 1990s, peacebuilding and prevention of conflict came to be viewed as new potential instruments of human security, particularly in those settings where a fragile peace accord had been negotiated but the peace process had not yet been consolidated. In his 1992 *Agenda for Peace*, UN Secretary-General Boutros Boutros-Ghali defined peacebuilding as a broad set of activities that 'tend to consolidate peace and advance a sense of confidence and well-being among people' (Boutros-Ghali, 1992: 55). He also argued that beyond peacekeeping the list of peacebuilding activities should include 'disarming the previously warring parties and the restoration of public order, the custody and possible destruction of weapons, repatriating refugees, [providing] advisory and training support for security personnel, monitoring elections, advancing efforts to protect human rights, reforming or strengthening governmental institutions and promoting formal and informal processes of political participation' (ibid.). Boutros-Ghali also suggested that the 'United Nations has an obligation to develop and provide . . . support for the transformation of deficient national structures and capabilities, and for strengthening democratic institutions' (ibid., 59).

The preventive aspects of peacebuilding have also been stressed by others. Former Australian Foreign Minister Gareth Evans defines peacebuilding as 'a set of strategies which aim to ensure that disputes, armed conflicts, and other major crises do not arise in the first place—or if they do arise, that they not subsequently recur' (Evans, 1993: 9–10). Evans suggests that there are two broad groups of instruments to promote human security: international regimes and in-country peacebuilding measures. International regimes are 'international laws, norms, agreements and arrangements—[which are] global, regional, or bilateral in scope—designed to minimize threats to security, promote confidence and trust and create the frameworks for dialogue and cooperation' (ibid., 9). In contrast, in-country peacebuilding refers to national and international efforts 'aimed at economic development, institution building, and, more generally, the creation or restoration within countries of the conditions necessary to make them stable and viable states' (ibid.).

What distinguishes peacebuilding from more conventional forms of international assistance, such as peacekeeping and humanitarian assistance, is its focus on the causes of conflict and the use of a wide range of multi-functional instruments to consolidate and entrench the peace process. Peacebuilding tries to transform the social and political context of conflict so that human beings can live in a stable and secure social, political, and economic environment. It recognizes that unless the peace process addresses the underlying causes of violence human security will continue to be threatened.

In the peacebuilding frame of reference, ethnic and intercommunal conflicts are seen less in terms of strategic security dilemmas and more in terms of sets of causal relationships in which the variables are poverty, socio-economic inequalities, the denial of human rights, due process of law, and liberal pluralist forms of democracy. Civic intolerance in the form of the denial of minority communal and religious rights may also be a major cause of conflict. Although establishing a respect for human rights and legal due process are critical to the peacebuilding enterprise, these activities have to be complemented by a wide range of military, non-military, economic, social, and political measures, which can help people in war-torn societies to rehabilitate themselves.

Another key tool for managing conflict and promoting human security is the concept of conflict prevention. In the words of the Report of the Carnegie Commission on Preventing Deadly Conflict:

> the need to prevent deadly conflict is increasingly urgent. The rapid compression of the world through breathtaking population growth, technological advancement, and economic interdependence, combined with the readily available supply of deadly weapons and easily transmitted contagion of hatred and incitement to violence, make it essential and urgent to find ways to prevent disputes from turning massively violent. . . . [P]reventing deadly conflict is possible. The problem is not [that] we do not know about incipient large-scale violence; it is that we often do not act. (Carnegie Commission, 1997: xvii)

The Carnegie Commission identified three broad aims or goals of preventive action: (1) to prevent the emergence of violent conflict; (2) to prevent ongoing conflicts from spreading; and (3) to prevent the re-emergence of violent conflict. Among the various strategies identified by the Commission to promote these goals, the principal ones involved the creation of 'states with representative governance based on the role of law . . . widely available economic opportunity, social safety nets, protection of fundamental human rights, and robust civil societies'; barriers or firewalls to prevent the escalation and spread of conflict by, for example, 'denying belligerents the ability to resupply arms, ammunition, and hard currency, combined with humanitarian operations that provide relief for victims'; and a safe and secure environment 'in the aftermath of conflict' through, for example, 'the rapid introduction of security forces to separate enemies, oversee disarmament plans', and 'restore legitimate political authority' (ibid., xviii).

Some now argue that conflict prevention should focus on the deeper causes of conflict, particularly economic causes. Horizontal inequalities that are the result of deliberate strategies by élites to hoard resources have created a culture of social and political intolerance among different groups in society. As noted by UN Secretary-General Kofi Annan, 'In recent years poor countries have been far more likely to be embroiled in armed conflicts than rich ones. But poverty per se appears not to be the decisive factor; most poor countries live in peace most of the time.' Rather, 'countries that are afflicted by war typically also suffer from inequality among domestic social groups. And it is this, rather than poverty, that seems to be the critical factor. The inequality may be based on ethnicity, religion, national identity or economic class, but it tends to be reflected in unequal access to power that too often forecloses paths to peaceful change' (Annan, 1999). Efforts to prevent conflict must therefore address these social and political inequalities if they are to be successful.

Sustainable Human Development

Unlike the humanitarian or 'safety of peoples' approach to human security, the sustainable human development conception of human security stresses the *non-military* threats to human security and the threats to human survival that have arisen from a wide variety of largely human-induced problems, such as unchecked global population growth, migration, disparities in economic opportunities (especially the widening income gap between the world's rich and poor), the rise of pandemic diseases (e.g., AIDS), environmental degradation, and new security problems that affect individuals and groups, such as drug trafficking and terrorism. This is a broad view of human security, but it is also one that stresses the distributive aspects of development and the fact that many of these problems are rooted in socio-economic inequalities and a lack of social justice. Accordingly, the sustainable development approach rejects the 'narrow' view of security, which defines the issue mainly in terms of the territory of the state and military aggression. It also tends to downplay the threat of nuclear war between states as a security challenge, because the Cold War—and with it the ideological struggle between the two superpowers—has ended.

Although the UNDP's *Human Development Report* (1994) provides the most coherent articulation of this new, enlarged concept of security, its origins date back to the 1960s. In the 1960s, the covenants on economic, social, and cultural rights, and on civil and political rights, further specified the link between 'fear and want' by expanding the range of rights defined in the Universal Declaration of Human Rights, as noted above. With these instruments, economic development, broadly defined, came to be seen, and crucially, as a right of the person. Security was mentioned specifically as the right to 'the security of the person' and 'social security' was explicitly guaranteed (Covenant on Economic, Social, and Cultural Rights, Article 9). With these small steps, security or its absence became part of the development agenda, not a consequence of its success or failure.

A further step towards the broadening of the concept of security was made at the beginning of the 1970s by the Food and Agriculture Organization's use of the term 'food security', which meant access by all people at all times to the food needed for a healthy and active life. The Independent Commission on International Development Issues (Brandt Commission), which delivered its report in 1980, argued that 'the arms race, in which each participant acts in the name of national security—too limited a view of national security—has produced a situation in which the extinction of mankind is a real possibility. . . . Our survival depends not only on military balance, but on global cooperation to ensure a sustainable biological environment, and sustainable prosperity based on equitably shared resources' (Independent Commission on International Development, 1980:

24). The Brandt Commission explicitly identified poor countries, i.e., the South, as one of the keys to international security: 'Much of the security in the world is connected with the divisions between rich and poor countries—grave injustice and mass starvation causing additional instability.'

Academic and policy reflections on the implications of environmental degradation also helped move the security agenda away from nuclear weapons and deterrence and narrow, territory-based definitions of security. The increased risks of conflict were associated with environmental degradation, particularly with the exhaustion of non-renewable resources (e.g., oil) and especially with the destruction of renewable ones, such as water. One of the catalysts in the growing debate about the role of the environment in human conflict was the World Commission on Environment and Development, chaired by former Norwegian Prime Minister Gro Harlem Brundtland. Its 1987 report coined the expression 'sustainable development', thus placing the requirements of sustainability, primarily if not exclusively environmental, at the core of the development agenda. Conflict was seen as a key factor in that sustainability and the report devoted a whole chapter to the linkages between peace, security, development, and the environment, arguing that 'environmental stress is both a cause and an effect of political tension and military conflict' (World Commission on Environment and Development, 1987: 290).

The main innovation in the burgeoning environmental security literature, however, involved conceiving environmental degradation as a security issue. A telling moment in that process was the discovery in the 1980s of stratospheric ozone holes over the South and North poles, and of an apparent warming of the planet, both linked to the by-products of human activity: the emission of CFCs into the atmosphere and the buildup of greenhouse gases. These environmental problems were seen as threatening the security of peoples and nations directly, without any need for a conflict intermediary, although conflict would almost certainly result from their consequences. Framed in these terms, even the most traditional state-centred security approach needed to make space for a wide range of environmentally based threats. In the steady evolution of the debate about the meaning of security, however, these new concepts joined an already crowded field of issues deemed 'security' problems, ranging from malnourishment, starvation, and poverty to nuclear war and overpopulation.

While intellectual challenges to the traditional concept of security were multiplying, a core component of the Cold War's political balance also was disappearing and was brought to an end by the surprisingly quick dissolution of the Communist bloc epitomized in the fall of the Berlin Wall in 1989, the subsequent reunification of Germany, and the collapse of the Soviet Union. Within a few years, democratically elected governments came to power in the countries in Eastern Europe and the ideological and strategic divide that had structured world politics for almost five decades vanished.

The 1992 United Nations Conference on the Environment and Sustainable Development proceeded to take stock of these changes and to define the agenda for the twenty-first century. The huge talkfest in Rio de Janeiro spectacularly ushered in a new age of international politics at the 'parallel summit', which brought together thousands of representatives from non-governmental organizations (see Timmerman, 1996). The NGOs and 'civil society' they claimed to represent asserted a legitimacy that was distinct and sometimes superior to that of governments. More than its plan of action (Agenda 21), this opening of the global political discourse is one of the legacies of the Rio summit.

During the 1980s and into the 1990s, there were calls to widen the security agenda to include more issues, to detach it from a narrow, state-centred outlook, to break the link between security and conflict, and to expand the number and types of players who could legitimately have a voice in security debates. Those calls for a redefinition of the very meaning of security, however, failed to come up with a new, shared definition of security. This logical next step emerged with the concept of human security. The central document was the UNDP's 1994 *Human Development Report*, which bluntly stated: 'The world can never be at peace unless people have security in their daily lives' (UNDP, 1994: 22). The *Report* argued that the concept of security should be viewed in terms of people and framed in terms of ordinary people and the security concerns they required in their daily lives:

> For most people, a feeling of insecurity arises more from worries about their daily life than from the dread of a cataclysmic world event. Will they and their families have enough to eat? Will they lose their jobs? Will their streets and neighborhoods be safe from crime? Will they be tortured by a repressive state? Will they become the victims of violence because of their gender? Will their religion or ethnic origin target them for persecution?. . . . In the final analysis, human security is a child who did not die, a disease that did not spread, a job that was not cut, an ethnic tension that did not explode into violence, a dissident who was not silenced. Human security is not a concern with weapons—it is a concern with human life and dignity. (Ibid.)

The *Report* names seven main categories or components of human security. They are:

- economic security, which requires a basic income from 'productive and remunerative work';
- food security, which means that 'all people at all times have both physical and economic access to basic food';
- health security, especially for the world's poor;
- environmental security, defined as a healthy physical environment;
- personal security in the form of reduced personal threats from violent crime;
- community security, i.e., security through membership in a group (provided that the social norms and behavioural practices of the group do not threaten the physical safety of the individual); and
- political security so that people 'live in a society that honors their basic rights' (ibid., 25–33).

These different aspects of human security are mutually reinforcing; conversely, the denial of one component may have adverse implications for the achievement of other components. There are many different kinds of threats to human security, particularly when defined in such multi-dimensional terms. The UNDP identified six principal challenges while suggesting that the 'real threats to human security in the next century will arise more from the actions of millions of people than from aggression by a few nations.' Unchecked population growth (along with diminished prospects for development) was cited as one of the main threats to human security in the twenty-first century. This was seen as one of the principal sources of human poverty, migration, and environmental degradation—although there is causal feedback among these problems, they tend to exacerbate each other.

Second on the list were disparities in economic opportunities as a result of growing inequality between the richest 20 per cent of the world's population and the remaining 80 per cent whose incomes have fallen steadily over the past three decades. Third were migration pressures resulting from growing population and limited economic opportunities in many developing countries. Fourth was environmental degradation, including harmful gas emissions, greenhouse gases, deforestation and destruction of wetlands, and accelerated destruction of coastal marine habitats. Drug trafficking, particularly in narcotic drugs, was fifth on the list of threats. The *Report* noted that drug trafficking posed one of 'the most corrosive threats to human security' because over the past 20 years the 'narcotics industry had progressed from a small cottage enterprise to a highly organized multinational business' (ibid., 36). Finally, the sixth global threat was international terrorism. Although the *Report* observed that the number of incidents of terrorism was dropping, the number of casualties continued to remain high (well over 1,000 people per year) and the focus of terrorist activity was now global as opposed to being limited to one or two regions in the world.

Strategies and Instruments

In proposing a new concept of security based on an expansive understanding of the different threats to human security, the UNDP argued for a transition in the security agenda that would involve two basic changes: a shift away from territorial security to a much greater stress on people's security and 'from security through armaments to security through sustainable development' (ibid., 23). The *Report* suggested that there was a clear link between human security and a strategy of sustainable human development: 'It will not be possible for the community of nations to achieve any of its major goals—not peace, not environmental protection, not human rights, not democratization, not fertility reduction, not social integration—except in the context of sustainable development that leads to human security' (ibid., 1). At the same time, it argued that the two were not synonymous: 'it is important that human security not be equated with human development. Human development is . . . a process of widening the range of people's choice. Human security means that all people can exercise these choices safely and freely—and that they can be relatively confident that the opportunities they have today are not lost tomorrow' (ibid., 23). In other words, human security is the result, not the cause, of a successful development process and one that is attentive to equity and social justice considerations. But the scope of the new concept could hardly be wider, as it includes economic security, food security, health security, environmental security, personal security, community security, and political security. Moreover, the threats to these different aspects of human security, such as AIDS, terrorism, pollution, poverty, and environmental problems, are global in scope, transcending the borders of the nation-state.

The *Report* called for the implementation of an action plan that would redistribute global wealth so as to 'ensure that people have basic capabilities and opportunities, especially access to assets and to productive and remunerative work.' It also recognized the importance of developing preventive strategies to alleviate poverty, social injustice, and environmental degradation, which are the root causes of conflict. The *Report* also called for a review and redesign of 'today's framework of global institutions' so that they could tackle the challenges of human security 'within the framework of a paradigm of longer-term sustainable human development'.

The policy implications of the UNDP *Report* exceeded by far the reach of the organization and were explicitly framed as an agenda for the World Summit on Social Development, held in Copenhagen in 1995. That Summit, however, refrained from endorsing the entire human security agenda, reaching at most a consensus on the issue of the investment of the so-called peace dividend (UN, 1995). Even so, the hopes for realizing the goals of sustainable development were sidelined by the explosion of regional and domestic conflicts in the 1990s. The radical marginalization of military issues by the UNDP was challenged by a growing sense that global chaos and disorder were the real legacies of the Cold War. As a result, while recognizing the need for, and importance of, human security, the Commission on Global Governance (1995: 80) gave military issues a renewed emphasis in its diagnosis of the security situation:

> The most pressing security challenge of the twenty-first century [is] preserving and extending the progress made in security states against the threat of war while finding ways to safeguard people against domestic threats of brutalization and gross deprivation and ensuring the integrity and viability of the life-support systems on which all life depends.

Comparing the Three Different Conceptions of Human Security

The three different conceptions of human security—rights/rule-of-law, 'safety of peoples', and sustainable development—are marked by different understandings about what constitutes the main threat to human security (see Table 2.1). They also offer different recommendations about what kinds of instruments and strategies are required to promote human security, although many of these recommendations are based on a shared understanding about the importance of political and legal norms in changing social behaviours. However, the referent or object of 'security' in these three different definitions is the individual, and, to the extent that international order is viewed as a global public good, the means to achieving that order is seen in terms of the needs and interests of the individual rather than of the state.

Table 2.1 Three Views of Human Security

Conception of Human Security	Key Elements	Strategies and Instruments	Object of Security
Human rights/ rule of law	Basic personal rights, legal rights, political and civil rights	Sanctions, co-optation, shaming, prosecution and conviction (criminal tribunals and International Criminal Court)	Individuals
Safety of peoples (humanitarian)	Basic personal rights, including subsistence rights	Military intervention, humanitarian and emergency assistance, peacebuilding, conflict prevention	Individuals
Sustainable human development	Economic, social, and environmental rights	Redistributive measures that address inequalities in wealth and income between rich and poor, new participatory governance structures at subnational, national, and global levels	Individuals

Definition of Threats

The rights and rule-of-law conception of human security holds the main threat to human security to lie in the denial of basic rights and 'due process' and the absence of democratic systems of governance. The denial of minority rights, under certain conditions, also poses a threat to human security, hence the need to strengthen international norms and provisions regarding national self-determination. Human security is at risk when these rights are not formally acknowledged and judicial and political systems of accountability are weak. Threats are therefore defined in terms of the absence of critical norms and judicial and political instruments to protect and promote human security. When these institutions are lacking or are found to be woefully inadequate, the risk of social and political anarchy increases and with it the threat to individual rights and freedoms. This conception of human security has little to say about the content of the threats to human security except perhaps by implicitly endorsing the traditional liberal position that social and political anarchy represent the true 'state of nature' when there are no judicial and political remedies to restrain the natural passions of human beings.

In the humanitarian or 'safety of peoples' conception of human security, war itself is seen as the main threat to human security because of the moral distinction that is drawn between civilians or non-combatants and combatants. Whereas combatants who are professional soldiers have in some sense agreed to place themselves in harm's way, civilians or 'innocents' have not. The obligation to help civilians when they are injured or when their health and physical safety are at risk and to conduct warfare in such a way as not to expose innocents to unnecessary risks derives from this moral distinction.

During the Cold War, interstate conflict between the two superpowers was considered to be the main threat to human security. Public concerns about the morality of nuclear weapons and deterrence grew after the Cuban Missile Crisis, which threatened to bring the world to the brink of nuclear annihilation. Many felt that because a nuclear war could not be fought without inflicting massive civilian casualties, the threat to use nuclear weapons was neither credible nor morally defensible. With the easing of political tensions and the fall of the Berlin Wall, the threat of a major nuclear war receded. However, with the increasing frequency of armed conflict within states in the late 1980s and early 1990s, many consider the main threat to human security as originating in 'failed' or 'failing' states. As noted in a paper prepared by the Canadian Department of Foreign Affairs and International Trade:

> A growing number of armed conflicts are being fought within, rather than between states. The warring factions in these civil wars are often irregular forces with loose chains of command, frequently divided along ethnic or religious lines. Small arms are the weapon of choice and non-combatants account for eight out of ten casualties. Once considered merely 'collateral damage', civilians are being thrust into the epicentre of contemporary war. (DFAIT, 1999: 1)

The incidence and severity of such wars, however, has been on the decline since 1992, although 1998 saw a significant increase in the number of wars, suggesting that there is little ground for complacency.

In contrast to the above two definitions, the sustainable human development conception of human security offers a very broad understanding of the array of threats that jeopardize human survival and well-being. This definition moves along three distinct axes: (1) the definition extends to a large number of problems that have not been traditionally associated with the concept of security; (2) the new understanding of these threats marginalizes those of an exclusively military nature; (3) those threats considered to be the most relevant—such as environmental degradation and population growth—are considered in a global context such that the national interest itself is a diminishing point of reference.

Although the individual continues to remain at the centre of the moral frame of reference, the problem of justice is cast in social/distributive as opposed to 'just war' terms as in the humanitarian conception of human security. One of the main threats to human security is underdevelopment and the widening income gap between the world's richest countries and the world's poorest. Poverty alleviation is considered to be essential to addressing these inequalities.

These two conceptions of security are also based on rather different understandings about whether war should be treated as a cause or a consequence of underdevelopment. In the 'safety of peoples' framework, war—and civil conflict, in particular—is the main cause of human insecurity, whereas in the sustainable human development framework conflict is a symptom rather than a cause of insecurity. There is some convergence in the two positions to the extent that peacebuilding and conflict prevention strategies in the 'safety of peoples' approach attempt to address the underlying causes of conflict, which include socioeconomic causes. But the order of priorities is reversed in these two approaches. The 'safety of peoples' approach to human security emphasizes the importance of disarmament, demobilization, and reintegration of former combatants and of tackling these problems first, before addressing social and economic problems, on the grounds that there can be no sustainable development unless the local security environment is conducive to reconstruction. In contrast, the sustainable human development approach to human security argues that economic issues have to be dealt with very early on in the peace process. This is because peacebuilding activities cannot and should not be carried out in a social and economic vacuum. There is a corresponding need for donors to play a larger role in the negotiation process so that economic issues are dealt with in a realistic manner and resources can be devoted to planning and to building collaborative relationships (Ball, 1996b). The sustainable human development conception of human security is also premised on the view that the resources devoted to peacebuilding and the reconstruction of war-torn societies should not divert from the larger development enterprise. This is because poverty alleviation, environmental degradation, and unchecked population growth ultimately pose greater risks to human security than violent conflict, which itself is viewed as a symptom rather than a cause of human insecurity.

Strategies and Instruments

These three different approaches to human security also claim somewhat different understandings about what kinds of strategies and instruments are appropriate to advancing and promoting human security, particularly at the international level. The human rights/rule-of-law approach to human security operates at the level of international regimes and norms. Intercommunal conflict and civil violence typically are viewed in terms of a set of causal relationships in which the key variables are the denial of human rights, due process of law, and liberal pluralist forms of democracy. The governance challenge, therefore, is to create participatory governance structures, develop new social and legal norms, and establish democracy and the rule of law. International institutions have an important role to play in addressing this challenge by promulgating universally agreed-upon norms and actively promoting these norms within states. As noted above, the mechanisms or instruments in this process are sanctions, shaming, and co-optation. Various actors and organizations in civil society also have a role to play in this process by mobilizing public support, documenting human rights abuses, and generating much-needed publicity (domestic and international) to pressure those who are guilty of abusing and violating the rights of others. These strategies are interventionist, but intervention is typically of the normative as opposed to coercive or military variety (with the exception of sanctions, which may inflict real costs on the parties concerned).

The 'safety of peoples' approach to human security has witnessed an important evolution in its understanding about the strategies and modalities of intervention necessary to advance human security in conflict settings. During the Cold War, humanitarian interventions typically aspired towards political neutrality. It did not matter who the injured or suffering party was because it was assumed that anyone in distress was morally worthy of emergency assistance and treatment. Neutrality was also considered to be critical if aid and relief workers were to be able to work in conflict settings without hindrance from the warring parties. Recent years have seen a growing awareness by those involved in the provision of humanitarian assistance of the potential impact of such interventions on conflict processes and the ability of conflicting parties to wage war. Ongoing efforts at peacebuilding and conflict prevention are also premised on the recognition that humanitarian assistance and limited peacekeeping operations are not sufficient to consolidate the peace in societies where the social, political, administrative, and economic fabric have been destroyed by prolonged civil strife. Beyond keeping the peace, the list of tasks includes reconstructing civil society at the both the national and local levels; reintegrating displaced populations in the society and economy; redefining the role of the military and police forces in the maintenance of law and order; building communities and allowing them to survive by bridging the gap between emergency assistance and development; rebuilding micro enterprises and instituting macroeconomic reforms; and addressing the needs of particularly vulnerable groups in society, such as women and children. Such an agenda is highly interventionist and goes well beyond efforts to exercise normative influence, as in the case of the rights/rule-of-law approach to human security. However, intervention is generally limited to those societies where there is an ongoing conflict or where conflict has ended but there are appeals for external assistance.

In the sustainable development conception of human security the potential array of strategies and instruments required to promote human security is as vast as the wide array of potential and actual threats to human security (population growth, environmental degradation, income inequalities, etc.). According to this view, the military has little role to play in dealing with most of the problems associated with human security. Instead, the appropriate instruments to deal with these problems are the tools of human development, particularly those that address socio-economic inequalities. Moreover, given the prominence of global threats among the sources of human insecurity, nation-states will be unable to tackle them alone, hence the growing emphasis on multilateral mechanisms, including both institutions and initiatives. Finally, at all levels, civil society and its organizations are reserved a special role in the development and implementation of human security policies. They must gain access to the definition of security within their particular organization, and security must be the core preoccupation of their policies and the implementation of these policies. Multilateral institutions displace some of the work of states because the global nature of these threats makes it impossible to deal with them at the national level. However, the current structure of these institutions is called into question by the need to reform them, to provide them with additional resources, and, in some instances, to create new ones to tackle these global problems.

The Individual as the Object of Security

Although these three different perspectives on human security are marked by some important differences in terms of what they see as being the main threats to human security and the strategies and instruments that may be required to deal with these threats, they do share a common point of reference. The point of reference or 'object' of security is not the nation-state and its territory but individual people in their daily activities, wherever they live, and humanity as a collective body in which all individuals are members. Although there is a globalization in the context and the meaning of security under these three different definitions—albeit with different degrees of emphasis—there is a common focus on the personal necessities and insecurities of individual human beings. This personalization of security entails a recognition that the interests of individual human beings are distinct from, and might even conflict with, those of states. The politics of security, i.e., the debate about who decides which threats are the most important, stems directly from this conflict, but it also has important implications about how we should think about international politics. These implications are the subject of the next chapter, where we examine how the human security paradigm of international politics differs from traditional realism and liberalism.

Note

1. The doctrine of sovereign inviolability dates to the Peace of Augsburg in 1555, which formalized the principle of *cuius region, eius religio* (the ruler decides his country's religion). This was subsequently reaffirmed and modified in the Peace of Westphalia, which marked the end of the Thirty Years War.

Chapter 3

Human Security as a Global Public Good

In this chapter we turn to the question of whether the three contrasting views of human security, when taken together, offer a view of international politics fundamentally different from the established paradigms that inform much of international relations theory. We argue that the human security vision of international politics is very much at variance with traditional realism and the neo-realist paradigm of international politics. The human security vision has considerably more in common with liberalism, and many of its assumptions, as suggested in Chapter 1, lie in liberal democratic theory. Even so, certain aspects of the human security vision also take their cue from socialist theories of international politics. This is especially true of the sustainable human development conception of human security, which puts a great deal of emphasis on social justice and the distributive aspects of international politics. To explain how the 'theory' of human security differs from other theories or paradigms of international politics, we will examine the concept in terms of public goods, which offers a useful perspective on the broader theoretical and policy implications of human security.

The Global Reach of Human Security

In traditional liberal democratic theories of the state, property rights, safety, and security are public goods provided by non-market mechanisms, usually the state. For example, the ultimate responsibility for maintaining law and order in domestic civil society rests with the state, which provides this public good. Early liberal theorists like Thomas Hobbes recognized that allowing private citizens to look after their own security was a recipe for social and political anarchy. Likewise, the various domestic legal institutions and instruments of the state could only in a real sense guarantee property rights. The large body of law that has developed in the area of contracts, for example, constitutes a kind of public good (see Olson, 1971). The legal rules and instruments of contract law not only guarantee reciprocity, but also permit private transactions to take place in an orderly and businesslike manner. As noted by Kaul, Grunberg, and Stern, 'Public goods are recognized as having benefits that cannot easily be confined to a single "buyer" (or set of "buyers"). Yet, once they are provided, many can enjoy them for free. Street names for example.

A clean environment is another. Without a mechanism for collective action, these goods can be underproduced' (Kaul et al., 1999b: xx).

Public goods can be broken into two main categories: so-called 'pure' public goods and joint goods (see Figure 3.1). Pure public goods have two main characteristics, jointness and non-excludability. Pure public goods are those whose benefits are consumed by all members of a community as soon as any one member produces them. Relevant examples of the polar case of pure public goods are hard to find but one is knowledge, a public intermediate input into the production function of all firms. Knowledge is both a non-rivalrous and non-excludable good (my consumption of knowledge does not diminish yours). But common property resources, e.g., the commons, are rivalrous even though they may be non-excludable (my excessive consumption or use of the commons will diminish your consumption and the consumption of others).

Figure 3.1 International Public Goods: Excludability and Jointness

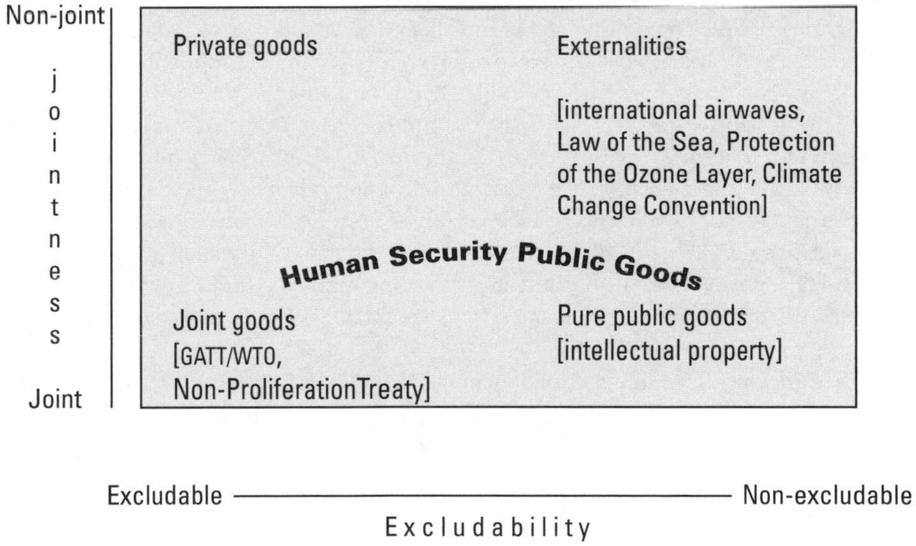

Joint or 'club goods' are characterized by their jointness and excludability. Since the benefits from club goods are excludable, normally through the price mechanism, they can be provided through the private sector, e.g., cable and pay television, movie theatres, recreational facilities. Club goods, by definition, can be extended or provided to somebody else without raising marginal costs. When jointness extends to the international level but benefits remain excludable, the optimal club size is international (Keohane, 1984).

In essence, the three different visions of human security presented in Chapter 2 all claim that human security (defined in terms of basic human liberties, certain political and civil rights, and equity and social justice) is a global public good, i.e., it should reach across borders to *all* peoples regardless of their ethnic or national origins, socio-economic status, religious beliefs, or political persuasions. And the marginal costs of extending the benefits of human security diminish once this good is created. However, given the current state of affairs, human security is very much an underprovided public good. Many states are their citizens' own worst enemy. Others suffer incapacities of various kinds (e.g., administrative, fiscal) and/or are racked by conflict. To the extent that human security is enjoyed as an international public good it is one that bears the hallmark of a club good, that is, its benefits are confined in large measure to citizens in rich democracies; some people in poor countries also are secure, but they are a distinct minority.

There are different explanations as to why human security is an underprovided public good. Whereas some scholars argue that the main sources of the human security deficit lie in the domestic and political failures of states, others argue that the sources of this deficit lie in the distributive failures of markets that perpetuate inequalities within and among states and that may, in some circumstances, exacerbate social and political tensions. According to the sustainable human development view of human security, there is need to change not just the political environment in which human security can be delivered but the economic environment as well. This broader view of human security is admittedly controversial, and some skeptics doubt whether there are explicit causal connections between socio-economic inequalities—especially at the global level—and conflicts within states and whether redistributive measures of the kind contemplated by human security advocates are achievable. However, an important and growing body of literature suggests that market and state failures do intersect and interact in significant ways that affect human security, as we see below.

Within the burgeoning human security literature, there is also an important debate about which are the most efficient, effective, and 'just' ways of dividing up the fixed (as opposed to marginal) costs not only of providing human security public goods, but also of creating new institutions that will themselves be the human security public good providers. Some argue that hegemonic actors (principally the United States) are the most efficient public goods providers because only they have the resources (economic and military) to provide these goods and discipline free riders and renegades. Others argue that international institutions are more effective because they have greater political legitimacy and that efficiency is not the only factor in the provision of these public goods. Still others argue that non-governmental actors are the most effective and legitimate providers of human security public goods because they are most sensitive to the different local conditions and to the needs of peoples for whom such goods ultimately are provided. The final section of this chapter examines these arguments.

Sources of Market and Political Failure in the Human Security Deficit

In exploring differences among the rights/rule-of-law, 'safety of peoples', and sustainable development approaches about the sources of market or political failure that contribute to the human security deficit, it is useful to contrast these views with more traditional liberal arguments about the demand for international institutions. This will help us understand why proponents of human security believe that it is an underprovided public good. We will begin our discussion with the maximalist definition or conception of human security—the sustainable human development conception—because it is, in some respects, the most controversial of the three.

Market Failures and the Problem of Global Equity

In classical liberal economics, as noted by Rao, 'global order and efficiency can be secured by the market system so long as nation states do not interfere in crossborder transactions among agents except to enforce property and contractual rights' (Rao, 1999: 74). However, this minimalist view of international governance is challenged in more recent neo-liberal accounts about the need and demand for international institutions. In much of the work of neo-liberal international relations scholars, international institutions or 'regimes' (defined as norms, rules, and principles of behaviour around which actors' expectations can converge) are seen as 'correctives' or institutional responses to a wide variety of international market or state-induced failures (Keohane, 1983, 1995; Yarborough and Yarborough, 1999). Where such failures exist, neo-liberal theorists recognize that some sort of governance response, either by private actors and/or by states, may be required to facilitate co-operation and provide the missing or underprovided public good(s). Governance structures in the form of international regimes are typically seen as devices through which political and economic actors can organize and manage their interdependencies (Schnieberg and Hollingsworth, 1988; Williamson, 1975).

In looking to the formation of international regimes and institutions, various scholars have identified different sources or 'causes' of market failure (for a more complete discussion, see Eden and Hampson, 1997). Some scholars emphasize the role of international transaction costs to explain the demand for international institutions, arguing that in an imperfect world uncertainty and a lack of information generate their own inefficiencies and diseconomies. International regimes are useful, therefore, when (1) a clear legal framework establishing liability is missing, (2) the market for information is imperfect, and (3) there are positive transaction costs. Regimes can be designed to reduce the effects of uncertainty (insurance regimes) and to create internal and environmental regularities, thereby reducing the incentives for opportunistic behaviour (control regimes) (Keohane, 1983). The notion of transaction costs focuses on the costs involved in market-making under uncertainty; state international governance structures or regimes can function as a way to improve market-making by reducing transaction costs (Casson, 1982). For example, the creation of international standards or the harmonization of national standards through the GATT/WTO and various bilateral treaties has helped to reduce transaction costs when national tax and tariff barriers have acted as barriers to international trade. Similarly, the elimination of border controls in the European Union has reduced interregional transaction costs.

Others have focused on structural failures involving macroeconomic instabilities to explain the demand for international institutions and new kinds of international governance arrangements. John Maynard Keynes was the first to argue that capitalist economies could get stuck in an underemployment equilibrium, and since the 1940s most developed market economies have made a formal commitment towards providing full employment, stable prices, and economic growth to their citizens. Clearly, domestic state governance structures are necessary to achieve these internal domestic goals, but domestic macroeconomic policies neither insulate economies from external shocks nor protect neighbouring economies from macroeconomic spillovers. The International Monetary Fund and World Bank were formed as part of the Bretton Woods monetary regime to cushion and control the effects of macroeconomic policies. As John Ruggie points out, under the 'compromise of embedded liberalism' in Bretton Woods, nation-states were supposed to pursue Keynesian macroeconomic policies internally without disrupting international stability (Gilpin, 1987; Ruggie, 1983). With its collapse, the Bretton Woods system has been replaced by an international monetary regime that consists of regional clubs (the European Monetary System and the G-7), unregulated markets (the Eurodollar market), old international organizations (the IMF and World Bank), and the Bank for International Settlements, which acts as the central bankers' bank, particularly for European banks (Andrews, 1994; Goodman, 1992; Goodman and Pauly, 1993).

Still others have focused on market failures involving externalities (defined as the unintended and uncompensated by-products arising out of transactions among private agents, households, and/or firms, i.e., so-called third-party effects) to explain the demand for international institutions and regimes. The externality problem is perhaps most severe in the case of common property resources: the 'tragedy of the commons'. An efficient property rights structure normally has four characteristics: universality (all resources are privately owned), exclusivity (no spillovers), transferability, and enforceability (Tietenberg, 1984). In the case of most externalities, the market failure lies in the exclusivity characteristic. However, for common property resources the universality characteristic also is not met. As a result, these resources tend to be overexploited, their scarcity rent dissipated, and the net benefit from these resources to society competed down to zero (Cowhey, 1990; Krasner, 1991; Hampson, 1995).

Sustainable human development proponents of human security argue that what is missing from most current international economic governance arrangements as well as from abstract arguments about why such institutions are needed— whether they take the form of formal international regimes or some other kinds of institutional form—are mechanisms and instruments that address the serious distributional inequities that arise from the operations of the global markets and the forces of globalization. They argue that most existing international institutions in the economic realm are directed at addressing efficiency and stability problems as noted by neo-liberal scholars. However, these institutions are insufficiently attuned to the distributional and social justice aspects of global and individual welfare. As Rao explains, 'the liberal position . . . ignores the role that inequality (or equality) may play in the construction of a political order. Equity and justice are neither necessary prerequisites nor necessary consequences of the order produced. . . . In such a world equity is neither a public good nor necessary for the provision of "proper" public goods' (Rao, 1999: 75).

The sustainable human development school argues that equity should be considered as a global public good and that equity and social justice must play a key role in international order. Although some attention has been given over the years to income differences between the rich, developed market economies and the poor, less-developed countries (LDCs), these advocates argue that many of these efforts have been largely ineffective. Foreign aid programs under the World Bank, LDC trade preferences in the GATT and the Lomé Conventions, and even debt rescheduling schemes through the World Bank, the Paris Club, and the Baker and Brady plans—all of which at one level constitute expressions of state concerns with income distribution—have failed to address the real economic vulnerabilities experienced by the world's poor. Thus, one study that examines the impact of the global political economy on development and underdevelopment argues that '[p]overty is the common denominator of economic insecurity' and the current 'paradox is that poverty is spreading in the most prosperous age in human history.' This is especially true in Africa, which has, for the most part, been bypassed by the forces of globalization and where '[b]etween one-half and two-thirds of the African population lives in a state of permanent destitution' (Nef, 1995: 40).

In the case of international markets, the sustainable development school argues that most are not competitive but also are dominated by small numbers of multinational enterprises that enjoy monopoly power. Large multinationals can create international market imperfections through monopoly pricing, market segmentation, the erection of barriers to entry, the truncation of subsidies, and the exertion of bargaining power over small countries, especially developing economies. States have also exacerbated the problem through strategic trade policies, the creation of national champions, and the competitive devaluation of currencies. Some have even formed domestic cartels as methods of shifting the terms of trade in favour of domestic producers. These non-competitive markets have both economic and political origins. However, international regimes that could be used to reduce and control multinational enterprise, such as tax treaties, foreign direct investment regimes, or voluntary codes of conduct (such as the United Nations code) have not been terribly effective and have done little to level the economic playing field between rich and poor countries.

The absence of adequate international institutional frameworks and mechanisms to provide equity and social justice is reflected not only in what is seen as a 'profligate per capita use of natural resources by industrial countries', but also the 'uncoordinated growth of exports from poor countries and from the protectionism of rich countries' and a financial system whose 'externalities can be grossly inequitable both domestically and internationally' (Rao, 1999: 72–3). Many argue that there is a relationship among deteriorating terms of trade, debt, and underdevelopment, which together have depressed living standards in many developing countries while also reducing their capacity to import. Further, there is growing recognition that worsening levels of health and epidemic diseases such as AIDS, which are ravaging many countries in the developing world, are partially rooted in the workings of the global economy and externally imposed structural adjustment policies that have directly contributed to a deterioration in public health systems and overall living standards (Leon and Walt, 2001). However, new concepts of distributive justice will only be achieved, argues Amartya Sen, when 'national particularism'—justice conceived exclusively in national terms and within a national policy context—gives way to more plural affiliations involving direct '*interpersonal* sympathies and solidarities across borders'. Such affiliations must have 'a cogency that can substantially transcend national particularism of the estranged polities' such that fairness and distribution are seen in more global but nonetheless interpersonal terms (Sen, 1999: 120). As Sen further notes, 'The freedom-efficiency of the market mechanism, on the one hand, and the seriousness of freedom-inequality problems, on the other hand, are worth considering simultaneously. The equity problems have to be addressed, especially in dealing with serious deprivations and poverty' (Sen, 2000: 119–20).

This concern with social justice and distribution is certainly not new in international relations. It has a distinguished pedigree dating back to the writings of Karl Marx, Lenin, and other socialists who focused on the material conditions of the lives of workers and the downtrodden. These theorists highlighted the importance of socio-economic factors in international relations in a way that distinguished them from mercantilists, realists, and even liberal thinkers. They provided important insights on the inequalities of the world's political economy, which, they argued, was a world defined by radically unequal economic terms (Doyle, 1997: 315–20).

What distinguishes the sustainable human development approach to human security from these earlier approaches to international poilitics is its focus on individual—as opposed to class-based—needs and its attention to equity considerations in market-based approaches to deal with poverty, resource scarcities (such as famine), and even problems like global environmental degradation (Sen, 1981; UNDP, 1994). Whereas Marx and his fellow socialists called for wholesale social and political revolution to achieve a fairer and more equitable distribution of wealth, human security proponents of the sustainable human development school believe that market reforms (not command economies) are the answer, but that such reforms will necessarily entail a major restructuring of global financial and economic institutions and the development of new distributive mechanisms and rules that are much more attentive to the needs, concerns, and choices of the world's poor than are existing institutions. Therefore, human development proponents stress institutional reform (as opposed to class-based revolution) and the development of participatory governance structures that give people real choices at the subnational, national, and international levels.

Although this particular conception of human security seeks to redefine the very nature of 'global' public goods by arguing that equity is (or should be) reclassified as a public good, another strand in this literature posits a direct link between socio-economic inequality and the delivery of public goods of the more traditional law-and-order variety. According to this view, 'horizontal inequalities' in a society increase the potential for violent civil conflict (i.e., the breakdown of law and order). Horizontal inequalities refer to inequalities among groups in their political, economic, and social dimensions. Such inequalities provide the basis for intergroup animosity and contribute to group mobilization processes around such cultural characteristics as ethnicity and religion.

According to Stewart, poverty and civil conflict have a tendency to feed on each other: eight of the 10 countries that scored lowest on the United National Development Program's human development index rating, and eight out of 10 countries with the lowest GNP per capita, have experienced civil wars in the recent past. Stewart also points out that about half of low-income countries have been subject to major political violence. Accordingly, '[c]ausality works both ways, as low incomes lead to conditions which are conducive to violence. But the evidence suggests that major civil wars are associated with markedly worse performance in economic growth, food production per capita and human indicators, such as infant mortality rates, school enrolment, and so on.' Thus, 'any comprehensive strategy to tackle poverty must give the prevention of conflict a central place. Policies to limit excessive horizontal inequalities are needed in all vulnerable countries' (Stewart, 2001; Stewart and FitzGerald, 2001).

The clear implication of this line of argument is that it is important to change the environment in which public goods, such as law and order, are produced by directly addressing socio-economic inequalities within and across societies, recognizing that there are important feedback effects between poverty and violence. This line of argument also resonates with some of the recent scholarly and policy literature on environmental change, which asserts that as competition for scarce 'renewable resources' (e.g., water) grows, so too does the potential for violence. Although the cause-effect link between scarcity and violent conflict is generally considered to be indirect, these analysts argue that such influences cannot be ignored in understanding why human security is threatened in some settings (see Homer-Dixon, 2000; Gleditsch, 2001).

Political Failures: International Anarchy versus State Failure

Whereas sustainable development proponents of human security tend to focus on distributional 'failures' in the international system to explain why human security is an underprovided public good (at least in terms of its equity and social justice components), others (the rights/rule-of-law and 'safety of peoples' adherents) argue that the significant failures are primarily *political* as opposed to economic or market-based. But, here again, there are some important differences between the human security view and traditional realist and liberal positions about what the main political 'failures' are in explaining why human security is an underprovided public good in international relations.

It has long been recognized that the anarchic structure of the international system may create a political demand for various international governance arrangements. This has frequently been referred to as the 'security dilemma', rooted in the absence of supranational authority in international politics and the fact that individual states are forced to provide for their own survival and welfare (Jervis, 1978, 1983; Waltz, 1979). Moreover, in the process of providing for their own security through various military measures, states may set in motion an escalatory dynamic as they seek to provide for their own security, but also to achieve a relative advantage over the military capabilities of other states (Solingen, 1994). This can lead to arms races and technological competition that can exacerbate political tensions and further heighten security problems (Downs et al., 1986).

Much of the debate between 'realist' and 'liberal' international relations scholars is not so much about the causes of international conflict per se. Both schools more or less accept the proposition that international anarchy is at the root of the problem, although they have somewhat different understandings about the meaning and content of 'anarchy' (see Milner, 1993). They differ about the kinds of institutional remedies that can best address the security dilemma (see Axelrod and Keohane, 1993). Realists argue that because the distribution of state power and resources (military and economic) generally tends to be unequal in the international system, it may be necessary for states to resort to balancing (or bandwagoning) strategies to maintain order and stability in the system (Waltz, 1979). Most balancing or bandwagoning strategies involve the creation of formal (or informal) military alliances as correctives to the power of large and powerful—especially preponderant—states in the international system (Walt, 1987). In the realist paradigm the way to achieve international order is through military alliances that can provide for a stable balance of power. Realists disagree as to whether a bipolar or multipolar system of alliances is more conducive to stability. Some realists also argue that technology has had an important impact on international order. In particular, they argue that nuclear weapons and strategies of nuclear deterrence contributed to international stability, especially during the Cold War (Mearsheimer, 1994).

Whereas realists favour alliances and military solutions to achieve international order, liberals believe that international institutions promote international peace and security and counter the anarchical tendencies of a state-based, international system. The 'collective security' viewpoint (which can be traced back to Woodrow Wilson and the League of Nations) stresses the contribution of international institutions over the domestic (i.e., democratic) character of states to achieve international order (Kupchan and Kupchan, 1991). The principle of collective security is premised on the assumption that sovereign states have an interest in maintaining international order and that international institutions can provide this public good through mechanisms that allow the members of the international community to take action against states that threaten the existing order. Unlike realists, who

believe that alliances are the best protection against external threats, liberal inter-
nationalists believe that international institutions provide the best form of protection insofar as they provide mechanisms for galvanizing the international
community against certain or would-be aggressors.

In the 'liberal' variant of the 'democratic peace' (which dates back to the writings of Immanuel Kant) non-democratic states pose the greatest threat to international peace and security in an anarchic international system (see Doyle, 1997;
Russett, 1993; Mansfield and Snyder, 1995). This is because relations between and
among democratic states will be inherently peaceful, being informed by democratic principles and respect for the rule of law. Authoritarian and autocratic regimes
are more likely to resort to aggressive behaviour and to threaten their neighbours
because they do not abide by these same democratic norms. Democratic states may
well have to defend themselves by going to war against these states, but they will
do so reluctantly. As Kant argued, their best defence is to establish a peaceful and
defensive democratic confederation.

Realists argue that the logic of collective action and the corrosive impact of
national self-interest tend to undermine the efficacy of universal, collective security
institutions. They point to the failure of the League of Nations and the difficulties
experienced by the United Nations (especially during the Cold War) in taking collective action as cases in point. However, some liberal thinkers argue that in the absence
of workable collective security arrangements, more modest institutional schemes can
be devised to curb the more pernicious aspects of the security dilemma. Arms control
regimes and confidence-building measures represent one kind of international governance response to the security dilemma of nation-states in an anarchical world. But it
is important to note that these regimes represent only one governance option in a
variety of possible responses (Price, 1995). The escalatory dynamics of the security
dilemma 'can [also] be checked by unilateral measures designed to reduce critical
uncertainties for the other side regarding its own actions' (George et al., 1988: 671).

Although realists and liberals have fundamentally different views about the
utility and efficacy of international institutions, they nonetheless share the view
that the central challenge to international peace and security originates in the
structure of the international system (see Keohane and Martin, 1995; Ruggie,
1995: Mearsheimer, 1995). Some states may harbour imperialist ambitions and
aspire towards systemic hegemony. Others may seek to defend their hegemonic
status by quashing their rivals. Still others may feel threatened by their neighbours
and look for allies to defend themselves against impending attack. Whatever the
motivation or reason, states themselves are the root of the problem, and as long as
we continue to live in an anarchic world comprised of nation-states the threat to
international order will never be eliminated.

In the rights/rule-of-law and humanitarian conceptions of human security, the
principal threats to international peace and security come 'from below' in the denial
of human security to the citizens in one or more states as a result of civil conflict,
or from strife within states, or from transnational economic forces that have marginalized certain groups in the world economy. International anarchy and the global

'system of states' do not pose the main threat to international peace and security; rather, the denial of fundamental individual liberties, rights, and socio-economic needs within states is the contemporary source of conflict. Thus, in the human security paradigm the problem of international order is redefined and shifted downward from the systemic (i.e., international) to the subsystemic (i.e., intrastate) level.

Proponents of human security argue that the nature of international conflict has fundamentally changed. They point to the fact that most of the wars in the second half of the twentieth century have been wars within states (Sollenberg et al., 1999), which are the result of ethnic, religious, or horizontal inequalities (i.e., the inequitable distribution of wealth and income among different groups within society), and not interstate wars. These conflicts are fought not by regular armies but between militias, armed civilians, guerrillas, and ethnic groups. These groups have been able to arm themselves with weapons that they obtain through the large international market for small arms.

During the Cold War, the two superpowers were all too willing to intervene in these conflicts. They helped arm and train rival factions and tried to manipulate the parties to expand their various spheres of influence. With the end of the Cold War, the superpowers withdrew from many of these conflicts and, perhaps as a direct consequence, the number of wars has actually declined since the late 1980s, as have the number of war-related deaths (Gurr et al., 2000). Nevertheless, as Ruben Mendez points out, these intrastate conflicts have generated 'massive negative externalities'. He further notes that '[a]t the end of 1997 there were more than 22 million refugees and displaced persons. This figure does not include movements of emigrants seeking to escape poor and deteriorating economic conditions.' As a result of their externalities and the consequences of globalization, such 'wars can no longer be considered private, national affairs. They are matters of concern to the entire world community' (Mendez, 1999: 396).

While some realists are prepared to concede that the nature of international conflict has changed with the end of the Cold War, they also argue that the dynamics of ethnic and communitarian conflicts are not all that different from the dynamics of interstate relations in an anarchic international system. Not only do ethnic communities experience the same kind of security dilemma as states when the domestic political order breaks down as a result of state failure, but the same kind of offence–defence escalatory spiral can occur as ethnic groups misinterpret the strategic intentions of other groups, thus intensifying the pressure to raise mass armies (Posen, 1993). Furthermore, the risks of war become greater as different nationalities become more densely intermingled with each other, populations become stateless, and borders are seen by the parties to the conflict as illegitimate and indefensible. If the boundaries of emerging states are compatible with ethnic boundaries, the risks of war will be correspondingly lower (Van Evera, 1994).

For these realists, the use of force and the balance of power play a central role in the resolution of ethnic and intercommunal disputes (Kaufmann, 1996). If ethnic groups are not to annihilate each other in their struggle for supremacy and control of the state, particularly if one side is militarily stronger than the other(s), then a new balance of forces has to be created, either by denying arms and resources to the stronger side or by providing arms and resources to the weaker side to compensate for its militarily inferior position (or some combination of the two). In some instances, direct military intervention by outside third parties may also be warranted to redress the balance and/or defend the weaker party.

Although the use of force and balance of power are considered pivotal to the resolution of ethnic and intercommunal disputes for these realists, the incentives for great powers to intervene in such conflicts are limited. According to these realists, relatively few situations justify the costs associated with military intervention, and such interventions should be limited to those conflicts that not only threaten to spill across interstate borders but also pose a direct threat to international peace and security (Haass, 1996; Luttwak, 1999; Nye, 1999).

Proponents of human security argue that force may have to be used to defend human rights and other human security values when they are threatened, even if international peace and security are not directly threatened. However, in contrast to realism (or its modified, post-Cold War variants), human security approaches see ethnic and communal conflicts less in terms of strategic security dilemmas and more in terms of a set of causal relationships in which the key variables are the denial of human rights, due process of law, and liberal pluralist forms of democracy. As Paul LaRose-Edwards argues, 'fear of [human rights] violations engenders self-defense and creates the security dilemma that drives escalation' (LaRose-Edwards, 1996: 10). Civic intolerance in the form of the denial of minority and communal and religious rights may also be a major cause of conflict (Little, 1996).

This particular view of human security stresses the rule of law and liberal norms as key ingredients in the establishment of a 'just' political order both domestically and internationally. Accordingly, it has its own unique view of the kinds of intervention strategies that may be required to contribute to a peaceful political order. In contrast to realism—which sees a role for force and the balance of power in the management of communal or ethnic conflict—humanitarian and rights/rule-of-law approaches to human security see the challenges of peacebuilding and third-party involvement largely in terms of the creation of participatory governance structures, the development of new social norms, and the establishment of the rule of law and democracy. Thus, in arguing that 'failed' or 'failing' states are the principal source of anarchy in contemporary international politics, these human security advocates also look to very different kinds of institutional responses and mechanisms for addressing these kinds of 'political failures'.

Unlike Kant, who was essentially non-interventionist when it came to promoting democracy and human rights in those states where such institutions were lacking, the proponents of the human security paradigm are much more inclined to be proactive and to favour interventionist approaches to defend and secure human rights, broader human security needs, and democracy. Many liberal thinkers other than Kant, of course, have entertained arguments about intervening with military instruments to defend democracy, human rights, and other human security values when they are threatened (see Smith, 1999). Even so, there is considerable disquiet in these debates about when intervention is desirable or the conditions under which force and other instruments of intervention should be used (see Hoffmann, 1998: 70–88). In the human security view of international politics, however, most of these reservations disappear and intervention, including that involving the use of force, is approved because human security is privileged over international order as a basic public good. When basic human security values are threatened, the presumption is that intervening will defend and promote this public good even it means risking international order and 'violating' the sovereignty of individual states in the process.

Providing for Human Security

In the human security approach to international relations, although international order is a desirable public good, *order* will not be achieved until basic human security needs are largely fulfilled. In this respect, the content of international order does matter and as long as the world is filled with 'failed' or 'failing' states where public institutions, governance, and the physical, political, and economic security of citizens are at risk or directly threatened, there is no real prospect for 'order' in the international system. The absence of interstate conflict in the international system—a condition that would presumably satisfy most realists and liberals and be considered a sign of health and stability in international politics—is not sufficient for advocates of human security. It may simply mask deeper problems at the intrastate or subsystemic levels. Genuine order will only be achieved when the majority of the world's human security needs are met. This underscores the point that well-founded order can contribute to human security and that there are reciprocal effects of meeting the human security needs of peoples and providing for a *just* international order.

However, if human security in all of its various dimensions is an underprovided public good, then which international institutions, mechanisms, and actors are best equipped to provide it and to help address these different kinds of political and market failures that are experienced at both the national and international levels? As we see in the discussion that follows, different arguments are advanced about how best to divide up the fixed (or up-front) costs of providing human security public goods. Some argue that states are ultimately the most efficient and capable providers of human security public goods. Others argue that these goods are best provided through international institutions. Still others argue that non-state actors, i.e., non-governmental organizations and various elements of civil society, are the preferred human security public goods providers not simply on grounds of efficiency but also on grounds of equity and social and political accountability. Although there tends to be general agreement that there are diminishing marginal costs of extending the benefits of human security public goods at the global level once these goods are created or provided, there is widespread disagreement about how best to absorb the fixed costs of creating these goods and what other values are involved in allocating these costs.

Traditional Realist and Liberal Views of Public Good Providers

There are three general schools of thought about how best to provide international public goods in the international relations literature (see Table 3.1). In the classical liberal framework, formal international organizations and institutions are the preferred instruments of collective management for providing international public goods, including international peace and security, exemplified in the League of Nations and the United Nations. In neo-liberal theories of international politics, formal international organizations are the preferred instruments for allowing states to overcome collective action dilemmas and market failures associated with rising transaction costs and poorly defined property rights (Keohane, 1983, 1984). The function of these institutions is to allow states to pursue strategies of reciprocity and to operate efficiently by 'providing information about others' preferences, intentions, behavior, standards of behavior, and causal knowledge' (Martin, 1999: 55). International organizations can also successfully address market failures of the equity and distributional kind by addressing the strategic dilemmas that arise when 'losers' exaggerate their losses/costs in order to seek greater levels of compensation and 'winners' seek to minimize their gains in order to avoid compensation. In these situations, international organizations can 'provide expert analyses of the claims of losers for compensation—say, by evaluating the extent of economic losses from participation in international agreements.' They can also 'set standards for contributions to the provision pools and publicize information about states that fall short of their obligations' (ibid., 58).

Table 3.1 Contrasting Views of Market and Political Failures and Public Good Providers

International Relations Paradigm	Type of Market/ Political Failure	Provider of Public Good
Liberalism	Systemic efficiency failures (transaction costs, uncertainty, macroeconomic instabilities, externalities)	International institutions and private (non-state) actors
Realism	Systemic political failure, i.e., international anarchy	Hegemonic leaders or 'minilateral' clubs
Human Security		
Sustainable human development conception	Equity and distributive failures at systemic and subsystemic levels	Contested view of human security public goods providers: International organizations/institutions versus states versus private/non-state actors
Human rights/rule-of-law conception and 'safety of peoples' conception	Subsystemic failure (failed or failing states)	

According to liberals, international organizations are best equipped to provide international public goods because they also enjoy political legitimacy—they have formal charters and their membership is comprised of states that are the dominant actors in the international system. International organizations also have the capacity to mobilize political and financial resources—resources that may be vital to the provision of certain kinds of public goods. International organizations can also collect, analyse, and disseminate information that may be critical to this purpose and can generate collective action to attain or protect certain public goods. International organizations also enjoy a kind of normative power that comes with their political legitimacy: they can articulate and promulgate new norms and standards of behaviour and thinking that may be essential to the development and acceptance of new rules by their members.

The second school of thought—the realist—has a different view about which actors are best able to provide international public goods. The classic realist position is that such goods can only be provided by a hegemonic leader who can, if and when necessary, punish and coerce those who threaten to defect from co-operative solutions or who free ride, a leader who can offer or withhold the necessary side-payments to get others to join in the regime. Others argue that hegemons are not necessary to the creation, maintenance, and continuance of international regimes that deliver public goods (Keohane, 1984; Snidal, 1985). Minilateral leadership by a group of states (usually great powers) provides an alternative solution to achieving co-operation and delivering public goods in quantity (Kahler, 1993). Such clubs provide rewards to their members in the form of direct benefits as well as enforceable penalties for non-compliant or recalcitrant behaviour even though their membership may expand later on in response to political pressures from within and without from non-members who wish to join the club. Given that all co-operative ventures are subject to strong and weak cheating pressures, a fairly high degree of trust and goodwill may be required at the outset to ensure that such ventures do not fail (Buckley and Casson, 1988).

A third school of thought argues that private actors can provide public goods, obviating the need for hegemonic leadership or formal institutions. It has long been recognized by economists that private firms can develop their own internal governance structures to compensate for different kinds of market failure. Such self-regulating governance structures range from low-control structures (vertically and horizontally integrated firms) to high-control structures such as trade associations and so-called 'peak' associations designed to 'promote and protect common interests by ordering, managing, and stabilizing both the relations within the industry as well as the relations between industry members and those whose strategies and activities can decisively affect the industry's fortunes' (Schnieberg and Hollingsworth, 1988: 4). In the area of environmental management, as noted by Elinor Ostrom, there is also sufficient theoretical and empirical evidence to demonstrate that many common-pool resource problems are solved by private individuals (or groups of private actors) developing co-operative norms and rules of behaviour on their own without the imposition of solutions by an external actor. Many of these institutions are neither purely private (i.e., market-based) nor state-based. Rather, they reflect a mixture of private-like and public-like institutions (Ostrom, 1990).

In international relations, similar kinds of theoretical arguments are advanced to argue that non-governmental organizations and various transnational actors can also provide public goods. For example, the work on 'epistemic communities' in the area of international environmental policy stresses the importance of the scientific community in generating and distributing a global public good, specifically, scientific knowledge about a wide variety of complex environmental problems ranging from transboundary air pollution to global warming, that has served as the basis for collective action (E. Haas, 1990; P. Haas, 1989, 1996). In the area of human rights, non-governmental organizations, such as Amnesty International, also are identified as playing important roles both as information providers of human rights abuses and practices in a wide range of different countries and in mobilizing public support and developing advocacy campaigns to change government policies and human rights practices (Forsythe, 1993; Korey, 1998: Donnelly, 1993).

The Human Security Debate about Public Good Providers

Among proponents of human security there is considerable disquiet about the ability of formal international organizations—the United Nations, in particular—to provide for human security in its various dimensions. They argue that international organizations and formal, intergovernmental institutions are unable to provide for human security for a variety of reasons. (1) They are paralysed or hamstrung by conflicts of interest among their most powerful (typically, state) members. (2) Many suffer from the corrosive 'logic' of collective action to which there are no effective or readily available institutional remedies. (3) Financial and other resourcing problems have effectively thwarted or hindered the ability of these organizations to provide these public goods. (4) Formal institutional and organizational mandates cannot readily be modified or changed to address the human security agenda and provide for this public good. (5) Many international organizations suffer from a lack of political leadership at the top and bureaucratic inertia or opposition from below, which has stifled any real movement or progress in meeting human security needs.

Although most human security advocates agree that existing international organizations and institutions are unable to provide this public good effectively, there are significant differences of opinion about what constitute the best or preferred alternatives—differences that largely mirror the more general debate between realists and liberals about which international actors or institutions are best able to deliver international public goods. For the purposes of simplification, and to isolate core assumptions and beliefs, the different positions in the ongoing debate about which actors and institutions are best able to promote human security may be characterized as follows (also see Table 3.2).

Table 3.2 Four Views of Human Security Public Good Providers

Approach to Human Security	Human Security Public Good Provider
Cosmopolitan	Non-governmental organizations, civil society, and social movements
Institutionalist	Reformed international organizations and institutions
Minilateralist	Hegemonic leader (US) and its allies
Middle-power multilateralist	Coalitions of the like-minded (middle powers and their civil society 'partners')

COSMOPOLITANS

The cosmopolitan school of thought argues that civil society, especially non-governmental organizations, and broadly based social movements that have been in a real sense empowered by modern communications technologies and that transcend national boundaries are the new champions of human security and providers of this public good. According to the cosmopolitan viewpoint, non–state actors are playing a key role in setting the international agenda by effectively using a wide range of media (television, radio, the Internet) to push their concerns onto that agenda and by lobbying and persuading governments to adopt new courses of action. They are also playing an important role in educating citizenry and facilitating social learning and, most importantly, in the promulgation of new human security norms through their various methods of information exchange and communication (see Hewson and Sinclair, 1999; Falk, 1995; Weiss and Gordenker, 1996).

These 'communities' of activists and policy-makers have, in a real way, been transformed and empowered by the forces of globalization (see Rosenau, 1990). As James Rosenau writes, 'The mushrooming of *social movements* in recent years offers still another instance of micro-macro interactions induced by globalizing dynamics' (Rosenau, 1997: 73). Rosenau also notes:

> [W]hether it be the environmental, feminist, peace, or Islamic movement . . . the symbols, membership, modes of interaction, and hierarchical arrangements are, at best, variable, and informal. Such movements tend to improvise from issue, sometimes circumventing national governments and sometimes working with them, but at all times eschewing efforts to develop and intrude formal structures into their deliberations and activities. (Ibid., 68)

Non-governmental organizations and social movements are seen by cosmopolitans as the inventors and providers of new social and political norms that are the building blocks of new forms of social and political discourse and, ultimately, political behaviours and institutions, national and international (see Czempiel and Rosenau, 1992; Lipschutz, 1992; Lipschutz and Mayer, 1996; Rosenau,

1990; Shaw, 1994). Although their presence is felt most acutely in the areas of human rights and environmental issues (see Falk, 1995; Haas, 1989), it is expanding into other issue areas, such as trade and investment policy (Dymond, 1999; Curtis and Wolfe, 2000).

But it is not just in the areas of agenda-setting and norm creation that these civil society actors are providing international public goods. They are also directly involved in providing for basic human needs (food, health, education, security, and economic development) and fulfilling those functions normally provided by the state itself or by international organizations. As Mary Anderson explains:

> Churches, civic groups, labor unions, private foundations, and millions of individuals have established organizations that usually operate as tax-free entities to support some group or some cause. While many of these operate within their own borders, a very large number of NGOs have defined their mission as working with people in other countries. (Anderson, 1996: 344)

They provide assistance in four different mandates: (1) provision of humanitarian relief to people in emergencies; (2) promotion of long-term social and economic development; (3) promulgation and monitoring of human rights; and (4) conflict resolution and management training and assistance.

According to the cosmopolitans, civil society is not just a poor substitute for the state when it comes to human security; it is in the vanguard of the provision of this public good. NGOs and various non-state actors are also both more efficient than states or international organizations and more attentive to considerations of equity and social justice in meeting human security needs (Anderson and Woodrow, 1989; Simai, 1995). This is not to say that non-governmental organizations are necessarily problem-free when it comes to providing these public goods (Anderson, 1996). Cosmopolitans merely argue that these non-state actors are better able to provide these goods because of their small size, organizational flexibility, and knowledge and experience with local conditions.

INSTITUTIONALISTS

Human security institutionalists tend to side with traditional liberals, and for the same reasons, in championing the virtues or comparative advantage of formal international organizations and institutions in the provision and maintenance of public goods, including human security. They believe that international organizations enjoy a much higher degree of political legitimacy and accountability than non-governmental organizations and non-state actors. This is because they tend to have universal or near-universal membership and also because they are state-based, i.e., intergovernmental. The intergovernmental nature and capacity of formal international organizations also mean that they can mobilize resources and the requisite political will on a vastly bigger scale than can most non-governmental organizations when it comes to defending human security values. Institutionalists also argue that formal international organizations have been remarkably successful in changing the expectations and behaviours of states through the promulgation of new norms, particularly in the context of human rights and the environment (Young, 1999). Institutionalists believe that when it comes to using force in the defence and protection of human security, international institutions typically enjoy a much higher degree of *collective* political legitimacy than states. When international organizations give their blessing to the use of force in the defence of human security values it is harder to challenge and criticize such interventions as being mere extensions of state power and selfish national interests.

Even so, few institutionalists of the human security persuasion believe that all is well with existing international organizations and the machinery of interstate co-operation. Foremost among the advocates for reform is the Secretary-General of the United Nations, Kofi Annan, who believes the United Nations has a unique role to play in halting human rights abuses around the globe and promoting human security values more generally. The Secretary-General questions those who assert that 'the Charter itself—with its roots in the aftermath of global inter-State war—is ill-suited to guide us in a world of ethnic wars and intra-State violence.' Instead, he argues that '[t]he Charter is a living document, whose high principles still define the aspirations of peoples everywhere for lives of peace, dignity, and development' and that '[n]othing in the Charter precludes a recognition that there are rights beyond borders' (UN Press Office, 1999). Specifically, the Secretary-General calls upon permanent members of the Security Council to have a wider conception of their national interests and to 'find far greater unity in the pursuit of such basic Charter values as democracy, human rights, and the rule of law.' The Secretary-General's view is also echoed in a wide range of reports and studies that argue for specific institutional reforms, not just of the United Nations but also of regional and subregional organizations, in order that they can more effectively promote human security.

There are also those who believe that a more radical set of reforms is required to ensure that international organizations promote human security values. For example, Richard Shell asserts that the assumptions underlying the structure of the GATT/WTO system and its current organizational structure are flawed when it comes to promoting equity and social justice in international relations and that new institutional structures are required to give standing to non-state actors (Shell, 1996). These new institutions should see their mission not just in terms of promoting free trade but also of providing fora where issues of fairness and social justice can be properly discussed. Similar kinds of arguments have also been advanced in the context of global environmental change, where many say that if a genuine moral discourse is to occur that is sensitive to human security concerns, 'new participatory structures are needed to give voice to hitherto unrepresented or underrepresented groups in society', particularly within international organizations (Hampson and Reppy, 1996: 251).

Minilateralists

Human security minilateralists believe that the main principles of the UN Charter (and of other international organizations) are on a collision course with the human security agenda. As Michael Glennon (1999: 3) writes, 'it is not only that the UN Charter prohibits intervention where enlightened states now believe it to be just— its problems run even deeper. For the Charter is grounded on a premise that is simply no longer valid—the assumption that the core threat to international security still comes from interstate violence.' According to minilateralists, although there are dangers from states acting independently to secure human security values when they are threatened because such interventions will necessarily be ad hoc and 'justice formed on the fly', the alternative—to do nothing—is worse and morally unacceptable. Because '[t]he failings of the old system were so disastrous . . . little will be lost in the attempt to forge a new one' (ibid.).

To deal with the problems of genocide, ethnic cleansing, and other egregious human rights abuses, minilateralists believe that the United States and other democracies must use military power if necessary to defend these values. Furthermore, to prevent intrastate wars from spilling across their borders with adverse consequences for international peace and security, the minilateralists sanction *early* intervention because the subsequent humanitarian costs are likely to be even higher than the initial costs of intervention (Lund, 1996).

Minilateralists, however, eschew unilateral intervention by great powers because such actions, even when taken with the best of intentions, will be misinterpreted as self-serving. As a safety measure, human security interventions should be multilateral in appearance, recognizing that most of the 'heavy lifting' in these situations will have to be done by the great powers rather than by their coalition partners. Thus, the 'hope is that building a multinational coalition will filter out the worst forms of national self-interest and keep them from playing a leading role in international intervention' (Glennon, 1999: 5).

Even so, minilateralism is no substitute for genuine multilateralism and interventions that have their basis in and can be legitimized through the rule of law. Under this approach *just* interventions will pave the way eventually to a new set of precedents for international law and a restructuring of international institutions: formal organizations and the system of rules and law upon which they are based will eventually catch up. As Glennon explains, '[a]chieving justice is the hard part; revising international law to reflect it can come afterward. If power is used to do justice, law will follow' (ibid., 7). Thus, minilateralism is the halfway house to a new normative order—a stepping stone but not a stopping place.

What is to be noted about this viewpoint is that, like traditional realists, human security minilateralists believe that traditional power is the key ingredient in international politics and that hegemonic involvement (in this case by the United States) is the key to establishing a new and more just international order. But whereas realists have traditionally argued that military power should be used only in defence of broader—and usually somewhat ill-defined—goals based on the national interest, human security minilateralists believe that power can and indeed should be used in the defence of human security values—a contention that most realists would dispute. Furthermore, political appearances, i.e., political legitimacy, do matter, hence the importance of assembling the 'sheriff's posse'—i.e., using the rationale of multilateralism—when force has to be used to protect or promote those values.

MIDDLE-POWER MULTILATERALISTS

Unlike minilateralists, middle-power multilateralists believe that 'coalitions of the like-minded' (middle and small powers) can deliver international public goods, including human security public goods. It is generally recognized that coalitions of middle powers can invent solutions and identify new institutional options in bargaining situations where the major actors are deadlocked and unable to arrive at a co-operative agreement, particularly with negotiations that occur within formal institutionalized settings. These actors provide a 'middle way' between major protagonists, not by 'difference splitting' but by providing 'a genuine alternative middle ground upon which the major actors [can] meet' (Higgott and Cooper, 1990: 628). Typically, bridging solutions are offered by coalitions of smaller states or middle powers who do not have structural power, that is, are not capable of providing a collective good on their own, but can compensate for a lack of structural power through the exercise of bargaining and negotiating skills directed at bringing competing interests together (Hampson, 1995).

Some argue that middle powers can project their influence outside of formal international institutions by tapping into the cosmopolitan sector and forming strategic alliances with non-governmental organizations and various transnational actors in civil society. Under this formulation, 'soft power'—defined as 'the art of disseminating information in such a way that desirable outcomes are achieved through persuasion rather than coercion' (Axworthy, 1997: 192)—is the key instrument of diplomacy and the means by which an alliance of middle-power state and non-state actors can promote human security values.

New information technologies, such as the Internet, are also considered by middle-power multilateralists to be valuable instruments for exchanging information and strengthening activities such as 'addressing human rights abuses or international crime, areas where the rapid exchange of information across borders is essential.' These strategies are also seen as being essential 'in helping to establish free media and counter hate propaganda, and so bolster democracy and reduce the likelihood of conflict in troubled regions' (ibid., 194).

The difference between traditional, middle-power multilateralism and the new multilateralism of human security is that traditionalists emphasize the importance of working through formal international institutions and organizations whereas the new multilateralists seek to work outside established institutional structures and to create new institutional fora, when necessary, to promote and advance the human security interests. Middle-power multilateralists also tend to be somewhat ambivalent about the utility of formal international organizations, such as the United Nations, in promoting human security values, because they recognize that entrenched state interests may be opposed to this agenda. They therefore seek to work more closely with civil society organizations because they believe that non-governmental organizations and the business sector (at least potentially) can be 'extremely effective partners in advocating the security of people' (DFAIT, 1999: 9). But whereas cosmopolitans argue that transnational civil society can provide human security public goods without the direct involvement of states, middle-power multilateralists generally believe that middle-power states have a constructive role to play in advancing human security by promoting human security values and norms to bring about much-needed reforms in those international organizations where they are formal members. Middle-power multilateralists also tend to be somewhat skeptical about the use of force in international politics because they believe that hard (i.e., military or coercive) power is of declining utility in the post-Cold War world where power 'is increasingly diffuse and malleable' (ibid., 193).

Sharing Costs and Managing Risk: A Portfolio Diversification Approach to Human Security

Because they view human security as an international public good, and therefore downgrade state sovereignty into a lesser global public good, human security advocates believe that state sovereignty should not be allowed to stand in the way of human security. But, as with any public good, the questions to be answered are: How costly is it to procure the good? Who is willing (or able) to pay for the fixed costs of public goods provision? Do the perceived benefits (local, national, and global) and the declining marginal costs of extending these benefits outweigh the up-front, fixed costs and risks? To the extent that values other than efficiency are involved in public goods provision (e.g., legitimacy, accountability, and distribution), there are also differing viewpoints about how to address value trade-offs. Theories may be universal but policy is about setting priorities, confronting difficult trade-offs, and making tough choices.

Cosmopolitans are inclined to think that it is preferable for human security to be provided on a voluntary basis and through the voluntary sector. They believe that this is most efficient and lends greater accountability and legitimacy to decision-making (because non-governmental organizations are more attentive to local needs and considerations). Further, to the extent that sovereignty stands in the way of the delivery of this public good, non-governmental organizations working with their counterparts in other societies are best able to circumvent and 'work around' state actors. While recognizing that international organizations, in their current, cash-strapped state, are financially incapable of meeting the vast array of human security needs and challenges, institutionalists nonetheless believe that international organizations are best positioned to make use of the available resources. International organizations also enjoy greater political legitimacy because of their mandates and membership—especially in the case of the global institutions such as the UN and its various affiliated agencies. With more resources, institutionalists believe that the barriers to meeting human security needs that international organizations currently confront would be significantly lowered. Minilateralists, in contrast, believe that only great powers are in a position to assume the costs of providing human security public goods, but they recognize that the political will to mobilize these resources (financial, economic, and military) is sorely lacking and that there are profound domestic obstacles to doing so. On the other hand, middle-power multilateralists tend to believe that resources per se are not the real problem, especially if one can bring about normative change that alters political behaviours and advances human security norms and values in the process. In other words, middle-power multilateralists believe that many, if not most, human security goals can be secured 'on the cheap'.

In the case studies of particular human security initiatives that follow we will explore each one of these arguments about which sets of actors or institutions are best able to provide human security as new kinds of global public good and at what price or cost. Are cosmopolitans essentially correct in thinking that human security is a global public good that can best be provided through the voluntary sector and through transnational civil society networks? Or are we still in a kind of realist world where human security can only be provided through minilateral approaches that circumvent the problems of collective action and engage and involve the world's great powers, especially the United States? And what are we to make of the argument that the new (and successful) champions of human security are coalitions of middle powers—the so-called new moral minority of international politics—who are playing a vital role in providing this public good? Finally, are international institutions—the United Nations, in particular—still needed in the quest to promote human security, or are they, as some argue, too constrained by their mandates and too committed to a world view of the past to play a useful role in the delivery of human security?

In taking up and evaluating these arguments, it will be demonstrated that there is no single mode of delivery and no 'preferred' path in the provision of human security. Rather, each actor (or set of actors) has its own strengths and weaknesses, but no single actor or set of institutions has a clear comparative advantage over the others. Because their advantages are complementary rather than exclusive, we maintain that a *portfolio diversification strategy* that builds on the capabilities of a wide range of institutional actors, and that spreads the costs and risks of intervention among them in order to maximize human security returns, is the most desirable.

In advancing this argument, we hold that a portfolio diversification approach to human security is also best suited to meeting the multi-dimensional aspects of human security. Because there is no clear, single source of market or political failure to explain the human security deficit in today's world, there is no easy or simple way to provide this public good. Furthermore, when the use of force is involved—as it sometimes is—it must be recognized that there is no simple formula in designing or deciding on an actual intervention. Human security values sit uneasily alongside more traditional values embodied in the principles of sovereignty and non-intervention in the internal affairs of states. Much of the difficulty with the human security enterprise frequently involves the reconciliation of these competing values in ambiguous situations where moral principles point in one direction and international law and established state practice in another. As we look to some of these cases in Chapter 7, we suggest that military interventions undertaken in the name of human security require institutional (and legal) legitimacy if they are to uphold the values on which they purportedly are based. In looking to the actual and potential role of international institutions, and of the UN in particular, it would be wrong to insist that they are not needed in the advancement of human security. Our discussion will show that they are needed more than ever both to co-ordinate and serve as strategic centres for the actions and activities of the growing array of civil society actors and to mobilize and manage the requisite political will and resources, thus providing further legitimacy for international action.

Chapter 4

Promoting Human Rights and the Rule of Law: The International Criminal Court

On 17 July 1998 in Rome, Italy, some 120 states agreed to sign a statute to establish an International Criminal Court. The signing followed lengthy negotiations at the United Nations Diplomatic Conference of Plenipotentiaries on the Establishment of an International Criminal Court, which had begun on 15 June. The Rome Statute signified the emergence of new norms in the international system. The Statute's preamble declares that the signatories recognize that international crimes 'threaten peace and security' and affirms that such crimes 'must not go unpunished'. States are to ensure an 'end to impunity' for individual perpetrators.

Thus, the Statute recognized the need both to further the creation of international criminal law and to establish a mechanism for its enforcement. Under the Statute, individuals are to be held responsible for the commission of human rights atrocities; as a consequence impunity is to be profoundly compromised.[1] The creation of the court posits that an internationally enforced rule of law has the power to order, and to judge, much of the conduct of international affairs.

The establishment of an International Criminal Court (ICC) is clearly a human security issue. The institution provides for non-military intervention based on the protection of individuals and their welfare. Individual perpetrators are held accountable for actions against their victims; these actions are defined as violations of international criminal law. It is this body of international criminal law, and in particular, international human rights law, that attempts to define and maintain the minimal conditions of human welfare. Further, the ICC is indicative of a normative shift towards human security, as the existence of interstate conflict is not a necessary precondition to the operation of the court's jurisdiction.

The establishment of the ICC falls under the rights/rule-of-law conception of human security. As discussed in Chapter 2, proponents of this conception view the absence of the rule of law and the denial of fundamental human rights as the main threats to human security. The creation of the ICC seeks to strengthen both the normative force and legal framework of fundamental human rights and human rights law. The Rome Statute attempts to achieve this objective by creating a permanent institution that will exercise and promote an internationally enforceable rule of law. Further, by including the enforcement of the laws and customs of war, the Rome Statute also addresses the concerns of proponents of the humanitarian conception of human security. In circumscribing acceptable methods and weapons of warfare, especially in relation to civilians, the ICC strengthens international law and promotes the safety of peoples.

The International Criminal Court as a Public Good

Proponents of the rule-of-law perspective argue that human security is under-provided because of a variety of political failures, and that these failures can be mitigated by the creation of institutions. Further, to the extent that institutions also embody democratic principles such as due process and the rule of law, the institutions themselves are public goods.

The Rome Statute has created a governance structure that allows for the management of problems created by conflict, international crime, and human rights violations. The ICC is also an inclusive institution, i.e., an open as opposed to a closed club; its signatories include a wide variety of states, many of which do not have the capacity to protect the security of their citizens on a unilateral basis. Further, the Rome Statute, and the method of its creation, embodies democratic principles, particularly respect for the rule of law and due process. Thus, future interactions between states and individuals within the ICC will be organized by these principles.

The rights/rule-of-law conception of human security considers the denial of fundamental human rights to be the main reason for human insecurity. Thus, to the extent that the ICC can strengthen the normative and legal force of international human rights law, it will provide the international community with an important public good. The institution's ability to provide for human security will be based on its ability to employ effectively such strategies as sanctioning, shaming, and co-optation. By deepening and entrenching the norms and principles embodied by international human rights law, the ICC has the potential to alter the political calculus of both governments and individuals.

Origins of the International Criminal Court

To the extent that the ICC is found to constitute and provide public goods, it is important to ask who is responsible for its creation. As discussed in Chapter 3, a plethora of actors, and groups of actors, are thought to have a role in the creation and delivery of public goods, including human security. Using the framework set out in Chapter 3, the actors and institutions relevant to the ICC case study will be discussed below.

Minilateralists argue that the leadership of great powers, and the hegemon in particular, is vital to the creation and delivery of public goods. Although the hegemon is best suited to take a leadership role, the involvement of other great powers serves to increase the credibility of the policy adopted. The quasi-multilateral nature of minilateral action has the potential to mute the elements of policies based on the national self-interest of a great power. Thus, in the context of the present case study, minilateralists would look to the United States, as well as to its allies, to explain the creation of the ICC.

Middle-power multilateralists look to coalitions of the like-minded to explain the creation of public goods. These coalitions involve small and medium-sized powers who can invent new solutions and bring forth policy options despite great-power discord or ambivalence. These coalitions compensate for their lack of structural power by working within institutions, adopting creative bargaining and negotiation tactics, and forging ties with civil society. Thus, in the context of the present case study, middle-power multilateralists would look to the coalition of like-minded states (LMS) to explain the creation of the ICC. This coalition was formed, in great part, by small and medium-sized states to promote the ICC's creation.

Institutionalists argue that public goods have their roots in the activities of formal institutions. If institutions are nearly universal and intergovernmental, they have a high degree of credibility to undertake influential action. Institutional actors are well situated to alter the expectations and behaviour of states. Further, institutionalists argue that reformers within institutions have the capacity to promote institutional change required for the realization of human security. Thus, in the context of the present case study, institutionalists would look to the activities of individual reformers within the United Nations in order to explain the creation of the ICC.

Finally, cosmopolitans argue that civil society actors have the capacity to create and provide public goods. Informal groupings of NGOs, epistemic communities, members of social movements, and individuals have the potential to work together for common goals. Through the exploitation of media and technology, cosmopolitan actors set agendas, facilitate social learning, promulgate norms, and provide public goods. Thus, in the context of the present case study, cosmopolitans look to civil society to explain the creation of the ICC. For example, cosmopolitans would consider the activities of NGOs, such as the Coalition for the International Criminal Court (CICC), and international jurists in seeking to explain the creation of the ICC.

The following account of the creation of the ICC will demonstrate that the roles and abilities of each set of actors described above are both complementary and necessary to the creation of this institution. However, as we see below, the need to integrate the interests of multiple actors prevented the creation of the kind of institution with enforcement powers that many within the international legal community felt was necessary to prosecute those charged with war crimes and other human rights abuses.

Early Attempts and Results

The idea of creating an internationally enforced criminal law is not a solely modern notion. In 1474, the Court of the Holy Roman Empire tried Peter von Hagenbach in Bresiach, Germany, for 'Crimes Against God and Humanity', for his torturing of civilians. At the Congress of Vienna in 1815, states debated the notion of holding trials to punish perpetrators of the slave trade. In 1872 the 'Peace Society in the United States' developed an International Criminal Code—the first attempt at outlining the jurisdiction of an international criminal court. Further, beginning in 1899, a number of second-tier powers, human rights groups, international jurists, and the media aided in the creation of the 'Hague Conference System' and The Hague Court of Arbitration (Best, 1999). It will be illustrated, however, that developments in the pre-Cold War era did not signify the acceptance of an internationally enforced rule of law.

It was not until the end of World War I that states seriously attempted to investigate and prosecute international crimes. The Allies established the Commission on the Responsibility of the Authors of War at the 1919 Paris Peace Conference. Articles 227 to 229 of the Treaty of Versailles envisioned the prosecution of Kaiser Wilhelm II and other German officials for war crimes and violations of the customs of war. Yet, although the Commission's investigations named 895 individuals against whom there was adequate evidence for prosecution, an Allied tribunal never was established.

Such a turn of events is not surprising when viewed in light of the political concerns of the Allies. The great powers explicitly placed the desire for political stability above the objective of punishing war criminals. The prosecution of German officials was thought to be antithetical to the stabilizing of the Weimar Republic; the detainment of the alleged criminals, and the information released through the trial process, could topple the government. As the Allies felt that peace in Europe could only be maintained through the consolidation of the Republic, no action was taken (Bassiouni, 1997). Similarly, the Allies were concerned about the burgeoning of the Bolshevik Revolution in Turkey. It was thought not wise to be antagonistic to Turkey, despite the original intent to prosecute Turkish nationals for offences against the Armenians.

The failure to establish an Allied tribunal was also the result of conceptual dilemmas underlying political considerations. For instance, the United States stymied attempts to have the Martens Clause of the 1907 Hague Convention serve as a definition of crimes against humanity upon which prosecutions would proceed (Bassiouni and Blakesley, 1992). The US was unwilling to further the codification of international law in this way, as such expansion was perceived as having the potential to constrain its national objectives in the future. The US was also reluctant to recognize officially that individuals, and particularly a head of state, could be held accountable for war crimes. The argument was that a head of state exercised sovereign power, such that only the domestic public that conferred this power could hold him accountable for any crime (MacPherson, 1998). Thus, the potential indictment of the Kaiser was viewed as a dangerous precedent.

Similarly, in the interwar period, states were not inclined to consider seriously the creation of an international criminal court. There was little political will or resources with which to proceed. The moral outrage that aided the creation of Articles 227 to 229 in the Treaty of Versailles had waned. Most states were concentrating on domestic reconstruction, and the United States, an increasingly powerful player in the international community, withdrew into a period of isolationism.

The League of Nations, however, was active in addressing the codification of international law and the development of a court, largely through the leadership of the League's Secretariat and the Assembly Committee System. These bodies worked closely with non-governmental organizations, and an Advisory Committee of Jurists to the League of Nations was created. Although these committees had few powers of enforcement, the open nature of deliberations served to identify vested interests and mobilize shame, often based on human rights considerations. This aided in the building of norms with respect to human rights and the corresponding normative restrictions on acceptable state action (Zimmern, 1969).

The work of the League's committees also resulted in a wealth of research and a number of conventions related to international criminal law. For example, in 1928, the League adopted the General Act for the Peaceful Settlement of Disputes, which encompassed the Geneva Protocol. Similarly, in 1937, the League passed the Convention on Terrorism. Annexed to this was a Protocol that provided for the establishment of a court to prosecute the crimes listed in the Convention. Thus, although the political will did not exist to create an international criminal court, the work of the League of Nations contributed to a growing base of knowledge that would be built upon following World War II.

The atrocities of World War II created an obvious need to revisit the notion of international enforcement of individual responsibility for criminal acts. The great powers examined the model created after World War I, the Inter-Parliamentary Union's 1925 Draft Criminal Code and the International Law Association's 1935 Plan for a World Criminal Code (White, 1951). In 1943, the United Nations War Crimes Commission was created, following discussions at the Palace of St James. Although the body produced 8,178 dossiers on alleged war criminals, it was largely overshadowed by the US-dominated International Military Tribunal (IMT) at Nuremberg and the International Military Tribunal for the Far East (IMTFE). The London Agreement of 1945 embodied a complete reversal of the prior American position regarding crimes against humanity. The IMT's jurisdiction was wide; crimes against humanity were included, as were 'crimes against peace', a concept with no entrenched legal meaning.

There has been much debate concerning how the evident zeal to create the IMT and IMTFE may be viewed as signifying the acceptance of the rule of law, individual responsibility, and the creation of an international criminal court. An examination of the operation of the tribunals, however, reveals that there was no clear triumph of law over politics; political imperatives remained persuasive. For instance, the abuse of prosecutorial selection in the Far East has been noted (Bassiouni, 1997). The decision not to prosecute Emperor Hirohito was based on a fear of destabilizing the region. Similarly, although the Italian Instrument of Surrender provided for the prosecution and extradition of Italian war criminals, no prosecutions ever took place. The Allies instead placed their faith in the reformation of the Italian fascists, given growing fear of the spread of communism in the region (Bassiouni, 1992).

Buttressing these arguments is the notion that the tribunals established following World War II cannot be accurately characterized as international courts in a strict sense. Rather, they were *ex post facto* tribunals that applied the law of the aggrieved retroactively. Instead of constituting a consistent affirmation of the rule of law, they were in large part 'victor's justice' imposed on the nationals of defeated states (MacPherson, 1998). The sovereignty of the defeated was not compromised, as it was deemed not to exist, and in many cases judicial process was not adequately observed.

Events in the pre-Cold War period illustrate that the actions and attitudes of powerful states are critical in explaining events related to the enforcement and development of international criminal law. As minilateralists would expect, strong states determined if and when individuals would be held accountable for international crimes and largely defined what was criminal. There was no acceptance of the rule of law or the norm of individual responsibility; such concepts were only appealed to if doing so satisfied political imperatives.

Strong states, however, did not make decisions regarding international justice without recourse to existing models. For example, as the victorious great powers negotiated how to structure the peace following World War I, The Hague Convention was used as a basis for their deliberations. Middle-power multilateralists would point to the fact that The Hague Convention was created in large part by the contributions of small and medium-sized powers, aided by the institutionalized nature of The Hague conference system. Further, the activities of middle powers and institutional reformers within the League of Nations created a body of codified international criminal law and served to build norms related to human rights. In this respect, cosmopolitan actors also had a role to play. Civil society actors, such as the Advisory Council of Jurists, contributed to the growing literature regarding an international criminal court and attempted to galvanize public support for the project.

The Cold War Era

The newly created United Nations affirmed the 'principles of international law recognized by the Charter of Nuremberg'. Using this as a starting point, the UN General Assembly (UNGA), as well as the International Law Commission (ILC), undertook numerous actions that served to further the development of international criminal law. For example, the 1948 Genocide Convention explicitly recognized the jurisdiction of a future international criminal court. Grave breaches of the 1949 Geneva Conventions were characterized as international crimes.

Members of civil society were integral to the progress made by the UN system. The UN Charter explicitly institutionalized the notion of social representation by allowing 'consultative status' for certain NGOs within the Economic and Social Council (ECOSOC). Groups also operated within the Human Rights Commission, its working groups, and the Human Rights Committee. NGOs facilitated norm-building by focusing attention on issues, setting standards, and monitoring compliance. Similarly, the creation of the ILC gave international jurists a forum within which to formulate ideas and programs. In sum, the postwar world witnessed a 'global associational explosion' (Fisher, 1997: 440). Civil society actors used the Cold War period to increase their organizational capacity and to adapt to the new institutional procedures created by the UN system (Korey, 1998).

In 1947, the UNGA gave the ILC a mandate for the codification of international criminal offences. The ILC was also to determine whether the creation of a court was desirable. There was little consensus within the ILC with which to proceed with the project. One report, written by Ricardo Alfaro, found the creation of a court to be both desirable and feasible. Another report, written by Emil Sandstrom, concluded that a court was not desirable given the lack of existing mechanisms for state co-operation. Although the ILC completed the Draft Code of Crimes Against Peace and Security in 1954, the body did not possess the consensus needed to develop a draft statute for the creation of an international criminal court (Morton, 1997).

This lack of consensus, however, was largely irrelevant given that the UNGA effectively removed the issue from the ILC's perusal. Progress was thwarted by state parties through the creation of an institutional 'catch-22': an international criminal court could not be created without the establishment of a Draft Code of Offences, and this could not be completed without the definition of aggression (Ferencz, 1992). State parties only concluded their work on aggression in 1974, long after the project had been effectively shelved.

There was a limited attempt to revive the project in the late 1970s, in large part due to the generally cohesive position of the international community against the apartheid regime in South Africa. During the creation of the Apartheid Convention, the eminent legal scholar Cherif Bassiouni prepared a report concerning an 'enforcement mechanism' for the UN Human Rights Commission. The resulting Draft Statute was considered at the UN's 6th Congress on Crime Prevention and the Treatment of Offenders. Favourable comments were viewed as giving the ILC a renewed mandate to study the creation of an international criminal court. Thus, the ILC appointed a special rapporteur to revisit the Draft Code of Crimes in 1982. This rapporteur issued reports from 1982 to 1988.

Despite these efforts, it was clear that the Code was going practically nowhere. The lack of progress must be viewed in light of the Cold War. The USSR and the US were not in favour of the creation of an international criminal court, given their involvement in their own spheres of influence. In addition, the USSR had a unique view of human rights, based on Communist ideology, that would have made agreement over jurisdiction and subject matter impossible. Preoccupation with Cold War imperatives thereby ensured that peace and justice remained both distinct and separate.

The Cold War experience illustrates the need for strong states to take a leadership role in order to effect international change. As minilateralists would suggest, the implementation of ideas and options created within the UN system was frustrated by the discord of the superpowers. Recognizing that the US and the Soviet Union would not agree to the creation of a court, the remaining states found it futile to proceed.

This is not to suggest, however, that other actors did not play important roles in developing international criminal law, and plans for an international criminal court, throughout the Cold War era. Institutional reformers and civil society actors worked in tandem to create a body of international law that would eventually become vital to the creation of the ICC.

The Post-Cold War Period

Several events in the late 1980s signalled a change in state attitudes. The first was the decline of US-Soviet hostilities that removed many of the political impediments for the creation of an international criminal court. In 1987, USSR General Secretary Mikhail Gorbachev expressed the desire for the creation of a global security plan in a letter to the UN. One hallmark of this proposal was the importance placed on the strengthening of an internationally enforceable rule of law. It was clear that Soviet opposition to the creation of an international court was deteriorating along with its domestic conditions.

Further, the end of the Cold War allowed states to recognize explicitly the need to provide legal mechanisms to control problematic transnational behaviours. States were increasingly concerned about 'new' security threats, such as drug trafficking, terrorism, and hijacking (Gilmore, 1995). A coalition of Caribbean states, led by Trinidad and Tobago, was adamant in its calls for the creation of a court to deal with such issues. The voices of these small and vulnerable states led the UNGA to request the ILC to prepare a report on international jurisdiction with respect to drug trafficking. Also at this time, an NGO Committee of Experts, chaired by Cherif Bassiouni, submitted a Draft Statute for the Establishment of an International Criminal Court to the 8th Congress on Crime Prevention and the Treatment of Offenders. The Congress responded favourably and urged the ILC to step up its work.

The United States also recognized the need to deal with issues such as drugs and terrorism. The 1988 American Anti-Drug Abuse Act gave an explicit mandate to the President to begin negotiations for the establishment of an international criminal court, tasked with prosecuting international drug traffickers. In 1989, the US House of Representatives passed a resolution encouraging the President to act in this respect. The President's mandate was encouraged and broadened by the 1991 Foreign Appropriations Bill. Congressional support was ensured by the active leadership of Republican Senator Arlen Specter and Republican Congressman Jim Leach, both members of the 'Parliamentarians for Global Action' organization (Anderson, 1991; Bassiouni and Blakesley, 1992).

Positive American attitudes were also secured by the Gulf War, which illustrated the ability of the international community to act collectively, albeit for a brief moment. An international criminal court seemed both desirable and feasible. Such a court would punish the 'Saddam Husseins' of the world and avoid extradition conflicts like the one the US was experiencing with Libya over the destruction of Pan Am Flight 103 (MacPherson, 1998). By 1994, the court had become a centrepiece of President Clinton's foreign policy agenda (Wedgwood, 1998).

Civil society actors were instrumental in creating, and maintaining, the momentum behind the creation of a court. The end of the Cold War had led to a proliferation of international human rights groups. These groups had transnational linkages and many reported increased contact with governments (Smith et al., 1998). The 1993 World Conference on Human Rights in Vienna illustrated that NGOs had expanded their influence and procedural repertoire; Vienna hosted 248 NGOs with consultative status and 593 NGO participants, and was attended by 1,400–1,500 NGOs (Nowak, 1994). Working with these groups, international jurists continued to agitate for the creation of the court. Development-oriented groups were also becoming interested in the creation of a court, as they experimented with truth commissions in nations torn apart by violent conflict (Edwards et al., 1999).

The international community (and its institutional machinery) responded rapidly to the softening of American attitudes. The ILC came under increasing pressure to consolidate its work; the ILC created an ICC working group in 1992 to identify how the ILC could proceed with the creation of a court. The first comprehensive Draft Statute was completed and submitted to the UNGA in 1993. The fact that the Draft was submitted to the UNGA before it was officially adopted by the ILC illustrates that its completion was viewed as a political priority. The General Assembly passed a resolution urging the ILC to continue its work and encouraging states to submit their concerns regarding the Draft Statute to the Working Group of the ILC, now chaired by an Australian, James Crawford. The revised Draft Statute of 1994 attempted to both identify and solve the political problems inherent in the creation of the international criminal court (Crawford, 1994; Wexler, 1996).

Support for the creation of a court was further buttressed by the Yugoslavian and Rwandan conflicts, which clearly invited an international response. International human rights groups worked with the media to sustain public pressure on national governments and international institutions to address this issue (MacPherson, 1998). The Security Council's creation of the International Criminal Tribunal for the Former Yugoslavia (ICTFY) and the International Criminal Tribunal for Rwanda (ICTR) affirmed the need for judicial structures to address atrocities committed in times of conflict. Yet the failed attempts of the Security Council to micromanage judicial processes in an ad hoc fashion contributed to 'tribunal fatigue'. This fatigue manifested itself in continued calls for the creation of a permanent international criminal court.

There was also growing momentum behind the project within UN machinery. The Ad Hoc Committee for the Establishment of the International Criminal Court, composed of state representatives, was formed in 1994, tasked with facilitating consultation between state parties regarding the ILC Draft Statute. Further, a Preparatory Committee (PrepCom) was created in 1995 to streamline the organization of formal negotiations. The PrepCom met six times, and was chaired by Adriaan Bos of the Netherlands. Each session organized discussions around specific issue areas, and permanent working groups were established for the definition of war crimes, general principles of international law, penalties, procedural matters, and state co-operation. The working groups were assisted by drafting committees, the latter assigned the task of compiling the bracketed negotiating test[2] (Hall, 1997, 1998).

Civil society actors were active in the PrepCom sessions; their ability to influence state behaviour and agitate for change had been clearly demonstrated by the conclusion of the landmines treaty (Cameron et al., 1998; also see Chapter 5). Non-governmental groups maximized and co-ordinated their influence through the creation of the Coalition for the International Criminal Court, led by the World Federalist Movement's William Pace. National and regional coalitions were also formed to lobby domestic governments. The CICC particularly sought to ensure that developing states, who feared that the court would become a tool of Western domination, would support a court. Civil society actors worked tirelessly to keep the creation of the ICC on international and domestic agendas and, using all technology available, publicized progress as it was made. Although NGO participation within the PrepCom sessions was curtailed as states focused on the most politicized issues, their efforts were rewarded. In December 1997, a PrepCom resolution authorized the UN Diplomatic Conference of Plenipotentiaries on the Establishment of an International Criminal Court to begin in June 1998.

As emphasized by minilateralists, events in the post–Cold War era clearly illustrate the importance of the leadership of strong states in the creation of public goods. It was not until the US signalled to the international community that the creation of the ICC was on its agenda that plans for its creation were created and formalized. Other actors, however, were vital in sustaining the momentum created by the US. Institutional reformers ensured that the machinery of the UN was focused on the creation of the court, thereby ensuring the continuance of the project. The LMS, led by small and medium-sized powers, worked to create a broad consensus behind the court. Further, civil society actors ensured that the ICC remained on domestic and international agendas.

The Rome Negotiations

With the onset of the Rome negotiations, there were three active coalitions: the conservative states, the restrictive states, and the like-minded states (Kaul, 1997; Kirsch and Holmes, 1999). The conservative states were concerned about how the proposed ICC would allow other states to interfere with their sovereignty. In particular, they were wary of creating a court with strong ties to the Security Council, as they felt that this body was incapable of representing their interests. The most active participants of the conservative states were India, Nigeria, and Mexico.

The restrictive states were also apprehensive about the scope of the ICC, but for different reasons. Consisting mainly of the United States, Russia, and China, this coalition sought to circumscribe the power of the ICC so as to ensure the continued influence of the Security Council, of which they are permanent members. The strength of the restrictive states was greatly weakened prior to Rome; the United Kingdom defected from the restrictive states to join the like-minded states after the election of Tony Blair in 1997.

The LMS coalition was characterized by its size and diversity. It included the majority of the European Union nations, the states of the Commonwealth, as well as a large number of African and Caribbean countries. These states were committed to the creation of a strong court, with independent powers and a wide jurisdiction.

Civil society actors were also extremely influential, virtually constituting their own coalition independent of state formations. After all, in addition to being included in various state delegations, some 222 non-state actors were accredited to the Rome Conference in their own right. Many of these organizations, such as the influential European Student Law Association, made presentations at the plenary sessions.

Further, non-state society actors continued to forge ties with important states and the institutional leadership. For example, the International Committee of the Red Cross worked closely with the leadership of New Zealand and Switzerland.

The CICC remained in close contact with the Canadian and British governments, who were increasingly adopting NGO positions as they took leadership roles within the LMS coalition. Non-state actors had also had strong ties with those individuals taking on a leadership role in the UN, such as Adriaan Bos and James Crawford (Kaul, 1997).

As opening statements in Rome began, the coalitions were faced with four major unresolved, and highly politicized, issues (see Table 4.1). The first of these issues was the funding mechanism for the ICC. The US insisted that the ICC be funded solely by contributions from state parties, whereas others argued that the ICC should be funded through the general UN budget.

Table 4.1 Comparison of Rome Statute and the US and LMS Positions

Issue	LMS Position (Multilateralist/ Cosmopolitan)	US Position (Minilateralist)	Rome Statute (Outcome)
Funding mechanism	UN funding	State party funding	State party funding; UN funding for Security Council referrals
National security information	Determination by ICC judiciary	Determination by state party possessing information	Determination by state possessing information
Subject matter	Broad subject matter and minimal chapeaus	Emphasis on subject-matter chapeaus	War crimes and crimes against humanity chapeaus
Triggering mechanisms	1. Inherent jurisdiction 2. ICC prosecution concurrent with national prosecutions 3. Strong independent prosecutor 4. No Security Council veto	1. State consent 2. National prosecution bars ICC action 3. No independent prosecutor 4. Security Council veto	1. National or territorial state must be party 2. National prosecution bars ICC action 3. Restrained prosecutor 4. Security Council renewable suspensions

The second issue was how the proposed ICC would handle the sensitive matter of national security information. It was clearly unacceptable for the ICC to compel evidence from states without restriction. The question then became: how would it be determined if the release of information was indeed a threat to the national security of a state? The UK contended that there should be an internal ICC process for determining what constituted information over which the ICC would be disallowed from exercising its jurisdiction. The US rejected this position, arguing that each state must have the individual right to define 'national security information' in each specific instance.

The final two (and most contentious) issues were fundamentally linked. The issue of subject-matter jurisdiction refers to the clarification of exactly what crimes the court has the jurisdiction to prosecute. 'Triggering mechanisms' refers to the determination of when the jurisdiction would become operative. Thus, a restrictive state may be satisfied by a court with wide subject-matter jurisdiction, if high triggering thresholds were created concurrently. The same state may be satisfied with a narrow subject-matter jurisdiction and low triggering thresholds. Both institutional designs would create a conservative court.

The US advocated a relatively wide subject-matter jurisdiction, although it now argued adamantly against the inclusion of drugs or terrorism. As expected, the US rejected the classification of the use of nuclear weapons as a crime against humanity. The US also joined others in arguing for the assertion of 'chapeaus', which serve to circumscribe the activation of the court's jurisdiction. For example, the US agreed to a broad list of war crimes, but asserted that these crimes must be committed pursuant to a 'plan or policy' if they were to be prosecuted. Similarly, the US was concerned about the scope of the ICC's jurisdiction over crimes against humanity. These positions were justified by the Pentagon's fear that American military personnel would become victims of politically motivated prosecutions. This, in turn, would hamper their ability to establish and maintain peacekeeping operations.

In terms of triggering mechanisms, the US insisted on high thresholds for ICC operation. The US accepted that the ICC should have jurisdiction over aggression, but only as defined by the Security Council. As a permanent member, the US also argued that the Security Council must have a veto over ICC investigations and prosecutions. The American proposal ensured that the US and other permanent Security Council members would, in effect, have a veto over the operation of the ICC. Consistent with such a stance, the US argued against the creation of a prosecutor with ex officio powers.

The US proposed an ICC that was triggered mainly by Security Council referral. State party referral was accepted, but in this respect ICC jurisdiction could only be activated on a case-by-case basis through a state 'opt-in'. For each crime, both the state of nationality and the territorial state must accept ICC jurisdiction. This would give states an effective veto over the prosecution of their nationals. The US also sought to ensure that the notion of complementarity had teeth; the ICC must not be permitted to supersede the operation of national laws. It was therefore suggested that the ICC would be required to defer to a state that declared a desire to prosecute unilaterally.

Thus, as formal negotiations commenced, the American attitude towards the court had become quite conservative. It was unclear how the US would deviate from its wish list; the US delegation failed to effectively articulate its bottom line to other states (Wedgwood, 1998). This confusion was largely due to internal divisions, as different departments and agencies presented divergent opinions on the creation of a court. Although President Clinton, Secretary of State Madeleine Albright, and Assistant Secretary of State for Human Rights Jack Shuttack were in favour of a strong court, they were not the only domestic actors involved. It has been reported that Clinton, preoccupied with his trip to China, allowed Department of Defense views to dominate the negotiations; Ambassador David Scheffer has been characterized as a 'Pentagon spokesperson' (Neier, 1998). Senator Jesse Helms made it clear that an ICC without a US veto would be 'dead on arrival' at the Senate Foreign Relations Committee (Hall, 1998). Personnel changes also took their toll, as the US Ambassador to the UN, Bill Richardson, was appointed to the US Department of Energy immediately prior to the beginning of negotiations, to be replaced by Richard Holbrooke.

The LMS, however, dominated negotiations, making concessions in an attempt to satisfy US demands (see Table 4.1). The strength of the LMS influence was largely bolstered by its close working relationship with the Bureau Committee of the Whole and the chairman of the Committee of the Whole, Canadian Philippe Kirsch, who was seen as being swift and creative, with the ability and experience to control and steer formal negotiations (Arsanjani, 1999). The Bureau was designed to aid the chairman in managing and organizing the working groups and drafting committees. The Bureau was largely composed of representatives of the LMS, and therefore served to maximize the coalition's influence in providing bridging solutions.

For example, the like-minded states had championed an ICC with inherent jurisdiction over genocide, war crimes, and crimes against humanity. Subsequently, however, South Korea, a member of the LMS, proposed the adoption of a state consent regime in an attempt to bring the US on board. The ICC would have jurisdiction over the enumerated war crimes and crimes against humanity where either the territorial, custodial, or national state had accepted ICC jurisdiction.

The LMS desire for a strong, independent prosecutor was also qualified by the creation of a Pre-Trial Chamber, which would act as a check on politically motivated prosecutions. American concern about the application of crimes against humanity was addressed by a Canadian proposal, which created a 'chapeau' on ICC jurisdiction. The chapeau required that the ICC could only prosecute crimes against humanity committed in the course of 'widespread or systemic attack'. Finally, Singapore continued to assert a compromise position, arguing for the ability of the Security Council to vote for the delay or suspension of ICC jurisdiction for 12-month periods.

Although these proposals engendered support, it was difficult for delegations to agree to certain elements of the court as they proceeded through the bracketed negotiating text. Indeed, Kirsch recognized that the bracketed approach was unproductive, given that it was a linear process; states were not willing to compromise on certain aspects of the court without knowledge of the content of the statute as a whole. Thus, given both time constraints and the interdependence of key issues, a 'package deal' was necessary (Kirsch and Holmes, 1999).

Kirsch and the Bureau adopted new procedures. Concerned about time pressure that was being exacerbated by filibustering, Kirsch instituted nighttime negotiating sessions. Further, on 5 July, the Canadian embassy in Rome hosted informal discussions attended by delegates of 30 interested states. Compromise positions were discussed and sticking points clarified, especially as between the LMS and the US. Based on this information, the 'Bureau Paper' was drafted.

The Bureau Paper outlined the issues that would have to be agreed upon in order to create the ICC. It identified key linkages between such issues and proposed a substantive package for the court. This initiative greatly increased the coherence of the negotiations that followed; although the working groups continued to function, discussions were increasingly held in private and were centred on the Bureau proposal. Subsequently, the Bureau refined the paper on 10 July. The second Bureau Paper was substantively tighter as the options for certain issues were narrowed by simply deleting the extreme positions. Further, subsequent negotiations were focused by the discarding of contentious but relatively minor issues, such as terrorism and drug trafficking.

Response to the Bureau's initiative was lukewarm. As the negotiations were drawing to a close, the Bureau was left with a difficult decision. They could begin preparations for a second session of formal negotiations, or they could put together a final package and force a vote. In choosing to put together the final package, the Bureau was aware that a high degree of consensus had to be achieved. Thus, the final package was as broad as possible. It contained a number of 'uneasy technical solutions, awkward formulations and difficult compromises that fully satisfied no one' (ibid., 11). Kirsch, however, gambled that the time was ripe and that continuation of negotiations would prove disastrous to the court's fate.

Civil society actors were largely responsible for ensuring that states signed onto the court. The activities of non-state actors ensured that a state's rejection of the court would entail a loss of face. Through the CICC creation of *Terraviva: The Rome Conference Newspaper*, NGOs were able to disperse information on the progress of negotiations and to chastise certain states for what they considered lacklustre performances. International jurists, such as Michael Scharf, pointed out inconsistencies in American positions (Scharf, 1998).

As negotiations moved to the final stages, non-state actors increasingly were shut out of the process; there were concerns that the ultimate statute may create a weak and unworkable court. Despite these concerns, the CICC, alongside the LMS, lobbied hard for Kirsch's 'take it or leave it' package, rather than gambling on a new round of negotiations. Although the Rome Statute was, in substantive terms, considerably less than their wish list, they were determined to create a court (CICC, 1998).

The package brought on side the majority of the other conservative states, but not the US. The US insisted on a veto over the court's operation and was extremely wary of an independent prosecutor. As negotiations proceeded, the US had become increasingly isolated, and ultimately rejected the court. It is clear, however, that American positions had an important impact on the substance of the Rome Statute.

For example, general UN funding of the ICC was limited to an assessment of the costs of Security Council referrals (Article 115). Determinations concerning national security information were left to the state in question (Article 72). On-site investigations can only take place if the state to be investigated consents (Article 54, Part 9). The subject matter chapeaus for which the US argued are found within the Rome Statute (Articles 7, 8). The US also influenced what is not in the Statute, namely, references to nuclear weapons, drugs, and terrorism. Further, although there is an expression of intent to include aggression within ICC jurisdiction, it will not be justiciable until it is acceptably defined by state parties, as outlined in Article 5(2).

The Statute gives complementarity teeth; the ICC must defer to national prosecution, unless the Pre-Trial Chamber decides that the national jurisdiction is unable to prosecute or if the decision to prosecute has been taken in bad faith (Article 18). The Pre-Trial Chamber will also act as a check on the prosecutor; a majority of justices in this Chamber must find a reasonable basis to proceed with investigations (Article 15).

The Rome Statute does defy the American insistence that states be able to opt in to ICC jurisdiction on a case-by-case basis. Once a state ratifies the treaty this means that it has accepted the court's jurisdiction. For the ICC jurisdiction to be invoked, either the territorial state or the state of nationality must be a party to the treaty (Article 12). In addition, the Security Council was given the power to vote for a delay or suspension of the ICC investigations and prosecutions for renewable one-year periods (Article 16), per Singapore's proposed compromise. Although this disallows a US veto through the Security Council, it does afford a great deal of Security Council input and control.

Thus, as minilateralists would argue, the leadership of the hegemon within the international system served both to provide leadership for the commencement of formal negotiations and to determine the outcome of these negotiations. This view, however, is overly simplistic when considering the key roles played by other actors. Middle-power multilateralists would point to the fact that the like-minded states were vital in ensuring that a court was created despite US objections and that there was a wide consensus behind the Statute. Institutional leadership was also necessary; throughout the process, the creation and manipulation of institutional processes and rules facilitated the creation of the court. Further, cosmopolitan actors, through their lobbying and 'shaming' activities, ensured that states signed onto the court.

Strengths and Limitations

The Rome Statute is an ambivalent document; both its structure and content seem designed to thwart its overall cohesion. Although new norms related to human security are emerging, it is clear that the entrenchment of these principles remains contested. In many instances, the emerging norms and traditional conceptions of state-based international relations coexist uneasily. Thus, both the content of the Rome Statute and its negotiating history demonstrate that institutionalizing human security norms and values within the ICC was a difficult task. There were both normative barriers to institutionalization and barriers related to power politics.

Normative barriers were a function of the fact that the rights of states, based on traditional conceptions of sovereignty, and the rights of people, based on conceptions of human security, are simply not always congruent. As discussed above, this barrier was overcome by allowing the Rome Statute to reflect the normative discord that currently exists. Although the post-Cold War era has witnessed a normative shift towards focusing on the rights of people, the shift is neither complete nor universally accepted. Only time will tell if the ICC will aid the triumph of human security norms and values despite the conservative elements of the Rome Statute.

Further, the Rome Statute clearly reflects the power politics behind its creation. The US position, largely influenced by domestic tensions, dictated the content of the Statute. American opposition, however, was not enough to thwart the creation of the ICC. Institutional reformers and middle powers ensured that the momentum behind the court's creation remained steady. Coalition-building and adept bargaining made the court's creation a certainty. Civil society actors also saw to it that the issue remained in the public spotlight, thereby forcing states to act and to participate in the negotiations.

Despite these many shortcomings, the ICC in many ways represents a public good insofar as it has the potential to provide for and enhance human security. The signatories of the Rome Statute created a governance structure based on democratic principles and the rule of law. Further, although there are restrictions on the operation of the ICC, the Rome Statute has the capacity to strengthen international and national norms and laws regarding fundamental human rights. What the institution lacks in its ability to sanction may be compensated for by its ability to shame and co-opt.

As the preceding account demonstrates, the roles played by each set of actors were in many respects complementary and necessary to the creation of the ICC. Although the involvement of multiple actors may be viewed as having weakened or strengthened the court (depending on one's point of view), the Rome Statute would not presently exist without the involvement of each set of actors.

From a minilateralist perspective, the United States played a key role in the creation of the ICC, notwithstanding its opposition to the direction the negotiations were leading in Rome. American leadership in calling for the creation of the ICC signalled to the international community that formal negotiations were both possible and desirable. US policies, in turn, were influenced by the Gulf War and the establishment of ad hoc tribunals in Yugoslavia and Rwanda. As we have pointed out, American promotion of the ICC was necessary to the launch of formal negotiations. Further, the US played a central role in defining the content of the Rome Statute. Although the United States government rejected the Statute that emerged in Rome—at least until President Clinton decided to sign it as one of his last acts in office—US opposition can largely be explained by an examination of domestic factors and forces. These forces will continue to be in play if the Statute is ever presented for ratification to the US Congress.

The position of middle-power multilateralists is also vital in explaining the success of negotiations leading to the creation of the ICC. Through the establishment of a broadly based LMS coalition, small and medium powers sustained the momentum of negotiations through to an agreement. The LMS also proposed a number of innovative bridging solutions, particularly in relation to triggering mechanisms and subject-matter jurisdiction, in order to forge a wide consensus for the court. The LMS worked effectively within the formal negotiating arena, exploiting bargaining tactics, such as the use of a negotiating deadline to ensure that the Rome Statute was completed and an agreement was reached. Finally, the coalition worked closely with civil society to promote the establishment of a strong court.

Similarly, international organizations and key individuals were vital to the success of the ICC. After President Clinton adopted the idea of an international court as a foreign policy goal, the UN ensured that the project continued even after Clinton effectively withdrew his country's support for the enterprise. Institutional reformers such as A.N.R. Robinson, James Crawford, Adriaan Bos, Cherif Bassiouni, and Philippe Kirsch also provided the right kind of intellectual leadership to move the process forward. The intergovernmental and universal nature of the UN system allowed these reformers to influence the positions and behaviours of key states during the negotiations.

Finally, the ICC case study clearly illustrates the necessity of the involvement of cosmopolitan actors in creating public goods. The support of civil society was integral to the creation of the ICC. Civil society actors, in particular the CICC, used media and technology to place the ICC firmly on the policy agenda of the international community. These non-governmental actors served an important educating function while also influencing the policies of key states. As has been noted, civil society actors forged and strengthened ties with institutional leaders and the LMS, thereby ensuring the creation of a court over American opposition. But it is also clear that civil society actors were shut out of the final round of negotiations as issues were narrowed to the most contentious and politicized topics. It should also be noted that cosmopolitan actors could not create the public good without the support of international institutions and the individuals and middle powers that took leadership roles within these institutions.

Civil society actors were most influential during the pre-negotiation stage as international attention came to be focused on the issue and states were formulating their interests, but their influence declined once formal negotiations were under way. However, with the conclusion of a formal agreement, the importance of civil society to the success of the ICC will grow. Human rights groups and the international legal community will be pivotal in implementing the human security norms and values embodied in the ICC. Considering the ability of non-governmental actors to promulgate norms, focus attention on issues, and gather information, these actors will be fundamental to the successful functioning and operation of the court. Further, although states and institutional actors must ultimately accept the court's jurisdiction through formal ratification in order to foster the legitimacy of the institution, civil society actors will be highly influential in getting states to do so.

The ICC experience illustrates that the creation of an international institution and the provision of human security public goods require a great deal of involvement from a wide range of different actors and interests. Without the involvement of non-governmental organizations, international institutions, and different states (great and small) working together, the ICC would not be a reality. And even when a great power defects from the process, if negotiations have sufficient momentum agreement can be reached. Thus, the ICC experience—its imperfections and problems notwithstanding—illustrates the importance of building on the capabilities of a wide range of institutional actors (governmental, intergovernmental, and non-governmental) in seeking to create institutions that provide for human security. In the next chapter we see how this process worked in the case of a 'safety of peoples' initiative, the international campaign to ban landmines.

Notes

1. Until the Rome Statute created a permanent institution charged with enforcing international law (as it relates to individuals) there was no such body. Thus, before the ICC, even if individuals committed recognized, i.e., codified international crimes, they could not be prosecuted directly under international law. The creation of the institution 'compromised' traditional impunity by making it possible in certain instances to prosecute an individual for an international offence in an international body.

2. The working groups each had a subject to deal with. Whenever agreement was not met numerous options existed: those provisions/words were bracketed (literally) for future negotiation. The drafting committees made sure that the texts represented the progress of the work within the working groups and then put the work of all the different groups together into one text. Only then could one see trade-offs in the different options between different areas.

Chapter 5

Promoting the Safety of Peoples: Banning Anti-Personnel Landmines

The 'Ottawa Convention' banning anti-personnel mines is often seen as a model of middle-power multilateralism at work and a successful illustration of how a coalition of like-minded middle powers, allied with members of civil society, can help create an international public good—in this case, the Convention itself, which promotes the greater safety of peoples by eliminating a class of weapons that has inflicted indiscriminate carnage on civilians during and after conflict. Since the negotiations were concluded in 1997, 137 countries have signed the treaty and 96 have ratified it. The Ottawa Convention has led to the destruction of 20 million stockpiled mines. As Canada's Foreign Minister, Lloyd Axworthy, one of the leading champions of the treaty, boasted to a Washington audience, 'Of the 54 states previously known to produce mines, only 16 continue to do so. Of the 34 countries known to export mines, all but one have instituted moratoriums or full bans on any further export. Casualty rates have dropped by more than 50 per cent in Cambodia, and by 90 per cent in Bosnia and Mozambique' (DFAIT, 2000).

But the statement that the landmines treaty, to quote Axworthy, 'represents a new kind of global politics—one in which governments, civil society and non-governmental organizations work together to effect positive change for people' may be somewhat of an exaggeration. As David Atwood, a close observer of the landmines treaty, argues:

> It may well be that the Ottawa Process will herald a useful path for future arms control negotiations. The cross-regional 'core group' process, the leadership of key 'middle' powers, the strategic collaboration between governments and NGOs, the global organizing capacity of the International Campaign to Ban Landmines, the movement away from the consensus rule, the emphasis on regional steps—all these are ways in which the Ottawa Process succeeded in moving an international concern within a very short period of time from near stalemate to a new international agreement enjoying broad support. . . . But it is important to remind ourselves of one factor which also probably facilitated this way of working, a factor which may be less present in other weapons control initiatives in the future. APMs are, even from the perspective of those who most ardently defend their continued possession, weapons of relatively minor importance from a military security

perspective. Their actual military utility has also been seriously challenged, even by military personnel. (Atwood, 1999: 44)

Even so, by seeking to eliminate a class of weapons whose humanitarian costs have been enormous and whose lingering presence in the fields and countryside of many developing nations has thwarted agriculture and rural development, this broad-based international coalition has attempted to provide an important human security public good. Both civil society and middle-power multilateralist elements are reflected in the negotiations that led to the Ottawa Convention. The negotiations most certainly—and undeniably—engaged many 'citizen diplomats', representing the various non-governmental organizations that lobbied hard to secure the treaty, but they also succeeded because of the efforts of a core group of states, namely, a middle-power coalition led by Canada and Norway, and because the Ottawa Process was actively supported behind the scenes by the Secretary-General of the United Nations, Kofi Annan. Before its own position became hostage to the Pentagon and President Bill Clinton caved in to domestic opponents of the treaty, the United States was a significant player—if not a vision leader—in those negotiations.

On the one hand, the failure of the United States (along with Russia, China, and India) to block the successful conclusion of the Ottawa Process can be seen in some respects as a victory for cosmopolitan/middle-power multilateralism and a defeat for great-power 'minilateralism'. On the other hand, the victory may be a hollow one given the importance of the above states to the worldwide production and trade in landmines. In the long run, the co-operation of these countries is clearly essential if the mechanisms set in place at Ottawa are to work and the scourge of landmines is to be eradicated from the face of the planet.

The reality is that minilateral (i.e., great-power) involvement and support are ultimately critical to the delivery of the human security public good envisaged by the treaty. But here the story is somewhat mixed and also somewhat surprising. As we see below, in spite of the fact it is not a signatory to the treaty, the United States has emerged, along with Norway, as one of the main financial contributors to the global campaign to eliminate landmines. The United States has further indicated that it intends to adhere to the treaty and hopes to be in a position to sign the Convention in 2006, the date set by President Clinton. One would have not predicted this kind of outcome given strong US opposition to the treaty that was signed in Ottawa. In this respect, the real story behind the Ottawa Process is not that the United States was the main 'spoiler'; rather, the United States was sufficiently embarrassed—some would say 'shamed'—by its position that it has been forced to contribute to the campaign in other ways even though it falls short of endorsing the full provisions of the treaty itself.

Early Catalysts

The first call for a landmines ban came from a quasi-intergovernmental body, the International Committee of the Red Cross. As John English, a close observer of the Ottawa Convention, notes, the 'origins of the ban movement lay in the attempt by the ICRC in the 1970s to reinvigorate the century-old tradition of international humanitarian law. These efforts led to the UN Convention on Certain Conventional Weapons (CCW) [of 1980], of which the second protocol dealt with the "Prohibitions or Restrictions on the Use of Mines, Booby-traps, and Other Devices"' (English, 1998: 122). ICRC officials who were pushing vigorously for the Convention were reacting to the devastating consequences of the use of landmines that Red Cross workers had observed in a wide variety of different conflict settings in Africa, Asia, and elsewhere. As English further observes:

> [the] ICRC is quasi-governmental and neutral and, from its earliest days, worked closely with national militaries to establish rights of wounded and the non-combatant. In the case of the landmines, the ICRC built upon its relationship with militaries throughout the world to involve them in the debate. The so-called ICRC Regional Conference held at locations as varied as the Philippines, Turkmenistan and New Delhi took advantage of ICRC's status to bring military officials together with representatives of governments and NGOs sympathetic to the landmine ban. Military officials from governments such as India, Pakistan and China which were opposed to the ban heard arguments from others, including military representatives from pro-ban countries. The most important ICRC document was, perhaps, the February 1996 report *Anti-personnel Landmines: Friend or Foe* to which a group of military experts gave their support. (Ibid., 127)

Along with the Red Cross, the other main champions for a landmines ban in the early years were American. The head of the Vietnam Veterans of America Foundation, Robert (Bobby) Muller, was so moved by his own encounters with landmine victims that he began to work closely with US Senator Patrick Leahy of Vermont to establish a fund to aid mine victims and to introduce legislation in the US Congress to ban the export of landmines. Although the resulting legislation, which was signed by President George Bush in 1992, initially called for a moratorium on American landmine exports, it continues to remain in effect (ibid., 122).

Realizing that he would need coalition partners, Bobby Muller forged links with Medico International and other humanitarian NGOs that were keen on banning landmines. In 1992, the International Campaign to Ban Landmines (ICBL) was formed, headed by the well-known activist Jody Williams. Williams, Muller, and ICRC president Cornelio Sommaruga were together to play a key role in lobbying governments around the world to support the idea of a ban.

Initially, the focus of the advocacy campaign was the United Nations. UN General Assembly Resolution 48/7 of 19 October 1993 requested the Secretary-General to submit a comprehensive report on the problems caused by mines and other unexploded devices. This resolution was followed by a second one on 16 December 1993 calling for a moratorium on the export of anti-personnel landmines. The resolution noted 'with satisfaction that several States have already declared moratoriums on the export, transfer or purchase of anti-personnel landmines' and called on all 'States to agree to a moratorium on the export of anti-personnel landmines that pose grave dangers to civilian populations' (UN General Assembly, 1993).

As international support for a landmines ban grew the government of the United States itself gave its support for a ban. In his 1994 address to the UN General Assembly, President Clinton called for a global ban on landmines. Backing up the President's call to eliminate landmines was a US State Department report, *Hidden Killers: The Global Problem with Uncleared Landmines* (1994), which painted a picture of an endless, perhaps insurmountable challenge. The report estimated that 80–110 million landmines were littered around the world and that although perhaps up to 80,000 of these were being removed on an annual basis, another 2.5 million were being planted.

In 1993 Handicap International mounted a major lobbying effort to get the French government to change its policies regarding landmines. In response, the French called for a Review Conference of the CCW to address the issues of landmines. The reason for this was that Protocol II of the 1980 UN Convention deals with Prohibitions or Restrictions on the Use of Certain Conventional Weapons which may be Deemed to be Excessively Injurious or to have Indiscriminate Effects, otherwise known as CUSHIE (causes unnecessary suffering or has indiscriminate effects). The Protocol both defines landmines and prohibits their use against civilians, and it also sets forth rules on deployment of landmines and restrictions on the certain kinds of mines, for example, remotely delivered mines, booby-traps, and so-called 'other devices', i.e., 'manually-emplaced munitions and devices designed to kill, injure or damage which are actuated by remote control or automatically after a lapse of time' (CUSHIE, 1980).

Many organizations, most notably the ICRC, were unhappy with the Convention because it focused on the military as opposed to the humanitarian aspects of these weapons (Fredenburg, 1997: 5). The Protocol did not contain provisions regarding the production, sale, or possession of landmines. It said nothing about use of these weapons in intrastate or civil conflicts and contained no verification or compliance procedures. In 1992 only 32 countries were signatories to these protocols.

Negotiations Begin

The first CCW Review Conference was held on 15 September–13 October 1995 in Vienna to discuss ways of strengthening the anti-personnel landmines (APL) protocols in the CCW. The UN's own estimate at the time was that there were 110 million APLs to be located and cleared in 64 countries and that the pace of mine deployment was increasing rather than diminishing (ibid.). The Review Conference was attended by 44 countries, with the ICBL and a number of NGOs attending as observers. In their briefings to the delegates and in their public statements to the media, the NGOs reiterated their call for a complete and immediate ban on landmines—a call that was supported by a number of countries, including Sweden, Norway, Germany, Mexico, Denmark, Ireland, and Austria. The conference did not make much progress in reaching a consensus on a ban or more stringent controls on the production, export, and use of landmines although it did reach an agreement on banning the use of laser-blinding weapons. Part of the reason for the impasse was that Western defence establishments shared the view that the humanitarian problem was caused by the indiscriminate use of landmines by guerrilla and non-professional armies who targeted civilians. They also were of the view that as older APL systems were replaced by self-neutralizing (SN) or self-destructing (SD) APLs—otherwise known as 'smart mines'—the risk to civilians and non-combatants would diminish. There was also a lack of consensus at the conference on how to verify a possible ban or more stringent restrictions on the production and use of landmines. Russia, China, and India were opposed outright to any kind of ban on landmines.

In spite of the lack of progress, advocates of the ban drew inspiration from President Ramos of the Philippines, who called for a landmine ban in December 1995. Coming from a government engaged in a major counter-insurgency operation against local guerrillas who were using landmines, Ramos's statement attracted considerable international attention. It should also be noted that at the G-7 summit in Naples earlier in the year, Canada's Prime Minister Chrétien discussed the issue of a landmines ban with his fellow leaders in spite of the fact that his own government had not formally given its support for a ban.

A second round of review meetings was held from 23 April to 3 May 1996. In the period leading up to this conference, the NGO campaign for a ban on landmines was clearly beginning to have some effect:

> With the understanding that the CCW would only continue to codify existing military practices, which would not stop the indiscriminate use of APLs, a concerted move began towards a total ban including [smart] SN/SD anti-personnel landmines. The theory was that if the ban did not include SN/SD types, which were more expensive than the older APLs, then a 'have' and 'have not' situation would result. Wealthy nations, who could afford the new APLs, would possess them and poor nations, who could not, would retain the old ones. (Ibid., 6)

In response to mounting public pressure, many countries agreed to institute a moratorium in support of the idea of a total ban.

Agreement was reached on 3 May on a series of amendments to Protocol II. Protocol prohibitions and restrictions were extended to cover 'armed conflicts not of an international character occurring in the territory of one of the High Contracting Parties', but they did not apply 'to situations of internal disturbances and tensions' of an 'isolated' or 'sporadic' nature. The parties also agreed that all 'mines, booby-traps, or other devices designed or of a nature to cause superfluous injury or unnecessary suffering' have to be cleared, removed, destroyed, or maintained under specified articles of the Protocol. It was further agreed that the 'indiscriminate use' of mines that 'is not on, or directed against, a military objective' is prohibited, as were weapons that 'may be expected to cause incidental loss of civilian life, injury to civilians, damage to civilian objects, or a combination thereof' (Article 1).

The agreed-upon amendments to Protocol II also required military forces to take 'All feasible precautions . . . to protect civilians from the effects of weapons to which this Article applies' and to provide 'Effective advance warning . . . of any emplacement of mines, booby traps, and other devices which may affect the civilian population' (Article 3). Other provisions included restrictions on the use of anti-personnel landmines other than remotely delivered mines (such as where they can be placed and provisions governing their removal and destruction) (Article 5); restrictions on the use of remotely delivered anti-personnel mines 'unless, to the extent feasible, they are equipped with an effective self-destruction or self-neutralization mechanism and have a back-up self-destruction feature' (Article 6). As well, the transfer of mines covered by the Protocol was prohibited (Article 8), detailed provisions required that information be recorded on minefields and mined areas (Article 9), and various requirements called on combatants to inform humanitarian workers concerning the placement of minefields or mined areas (Article 12).

Although some of the parties may have felt that this was progress, this was not the mood outside the negotiating room. The ICBL criticized the amendments because they failed to ban the use of dual-purpose mines, including anti-tank mines that have dual uses. The revised protocols also left a large loophole for scatterable mines and permitted the production of smart mines. ICBL members also pointed out that states were given too much latitude in determining whether internal conflicts were governed by the Protocol's provisions. As one account of what proved to be a key turning point in the negotiations chronicles:

> The disappointed gathered on the evening of 22 April 1996 over bean soup at the home of Quaker activist David Atwood. Not only were the members of the NGOs at this rather surreptitious meeting but also representatives of 12 states including Austria, Australia, Belgium, Canada, Norway, New Zealand, and Peru. They considered alternative courses and one was another conference. When the Amended Protocol was adopted on 3 May, Canadian Ambassador Mark Moher announced that Canada would hold a strategy conference of states [supporting] a total ban in Ottawa later that year. To prevent opponents derailing the conference, organizers developed a process of 'self-selection' whereby a Final Declaration was circulated prior to the conference. Those who could sign on were invited as participants; those who would not came as observers. The device was of critical importance in creating the Ottawa Process. A group of 'core partners' was formed, and these states worked closely with the ICRC and ICBL to rally support for the ban. (English, 1998: 123)

The Ottawa Process

As the review sessions of the CCW proceeded at their own glacial pace, a series of backroom meetings between NGOs and government officials aimed at widening and strengthening the ban took place. There was gathering support at these meetings for creating a second track that would take the negotiations outside of the CCW framework. Those in favour of this second track realized all too well that the consensus-based rules governing the negotiations in the CCW meant that agree-

ment would fall to the lowest common denominator, allowing those states opposing a ban to effectively block the will of the majority. At the first of these meetings, in January 1996, only eight governments were in attendance, but by the
second, in April of that year, the number had grown to 14. Canada was the host of
the third meeting, which examined the modalities of an international meeting to
take place in Ottawa later in the year.

> At these meetings various themes emerged that would subsequently evolve into
> core tenets of the Ottawa Process: first, the need to highlight the debate around
> the military versus the humanitarian impact of AP mines in order to 'contribute to
> the development of new global norms with respect to landmines'; second, the
> importance of regional initiatives such as 'mine-free zones' and regional institu-
> tions; and third, the importance of educational actions designed to attract wider
> official and public interest in the AP mine campaign. (Dolan and Hunt, 1998: 402)

As support for moving the negotiations to a second track grew, there was
much jockeying to keep the negotiations in Geneva. The United States worried
about losing control of the agenda and therefore argued strongly in favour of keeping the negotiations within the Conference on Disarmament (CD) in Geneva.
Signalling its qualified endorsement of a ban, it announced that it would introduce
a new policy on AP mines that would seek the removal of so-called 'dumb mines'
around the globe (with the exception of the Korean peninsula, where the US military firmly believed that landmines were still needed to help defend South Korea)
but allow the continued use smart mines. Australia allied itself with the United
States, arguing that any treaty negotiated outside the CD would be neither credible nor verifiable. There were no takers for a second track among the other permanent five (P-5) members of the UN Security Council. However, among the
members of the European Union there was growing support for moving negotiations outside of the CD arena so that an agreement on a total ban could be reached.

The challenge was to galvanize enough support for a second track so that
when the proposed meeting took place in Ottawa there would be a big enough
turnout that the process would have both credibility and legitimacy. The ICRC
took the important step of convening a series of regional meetings that brought
together NGO and government representatives and military officials to discuss the
landmines issue. The ICRC also commissioned a study that raised real doubts about
the military effectiveness of landmines, arguing that the military benefits were
vastly outweighed by the humanitarian costs.

On 1 October 1996, the European Union decided to implement a joint action
plan directed at the total elimination of AP mines. Under this plan, the members of
the EU committed themselves to 'ensure full implementation of the results of the
Review Conference of the 1980 Convention on the one hand, and support for
international efforts to ban AP mines on the other hand'; to seek 'the total elimination of AP mines and [to work] actively towards the achievement at the earliest possible date of an effective international agreement to ban these weapons worldwide';
and 'to raise without delay the issue of a total ban in the most appropriate interna-

tional forum' (Chairman's Agenda for Action on Anti-Personnel Mines, 1996). At the same time, the member states agreed to implement a common moratorium on the export of all AP mines to all destinations and to refrain from issuing new licences for the transfer of technology to enable the manufacture of AP mines in their countries. The EU set aside 7 million ECUs[1] for initiatives, to be launched in the period up to the end of 1997, in the form of contributions to the UN Voluntary Trust Fund for assistance in mine clearance and/or specific EU actions providing assistance for mine clearance in response to the request of a regional organization or a third country's authorities. It was clear that the tide of support for a landmines ban was rising.

On 3–5 October 1996, the first international strategy conference for a land-mines ban was held in Ottawa. The purpose of the conference 'was to catalyze practical efforts to move toward a ban and create partnerships between states, international organizations and agencies and nongovernmental organizations' (ibid.). At the Ottawa meeting 50 countries pledged their support 'to work together to ensure the earliest possible conclusion of a legally binding international agreement to ban anti-personnel landmines'. France and the UK were among the signatories of the Ottawa Declaration that came out of this meeting. Nonetheless, there were rumblings of discontent among the 24 observer countries and from the NGOs.

> The mood among NGOs and others who attended the conference was one of frustration. Reflecting that frustration, Axworthy ended the conference with an unexpected invitation. Come back to Ottawa at the end of the year and sign a ban on the export, production, transfer, and use of landmines. . . . Many, including the United States and Australia, were shocked and, according to some reports, furious about what they claimed as Canadian grandstanding. Axworthy's invitation meant abandoning the CD, the traditional practices of verification and the normal relationship between NGOs and states. (English, 1998: 121)

The Ottawa Declaration called for:

> the earliest possible conclusion of a legally-binding international agreement to ban anti-personnel mines; progressive reductions in new deployments of anti-personnel mines with the urgent objective of halting all new deployments of anti-personnel mines; support for a UNGA . . . resolution calling upon member states, inter alia, to implement national moratoria, bans or restrictions, particularly on the operational use and transfer of anti-personnel mines at the earliest possible date; and regional and sub-regional activities in support of a global ban on anti-personnel mines; and a follow-on conference hosted by Belgium in June 1997 to review the progress of the international community in achieving a global ban on anti-personnel mines. ('Towards a Global Ban', 1996)

On 10 December, UN Resolution 51/45S, passed by the General Assembly by a vote of 156–0 with 10 abstentions, welcomed the adoption of the Ottawa Declaration and recognized the 'need to conclude an international agreement to ban all anti-personnel landmines as soon as possible'. It 'urge[d] states to pursue vigorously an effective, legally binding international agreement to ban the use, stockpiling, production, and transfer of anti-personnel landmines with a view to completing the negotiation as soon as possible' and also called for 'states that have not yet done so' to accede to the CCW and its Protocol II (UN General Assembly, 1997).

As the coalition of countries supporting the negotiation process initiated at Ottawa grew, there was the problem of what to do with the 'official' CD track in Geneva. One of the main obstacles was that the landmine issue was not placed on the CD agenda for 1997. As Dolan and Hunt (1998: 405) explain:

> The rupture of the landmine issue involved a complex arrangement of states— some who feared that the CD would derail the Ottawa Process, some who used the CD to deflect pressure to sign the Ottawa Convention, and yet others who wanted nuclear disarmament to be the top priority for the CD. So in the end, the CD track ended in deadlock. The closest the CD came to agreement was the appointment of Ambassador John Campbell of Australia as special co-ordinator on landmines, essentially to 'conduct talks about having talks'.

In the end it did not really matter what happened in Geneva. The Ottawa Process had gathered sufficient diplomatic and political momentum of its own that Axworthy's vision of an agreement within the year was fast becoming a reality. Austria, which had been tasked with the responsibility of drafting the landmines treaty, had a draft ready to be circulated in November 1996 and then hosted the first 'meeting of experts' in Vienna on 12–14 February 1997 to discuss its draft text. Attending this meeting were representatives from 111 countries. During the discussions some countries continued to press for exceptions on the grounds that AP mines were a necessary tool for self-defence. The draft text called for a one-year period to destroy stockpiles, which some countries objected to, arguing that longer phase-in times were required. Many countries also opposed the intrusive verification regime called for in the text. The devil was clearly in the details.

In retrospect, a series of regional conferences held around the globe and organized by the ICBL, host states, and the ICRC were essential to building international support for a treaty. These conferences not only helped to raise the political profile of the campaign but also strengthened the coalition in favour of a ban. The ICBL held its fourth international conference in Maputo, Mozambique, 25–8 February 1997. Attended by some 450 delegates from more than 60 countries, the sheer size of the conference was impressive. The conference was co-hosted by the Mozambique Campaign to Ban Landmines. Efforts prior to the meeting helped to strengthen the NGO ban campaigns in Angola, Zambia, Zimbabwe, Kenya, and Somalia. Adding to the drama was the fact that just before the conference South Africa, which was a major producer, exporter, and user of landmines, announced that it was immediately introducing a comprehensive ban on landmines. Not to be upstaged by its neighbour, Mozambique, the conference host, announced during the conference that it, too, would ban the use, production, import, and export of anti-personnel landmines. The conference helped to build NGO and pro-ban government partnerships. Seventeen governments addressed the conference during the plenary sessions and two countries—Malawi and Swaziland—announced their support for the ban. The final declaration stated that 'the Ottawa Process is the most clear expression of the will of the international community as stated in the December 10, 1996 United Nations General Assembly resolution calling for the conclusion of an international ban treaty "as soon as possible" and that other negotiating fora, such as the Conference on Disarmament, will not fulfill that will in a timely fashion' (DFAIT, 1997a).

A second major conference, the regional seminar for the states of the Southern Africa Development Community (SADC), sponsored by the International Committee of the Red Cross in co-operation with the Organization of African Unity and the Republic of Zimbabwe, was held in Harare, 21–3 April 1997. Echoing some of the same themes of the earlier ICBL meeting, the final declaration called for the immediate launch of an initiative by the SADC for the establishment of a regional mine-free zone. Some of the concrete initiatives taken at the meeting included the establishment within the SADC Organ on Politics, Defence, and Security of a Sub-Committee on Landmines supported by a working group of experts to promote and co-ordinate 'as a matter of urgency' the planning for humanitarian mine clearance; joint training of mine clearance personnel; technological co-operation to facilitate more rapid and cost-effective clearance operations in the region; adoption of an SADC code of ethics and standards for humanitarian mine clearance; mine awareness campaigns; support of national programs for victim assistance; creation of an SADC database on landmine matters; and funding for humanitarian mine clearance, victim assistance, rehabilitation programs, and mine awareness. Importantly, the participating countries committed themselves 'to end all new deployments of anti-personnel mines and to establish national prohibitions, such as those already adopted in the region, on their production, stockpiling, transfer and use' (Regional Seminar for the States of the SADC, 1997).

The first continent-wide Conference of African Experts on Landmines was held in Kempton Park, South Africa, 19–21 May 1997. The conference was attended by 40 member states of the OAU, UN specialized agencies, and representatives of donor community and non-governmental organizations. The conference discussed African policies on anti-personnel landmines and stressed that the problem be addressed 'in a coordinated and multifaceted manner'. It adopted as its goal 'the elimination of all anti-personnel landmines and the establishment of Africa as an Anti-Personnel Landmines Free Zone'. It also called on all African states to 'end deployments of anti-personnel landmines in Africa and to establish national prohibitions such as those already adopted on the African continent, on their use, production, stockpiling, transfer and their destruction' ('Plan of Action', 1997).

Another important meeting was held in Tokyo on 6–7 March 1997 at the initiative of Japanese Prime Minister Ryutaro Hashimoto. The conference was attended by 27 countries, the European Union, and 10 international organizations. Participants undertook a comprehensive discussion to strengthen international efforts on the problems of anti-personnel landmines. Some of the main points to emerge were that mine-infested countries should themselves play a key role in demining efforts; the UN should serve as a focal point for co-ordinating and assisting demining activities; the international community should consider the impact of the anti-personnel landmine problem in reconstruction and development; and the international community should strengthen efforts to develop usable and cost-effective demining technologies, recognizing the imperative of a 'two-track' approach: combining the most effective, existing technologies in the short term and developing new technologies over the medium term. The participants also called on the UN to develop a technology registration database on demining technologies. The meeting underscored the importance of developing a comprehensive approach to victim assistance and the establishment of mine information systems to collect and analyse information at the local level in order to assist victims ('Tokyo Guidelines' and 'Chairman's Summary', 1997).

On 10–12 June the Central Asian Regional Conference on a Global Ban on Anti-Personnel Mines was held in Ashgabat, Turkmenistan. Participants met to explore regional and global issues related to landmines, calling on the 'world community to do its utmost for mine clearance, rendering of humanitarian aid to mine victims and creating conditions of normal life for the civilian populations' ('Final Communiqué', 1997).

By the spring and early summer of 1997, the key elements of a landmines treaty were falling into place. A second meeting of experts was held in Bonn, 24–5 April, with 120 countries attending. Discussions continued after the Bonn meeting and a final draft of the treaty was ready to be presented in Brussels in June. The new draft dropped some of the verification and compliance requirements in the earlier versions of the treaty, relying instead on voluntary compliance mechanisms. At the Brussels meeting 154 countries attended either as participants or observers. On 27 June 1997, 97 countries signed the Brussels Declaration (with 10 more signing shortly afterwards). The Declaration urged 'the vigorous pursuit of "an effective, legally binding international agreement to ban the use, stockpiling, production and transfer of anti-personnel landmines"' and affirmed that 'the essential elements of an agreement should include: a comprehensive ban on the use, stockpiling, production, and transfer of anti-personnel landmines; the destruction of stockpiled and removed anti-personnel landmines; and international cooperation and assistance in the field of mine clearance in affected countries' ('Declaration of the Brussels Conference', 1997).

Signalling a major change in P-5 attitudes towards the ban, France and Britain, partly as a result of growing domestic political pressure (coupled with the change of government in Britain), came out strongly in favour of the treaty. The ban was also getting some high-level celebrity endorsements, most notably from Diana, Princess of Wales, whose highly publicized trips to Africa to meet with landmine victims helped galvanize worldwide public attention and concern.

One month before delegates met in Oslo to hammer out the final provisions for a treaty, the United States in an abrupt reversal announced that it would attend the conference and essentially 'buy in' to the Ottawa Process. This change reflected the mounting public pressure on the White House to support the fast-track approach towards a landmines ban. However, a number of key holdout countries—Russia, Pakistan, China, and India—decided that they would not participate in the negotiations in Oslo.

When the Oslo Diplomatic Conference finally convened in September, some 87 countries were there as full participants with another 33 others participating as observers. Their goal was to turn the draft Austrian treaty into a final text that would be ready for signature in time to meet Lloyd Axworthy's deadline. The extremely able conference president and chair was Jacob Selebi, a South African. The rules of the conference were that all decisions would be taken by a two-thirds majority, thus effectively making it impossible for any one state to block agreement and marking a significant departure from the way negotiations were handled in the CD, where decisions were made by consensus.

The US made it clear at the outset that it was seeking an exemption from the treaty for Korea and a redefinition of anti-tank mines to fit with the US definition of 'mixed-mine systems' (English, 1998: 124). Although anti-tank mines were excluded from the treaty, those containing anti-handling devices were included. The US wanted the definition of anti-personnel mines to exclude anti-handling devices and self-deactivating mines. The US proposed a number of major changes to the Austrian text that would permit the continued use of smart mines along with landmines deployed on the Korean peninsula. The US also favoured an opt-out clause that would allow any state that found itself involved in armed conflicts to be able to withdraw from the treaty on short notice. The other major amendment sought by the United States was a nine-year delay provision for any signatory to the treaty before it would have to carry out its obligations under the treaty. The proposed amendments did not sit well with the other negotiating parties and were vociferously opposed by the ICBL, which was closely monitoring the negotiations. The US government was only able to gather a handful of supporters for its proposals, e.g., from Japan, Australia, Spain, Ecuador, and Poland, but even then support was lukewarm. Many countries opposed the US-proposed amendments, arguing that there should be no loopholes or exceptions to the treaty. They felt that a longer transition period and a pull-out option from the treaty would leave too many loopholes and undermine the treaty's basic premise, which was to implement a comprehensive and complete ban.

As negotiations with the United States reached an impasse, Canada and Germany worked hard to strike a compromise that would allow the US to become a signatory to the treaty. Even so, the US decided to up the ante by threatening to pull out of the negotiations. At the same time, Canada found itself coming under strong pressure from the NGO constituency not to allow the treaty to be watered down by accepting US demands. In the end, the US offered a number of minor modifications to its original demands—it dropped the specific reference to Korea and its demand for a reservations clause. However, under the new proposals the US would still effectively have been allowed it to keep its mines in Korea for a nine-year period and to find a replacement for AP mines. Failing to find a replacement, the US could still withdraw from the treaty after nine years or if an ally became involved in armed conflict. The modified US proposal had few takers and on 18 September, when the treaty was formally adopted by the conference participants, the US was notably absent. Following the conference, President Clinton announced that the US would stop using landmines in 2006. Russian President

Boris Yelstin offered Russia's commitment to stop exporting landmines and to sign the treaty when his country was in a strong enough economic position to be able to do so. Japan, which earlier supported the US position, indicated that it would support the treaty and Greece and Australia also offered their support.

In December when they met in Ottawa, 122 countries signed the Convention on the Prohibition of the Use, Stockpiling, Production, and Transfer of Anti-Person-nel Mines and on Their Destruction, as the treaty was formally called. Axworthy declared at the signing that the conference was 'undeniable proof that this coalition of governments, NGOs, international institutions and civil society can set a global agenda and effect change' (quoted ibid.). Even so, there were some notable absen-tees at the signing, the foremost being the United States. As US Senator Patrick Leahy (D. Vermont), a strong champion of the treaty, explained with obvious embar-rassment, 'There is no doubt in my mind that he [President Clinton] wanted to sign the treaty. He searched hard for agreement in Oslo, but time ran out. The excep-tions demanded by the Pentagon were not simply minor modifications as some have claimed. They would have seriously weakened the treaty and delayed its implemen-tation for another decade. They were totally unacceptable' (Leahy, 1997).

The Ottawa Convention and Its Consequences

The preamble to the Ottawa Convention states that its chief goal is:

> to put an end to the suffering and casualties caused by anti-personnel mines, that kill or maim hundreds of people every week, mostly innocent and defenceless civilians and especially children, obstruct economic development and reconstruc-tion, inhibit the repatriation of refugees and internally displaced persons, and have other severe consequences for years after emplacement. . . .

These goals are justified on the basis of humanitarian law:

> that the right of the parties to an armed conflict to choose methods or means of warfare is not unlimited, on the principle that the employment in armed conflicts of weapons, projectiles and materials and methods of warfare of a nature to cause superfluous injury or unnecessary suffering and on the principle that a distinction must be made between civilians and combatants. . . .

The Convention makes it clear that its goal is to eliminate anti-personnel mines by prohibiting their development, production, stockpiling, transfer, and use, includ-ing 'smart mines', which were permitted under the amended Protocol II to the CCW. Each state party to the Convention agrees not to use anti-personnel mines; not to develop, produce, otherwise acquire, retain, or transfer to anyone, directly or indirectly, anti-personnel mines; and not to assist, encourage, or induce, in any way, anyone to engage in any activity prohibited under the Convention. States are also obliged to destroy their stockpiles of anti-personnel mines within four years of the

Convention going into force. All states must also destroy all anti-personnel land-mines in mined areas under their jurisdiction within 10 years of the treaty going into force. The Convention also provides for a variety of transparency, facilitation, and compliance measures (Articles 7–13), although it does not contain intrusive verification measures, which many states opposed on the grounds of their intrusiveness and cost. Provisions regarding mine clearance, victim assistance, and rehabilitation are also contained in the treaty.

By 1999 enough countries had ratified the treaty that it went into force, establishing, in the words of one observer, 'a powerful new international norm which will help make possible meaningful inroads into ameliorating the human suffering APMs have caused' (Atwood, 1999: 47). However, a number of potential loopholes in the treaty have concerned some critics. Although smart mines are covered by the treaty, under Article 2, paragraph 1, 'Mines designed to be detonated by the presence, proximity or contact of a vehicle as opposed to a person, that are equipped with anti-handling devices, are not considered anti-personnel mines as a result of being so equipped.' This means that mines that could be used against lightweight vehicles, and that essentially operate like anti-personnel mines, could fall outside of the Convention. Critics also fear that by permitting the use of anti-handling devices, civilians or any innocent bystander could be hurt by such mines. Although the diplomatic record of the Convention suggests general agreement that any device that operates like an anti-personnel mine should be classified as such, the Convention, in the eyes of some, contains enough wiggle room to be a source of concern (ibid., 48).

The success of the Convention can be measured in a number of ways. First, almost 100 countries have ratified the Convention, with the first meeting of states parties to the Convention being held in Maputo, Mozambique, in May 1999. However, there are (and will continue to be) some key holdout states. The list of non-signatories includes Russia, China, the United States, India, Pakistan, Turkey, Finland, North Korea, South Korea, Egypt, Israel, Syria, Iraq, Iran, and most other Middle Eastern states. Some countries, like Russia, argue that they are not in a position economically to sign on to the treaty, but others argue that landmines are critical to their national defence, particularly if their hostile neighbours still have landmines.

Since the treaty was signed a large number of follow-up meetings have aimed at educating and addressing the concerns of states. They include the 'Baltic-to-the-Balkans' regional conference held in Budapest in March 1998, a number of other regional seminars and workshops, and 'conditionality arrangements' for international assistance in mine clearance and victim assistance. The relationship between the Ottawa Convention and the CCW and the CD still remains in some doubt. On the one hand, the Ottawa Convention was designed to be complementary to the amended Protocol II of the CCW so that the two mechanisms can eventually be merged. However, this will require states that have signed the Mine Ban Convention to sign and ratify Protocol II of the CCW. This will eventually pave the way to greater consensus when the next Review Conference of the CCW is held in 2001, and possibly will help to reinforce the primacy of the stronger provisions in the Ottawa Convention (ibid., 53).

One of the criticisms of the treaty is that it has no formal compliance and monitoring mechanisms other than the fact that states parties to the Convention are required to submit periodic reports to the UN Secretary-General. The ICBL has established an international reporting network and database to monitor treaty compliance by individual countries in the areas of mine production, transfers, stockpiling and destruction, use, mine clearance, etc. Co-ordination mechanisms have also been strengthened: the UN Department for Peacekeeping Operations is responsible for co-ordinating all UN activities concerning landmines. At the Ottawa Conference in December 1997 some $500 million was pledged by signatory states and these and other funds have been used to set up a wide range of programs. In the long run, however, the success of the Ottawa Convention and subsequent efforts to strengthen the international regime it represents will be determined by a number of factors, including, as noted by Atwood, the 'effective allocation of resources' (especially financial) to areas where they are needed; a sustained and continued commitment of financial resources; capacity-building, especially at the regional, national, and subnational levels; the development and exchange of data on the number and location of mines; and the successful integration of 'lessons learned' into mine clearance, victim assistance, and public education and awareness (ibid., 56–7).

Figure 5.1 Mine Action Contributions by Country, 1993–1999

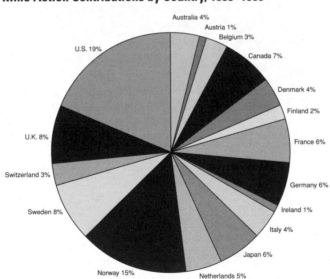

Source: *Landmine Monitor Report 1999: Toward a Mine-Free World:*
http://www.hrw.org/reports/1999/landmine/execsum/Execweb1-05.htm#P633_98552

As Figure 5.1 shows, the chief contributors to the global mine action campaign are a handful of advanced industrial countries, led by the United States and Norway. The size of the US contribution is somewhat surprising given the stiff opposition mounted by the United States government in the negotiations and that the US, at the end, was on the outside as a non–signatory looking in. Figure 5.2 shows that the size of the US contribution to the mine action campaign continued to rise after the Convention was signed but has fallen (marginally) since 1998, when it reached its peak. However, the same is true for Norway (a strong supporter and participant through the entire Ottawa Process) as well as for most other contributing countries (with the notable exception of the UK). This may be a worrisome indicator of declining interest in the treaty which was preceded by a highly visible international public campaign and considerable media hype. Figure 5.3 shows that the bulk of contributions by individual donor countries over the years for which figures are available has gone into mine clearance. Although contributions to public awareness/education/advocacy are also a priority for most countries, the same cannot be said for victim assistance, which does not even figure into the budgetary contributions of three key contributing countries: the UK, the US, and Sweden.

Figure 5.2 Total Mine Action Donor Contributions, 1993–1999

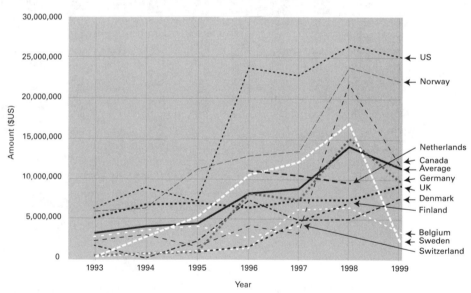

Sources: *Landmine Monitor Report 1999: Toward a Mine-Free World:*
http://www.hrw.org/reports/1999/landmine/execsum/Execweb1-05.htm#P6333_98552;
UN Department of Peacekeeping Operations, Mine Action Investment Database:
http://webapps.dfait-maeci.gc.ca/mai/frameset.asp

Some critics of the Ottawa Process argued that the treaty would not add one more dollar to mine clearance and that the exercise was simply a public relations gabfest. This is obviously not so, given the sizable resources that many governments, including the US government, have devoted to the global mine action campaign. In fact, it is arguably the case that the negotiations themselves and the publicity that surrounded them did much to galvanize the international community and open national cheque books. However, there may be some danger that international inter-est in the mine action campaign is subsiding in the aftermath of the treaty's signing and going into effect. The low priority assigned to victim assistance by some major donors (at least as measured by budgetary expenditures) is also a source of concern, particularly since this was a key priority in the Ottawa Convention. In sum, although there is good reason to conclude that the treaty has been a 'success' according to some of the above-mentioned indicators, it is by no means an unqualified success and some trends, particularly on the financial side of the picture, should raise some red flags.

Figure 5.3 Donor Budget Allocation, 1993–1999

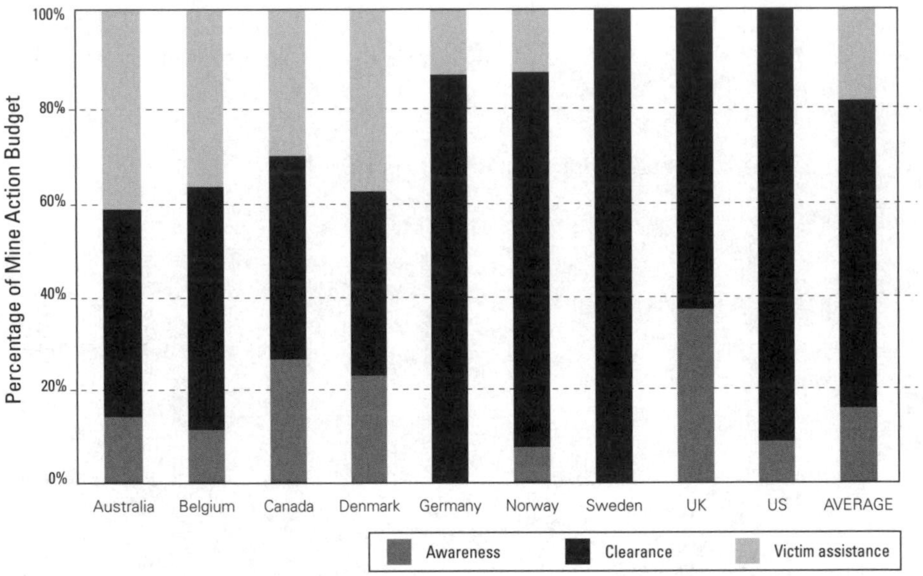

Source: UN Department of Peacekeeping Operations, Mine Action Investment Database:
http://webapps.dfait-maeci.gc.ca/mai/frameset.asp

Conclusion

As a limited global undertaking directed at creating a public good that in many ways spans 'safety of peoples' and 'sustainable human development' conceptions of human security, the Ottawa Process is a noteworthy achievement. Not only did the negoti-ations leading up to the treaty galvanize public attention and concern, but they also have generated real resources that are being directed (though not in equal measure) at the three main goals of the treaty that was signed in Ottawa in December 1997: mine clearance, mine awareness and education, and victim assistance. But in regard to the question of who provided (and is providing) this global public good, there is no simple or straightforward answer. On the one hand, the global landmines action campaign was a largely, though not exclusively, civil society or cosmopolitan under-taking. Even so, this campaign to a large extent had North American and European roots and sponsors. A survey of delegates attending the Ottawa Conference showed that the majority of NGOs participating were North American (and primarily American, not Canadian). Non-European or non-North American NGOs accounted for only 20 per cent of the sample (English, 1998: 128). We should also not forget that international organizations, in particular the ICRC, played a key role in launching the landmines campaign and working alongside the ICBL in raising the profile of the issue around the globe, thus lending support to the institutional perspective on global public goods and their creation. UN Secretary-General Kofi Annan was a key supporter of the Ottawa Process and helped generate international support while offering the legitimacy of his own office for this second negotiating track.

On the other hand, it must not be forgotten that the parties to the Ottawa Convention were and are states and that the governments of some states (Canada and Norway) played a key role in lobbying other governments to join the Ottawa Process and sign the treaty. It is therefore much closer to the truth to view the Ottawa Process and Convention as a confirmation of the growing influence and impact of middle-power multilateralism.

But the Convention represents only one element (admittedly an important one) of the human security public goods and goals that it seeks to achieve. The provision of most public goods also requires a corresponding commitment of financial resources. Here the picture is more complex and includes some important minilateral components. This is because one of the principal non-signatories, the United States, has been one of the most important financial contributors to the global mine action campaign. In view of strong US opposition to the treaty itself, the extent of US financial support is perhaps somewhat surprising, although some would argue that the US position—being the biggest operational player, but being reluctant to join the normative bandwagon—is consistent with deeply rooted strains in the history of American diplomacy and culture (Luck, 1999a). What is also somewhat surprising, if for somewhat different reasons, is that a small country like Norway, which was one of the champions of the treaty, is a relative superpower when it comes to the level of resources it has committed to the mine action campaign. By comparison, Canada's contribution is relatively modest.

The real lesson of the landmines campaign, therefore, is that human security public goods (and the social and political change that necessarily precedes their delivery) can only be provided if governments, non-governmental organizations, and international organizations work together in pursuit of common goals and a shared agenda. As the Ottawa Process demonstrates, middle powers can be leaders in this process by changing the agenda and forging new international coalitions. But the provision of most public goods, including those of the human security variety, also requires a commitment of real resources and not just good intentions. For this, the support of great powers, including the United States, will be crucial.

Note

1. An ECU was a European currency unit, which consists of a weighted basket of European currencies. It has been superseded by the 'euro'.

Chapter 6

Promoting the Safety of Peoples: Controlling Small Arms

Riding high on the success of the signing of the 1997 Ottawa Convention banning anti-personnel mines, Canadian Foreign Minister Lloyd Axworthy and Red Cross president Cornelio Sommaruga called for a coalition of like-minded states and civil society actors to address the small arms and light weapons problem.[1] At a workshop immediately following the signing conference in Ottawa in December 1997, an NGO-inspired proposal for a convention to prohibit civilian access to military-style arms and curb intergovernmental transfers was advanced as a successor to the just-signed Landmines Convention. It was thought that the same grouping of middle-power and civil society actors behind the success of the landmine treaty could extend their momentum into the field of small arms proliferation. Three years later, Axworthy appeared to have largely abandoned the effort. In fact, the plan did not receive widespread support and roused considerable criticism from both the government and NGO sectors. This state of affairs would suggest that the effort to create a small arms regime will not come so easily.

At the same time, curbing the flow of small arms is perhaps one of the clearest and most pressing human security concerns facing the international community today. With the shift from interstate to intrastate conflict since the 1960s, the ready availability of small arms has made them the weapons of choice for today's combatants. Consequently, small arms have also become the main instruments behind civilian casualties and account for much of the human misery and economic and social disruption in societies wracked by armed conflict (see Figure 6.1). The very high level of civilian death and suffering in recent conflicts is no longer considered as simply a side effect of these conflicts. Instead, the impact on civilians is now considered to be a consequence of inadequate or non-existent management of the flow of small arms. Accordingly, small arms control falls squarely under the humanitarian or 'safety of peoples' concept of human security since it affects the well-being of non-combatants in violent conflict. The focus of efforts to date has been on curbing the illicit trade and on limiting legal arms transfers and availability—especially in circumstances where humanitarian principles are being violated.

Figure 6.1 Survey of Red Cross Workers:
Which Arms Cause the Most Civilian Casualties?

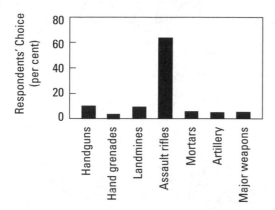

Source: http://www.armscontrol.org/ACT/augsep98/mkas.htm

However, judging by the wide array of actors, institutions, and interests involved in the manufacture and trade of small arms (see Figure 6.2 and Table 6.1), it has been less clear how best to provide for this public good. Current efforts to control small arms are characterized by a patchwork of international and regional initiatives involving a multitude of state actors and organizations with varying interests and objectives. Great powers either have not taken the lead or have only been grudging participants in efforts to curb small arms flows and have focused largely on the illicit trade. Like the drive to ban landmines, efforts at building a small arms regime involve both civil society and middle-power multilateralist actors. Many NGOs have designed proposals to control the trade, have begun grass-roots campaigns to remove small arms from circulation, and have been applying pressure on reluctant governments to take the small arms problem more seriously. Many see the Ottawa Process—where like-minded states joined with civil society actors to forge a new norm—as a precedent that can be applied to efforts to institute a small arms regime. As during the Ottawa Process, middle powers, including Belgium, Canada, Norway, and Sweden, have been collaborating with civil society in an effort to address the small arms issue. However, in a somewhat different vein from the Ottawa Process, efforts to negotiate a small arms control regime are occurring largely within formal international organizations. As yet, there is neither the political will nor the desire to create a separate track that would move negotiations to a different forum, as occurred during the Ottawa Process.

Ultimately, issue complexity differentiates small arms from other types of arms control and makes it inherently difficult to provide for a small arms control regime. As UN Secretary-General Kofi Annan concluded: 'there is probably no single tool of conflict so widespread, so easily available, and so difficult to restrict, as small arms' (quoted in Regehr, 1999b: 2). As is not the case with anti-personnel landmines and weapons of mass destruction, national governments, militaries, police forces, and even civilians can demonstrate a far greater legitimate need for small arms to provide for national and personal security. Many states, including the major powers and many developing states, also view small arms as legitimate commodities of commerce and are therefore hesitant to welcome measures that would restrict their trade.

Figure 6.2 Worldwide Small Arms Manufacturers

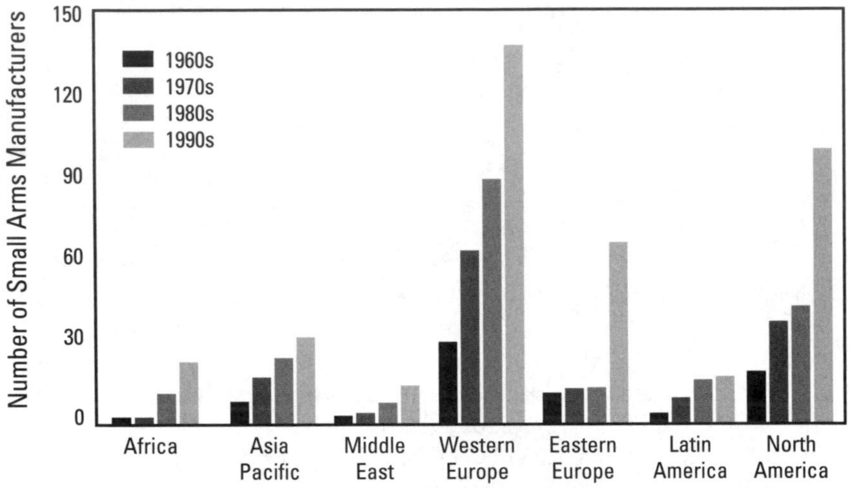

Source: http://www.armscontrol.org/ACT/augsep98/mkas.htm

Simply stated, the problem presented by small arms proliferation affects more regions of the world and is underpinned by stronger political and economic interests. The actors engaged in the small arms trade are also more numerous and harder to control than those involved in the manufacture of other types of weapons. In addition, because small arms are so widespread and represent such a myriad of weapon types, efforts to control small arms lack the advantage that the landmines campaign had in that international attention was able to coalesce around a distinct weapon of questionable military value (Dyer and O'Callaghan, 1998: 31). Even in the case of landmines, although an international norm has been established, it will take several decades of devoted effort to universalize the Ottawa Convention, to clear existing mines, and to assist the victims before the process can be said to be fully successful.

More to the point, the nature of small arms is such that practical initiatives to restrain and manage these weapons will not come easily. As Michael Renner (1997) observes, 'The tools and assumptions of traditional arms control and disarmament, focused as they are on nuclear and major conventional arms, and tailored to the needs and circumstances of Cold War protagonists in North America, Russia, and Europe, have little relevance for dealing with the spread of small arms and the peculiar set of internal conflicts in which they are used to devastating effect.' Although international concern over small arms has grown in recent years, the fact remains that few practical efforts have been made to control effectively their transfer or production.

Table 6.1 Fifty Conflicts Around the World

Region in Conflict in 1998, 1999, or 2000	Soldiers and Rebels Under 18		Known Weapons Suppliers
	Total Number	Lowest Age	
Afghanistan	100,000 – *	10	Russia
Algeria	100 – *	15	Russia
Angola	7,000 +	8	Russia, France, US, private dealers
Bangladesh	100 +	16	
Burundi	8,000 +	8	private dealers
Cambodia	7,000 +	5	France, Russia, China, South Africa
Central African Republic			
Chad		12	US, France
Chechnya	1,000 – *	11	
China			
Colombia	19,000 +	8	US, Germany, Russia
Comoros		13	
Congo (Brazzaville)		14	Italy, black market
Congo (Kinshasa)	6,000 +	7	China, France, US
East Timor	1,000 +	15	US, UK, Germany, France, Russia, domestic
Egypt			US, France
Eritrea	100 +	11	
Ethiopia		12	
Georgia			
Guatemala	1,000 –*	11	
Guinea-Bissau	50 +	17	
Haiti			
Honduras	1,000 – *	13	
Kashmir	100 – *	12	China, Russia, UK, France, Germany, US, domestic
Kenya			US, Belgium
Kosovo	100 –*	13	
Kurdistan (Iraq, Iran, Turkey)	3,000 +	7	France, China, Brazil, US, Germany, Russia, independent transfers, Israel, UK, domestic
Kyrgyzstan			
Lebanon	100 – *	9	
Lesotho			
Liberia	12,800 *	6	
Mexico	1,000 – *	6	
Mozambique			
Myanmar	50,000 +	6	China, domestic
Nepal			
Niger			
Nigeria			
Northern Ireland		16	
Palestine (Occup. Territories)	1,000 – *	12	
Peru	2,100 +	9	Russia, US
Philippines	1,000 +	10	US, UK, domestic
Rwanda	20,000 +	7	China, Israel, South Africa, US
Senegal			
Sierra Leone	5,000 +	5	US
Somalia	1,000 – *	11	
South Africa			US, Israel, France, UK, Germany, domestic
Sri Lanka	1,000 – *	8	China, US, Israel, black market
Sudan	25,000 +	7	China, France
Tajikistan	100 – *	16	Russia
Uganda	8,000 +	5	US, Russia

*1996 estimate (other figures are for 1998–2000).
Note: Information on child soldiers and leading arms suppliers is noted where available.
Source: http://www.iansa.org/news/2000/may_00/scourge_sciam.htm

Specifically, if the international community is to address small arms proliferation with any success, it will likely have to move beyond efforts to restrict trade and circulation and focus on future production. With previous arms control efforts having largely focused only on the possession or deployment of weapons, creating restraints on production is a concept largely foreign to policy-makers. Indeed, only a very few weapons have been banned in the past century, including chemical weapons and, most recently, landmines. One of the lessons to be drawn from the landmines process is that creating the political will to contain production is possible only if the widespread availability of a weapon is seen as more of a nuisance than a benefit.[2] Of course, the question is whether small arms can be classified in a similar fashion, thus creating the momentum necessary for political change. However, upon consideration of the small arms debate, it is not clear if this is happening.

Small Arms and Human Security

The small arms issue is intimately related to the changing nature of warfare and security. Since the latter half of the twentieth century, there has been a trend away from interstate wars fought between states to intrastate conflicts where communal groups have become the main belligerents. Since the end of the Cold War, these wars have caused the deaths of millions of people and created tens of millions of refugees and displaced persons. Such conflicts have included a broad array of actors, including regular armies, insurgent groups, militias, ethnic groups, social classes, criminal squads, and mercenaries. Intrastate conflicts tend to involve the indiscriminate use of violence against civilians, occur on non-traditional battlegrounds, are 'low intensity' and typically protracted over a long period of time, and occur largely in the developing world. In fact, during the 1990s, close to half of the world's least-developed countries endured conflict directly and countless others faced refugees from neighbouring countries. This trend towards intrastate warfare and, specifically, the characteristics that define it correlate strongly with the intensification of the small arms problem.

Of course, the causes of communal conflict are complex and varied, often involving political and economic grievances, the actions of self-aggrandizing leaders, security dilemmas, and the lack of democratic process. Although not the cause of conflict, the rampant and wholesale accumulation, diffusion, and transfer of small arms have served to heighten the degree of intrastate conflict. For instance, a strong correlation has been noted between the worsening of the conflict in Kosovo and the pillaging of close to a million weapons from neighbouring Albania. Further, small arms have had a direct impact on the probability and duration of conflicts and the ability of affected societies to foster peace in the aftermath of negotiated peace settlements. As Jeffrey Boutwell and Michael Klare (1992: 2) explain, there are several reasons for this symbiotic relationship between small arms trafficking and contemporary conflict.

First, small arms are comparatively cheap to make and buy since they require little technological ingenuity, and they are also easy to manufacture. As compared to an F-5 jet fighter, which requires an inventory of about 60,000 spare parts, an AK-47 Kalashnikov only has 16 moving parts. In fact, many subnational groups, among them the Irish Republican Army and the Palestine Liberation Organization, possess the ability to manufacture their own small arms. Further, there is a major glut in the small arms market, due largely to the high level of arms transfers during the Cold War but also because there are many manufacturers, as many countries have acquired the requisite expertise and licences to produce them. For example, approximately 400 firms are now producing small arms in over 60 countries worldwide, representing an increase of over 500 per cent since the 1960s (see Table 6.2).

Table 6.2 Proliferation of Small Arms Production, 1960-1999

		Africa	Asia/ Pacific	Western Europe	Eastern Europe	Middle East	Latin America	North America	Total
1990s	Firms	22	31	137	66	13	17	99	385
	States	7	14	15	15	6	5	2	64
1980s	Firms	10	23	88	12	6	15	42	196
	States	5	14	15	7	4	5	2	52
1970s	Firms	2	17	63	12	4	8	36	142
	States	2	10	16	7	2	4	2	43
1960s	Firms	1	7	29	10	2	3	17	69
	States	1	5	14	6	2	2	2	30

Source: Lumpe (2000: 82), based on information from *Jane's Infantry Weapons, Jane's Security & Counter Insurgency Equipment, British Defence Equipment Catalogue, International Defence Equipment Catalogue*, technical and advertising brochures from law enforcement equipment manufacturing companies, and the Omega Foundation's database of military, security, and police companies.

Second, small arms provide an extremely lethal punch relative to their size and cost. With some weapons—such as the AK-47, selling in Angola for $10–$15 on the black market—firing hundreds of rounds per minute, small arms are a particular menace to individual security (Boutwell and Klare, 2000: 3). Modern assault rifles can discharge hundreds of rounds per minute, providing a single gunman with enough firepower to slaughter dozens, and perhaps hundreds, of people in a very short time.

Third, small arms are simple to operate, as evidenced by the number of children using them. The new brands of ultralight weapons can be fired by children as young as nine, differentiating small arms from their counterparts of earlier eras, which required precision aiming and sheer strength to be used effectively. They are also highly durable, often remaining operational for 20 to 40 years.

Fourth, small arms are highly portable and easy to hide, making them ideal for smuggling. They can be transported by a single soldier or light vehicle and thus are relatively easy to introduce into areas of conflict. Finally, unlike other types of weapons systems, small arms have legitimate uses for military and police forces. In fact, depending on a state's national laws, citizens are able to own small arms ranging from pistols to automatic rifles. In other countries there has been a dramatic rise in the number of militias or private security firms, which are often equipped with small arms.

The above attributes make small arms highly adaptable to today's conflicts where the combatants are typically poor and lack access to major weapon systems, lack professional military training, and must operate in remote areas. In other words, small arms are not simply a smaller and less costly version of major weapons systems. Rather, they are a separate class of weapons with unique qualities and characteristics. Whereas small arms are personal weapons intended for the use of individual combatants and require no real expertise, training, wealth, or logistical capacity on the part of the user, major conventional systems are intended for teams of combatants belonging to professional military structures. The use of such weapons usually entails months of training, frequent servicing by technicians, and an elaborate supply line. This difference sets small arms apart from other weapons and makes them a particular threat to human security.

Aside from their qualities, the modes of acquisition of these weapons have also added to their adaptability to today's conflicts. As in the Cold War, much of the supply and acquisition of small arms are arranged through legitimate channels and are not 'contrary to the laws of States and/or international law' (UN, 1991). Likewise, states can legally strengthen their own security and power by supplying subnational groups with small arms, as has occurred in South Africa, Mozambique, Colombia, Guatemala, and Albania. However, and unlike the Cold War, a large part of the trade in small arms could be seen as no longer complying with the definitions of the legal trade. Specifically, with the end of the superpower rivalry, the major producing states have been left with large surpluses of small arms and, as they have downsized their armed forces, many of these weapons have found their way into developing countries experiencing conflict.

In contrast to the diminishing trade in major conventional weaponry since the end of the Cold War, the small arms trade is bigger than ever.[3] Governments continue to trade massive quantities of small arms, both through open and accepted military aid programs and through covert operations. As militaries have diminished since the end of the Cold War, both Western and post-Communist countries have sold off their surplus weapons to practically any interested party. However, most arms are sold by private firms legally through ordinary trade channels. Although these channels are presumably regulated, few countries actually pay much attention. The United States likely has one of the strictest national control regimes, but even so, it sold or transferred $463 million worth of small arms to 124 countries in 1998 alone (Boutwell and Klare, 2000: 2). Of these countries, approximately 30 were at war or experiencing significant civil violence during the same year—in at least five of these conflicts, US or UN soldiers on peacekeeping duty have come under fire or were threatened with US weapons.

There has especially been a rise in the illicit small arms trade, confounded by the above characteristics of this class of weapon. In the black market, private dealers consciously defy the arms sales policies of source, transit, and/or recipient states for economic profit. In fact, few if any non-state groups or even repressive governments produce their own weaponry. Most rely on the illegal market for their small arms needs. There are at least three kinds of illegal acquisition in areas of intrastate conflict. The first involves the covert transfer of weapons to a government or non-state actor from another government. A second type of illegal transfer relates to the black market. With the increasing number of United Nations arms embargoes and the involvement of non-state actors in conflict, black market channels have become the source of arms for states and groups that are barred from obtaining arms through normal conduits. A third variation involves illegal national circulation, including theft from government arsenals, ambushes to seize weapons from opponents, and subnational groups conducting arms deals with one another. Accordingly, although much of the trade in small arms is perfectly legal, recent events would suggest that the illicit trade has had a major effect on contemporary conflict. Nonetheless, legal and illegal transfers are typically so interconnected that deciphering between the two is next to impossible.

At the same time, the technology to manufacture small arms is no longer confined to the traditional supplier states such as the United States, Russia, China, and France. Over the past few decades many countries have developed the infrastructure and expertise to build small arms. Other countries have manufactured certain weapons or components under licence from companies in Europe and North America and, over time, have acquired production rights. Of worry to proponents of arms control has been the fact that much of this indigenous production is occurring in developing countries, and Brazil, Egypt, Israel, and China have become significant exporters. In fact, it is estimated that over 20 developing nations now manufacture light weapons. Further compounding the proliferation problem is the fact that companies in the developing world operate and export with less oversight than their counterparts in the North, where national governments issue the production licences.

Consequently, through a combination of legal export from supplier states, a burgeoning market for black market weapons, and indigenous manufacture, it is estimated that there are roughly 500 million military-style firearms in current use along with hundreds of millions of guns designed for police and civilian uses. Even if all new deliveries were to stop tomorrow, the sheer number of small arms in circulation has the potential to create mayhem for decades to come—and mayhem they are creating. Although the amount of money spent on small arms pales in comparison to the roughly $800 billion spent annually on military forces around the world, the money for small arms has had a vastly skewed impact on human security. In fact, although it is hard to arrive at an exact figure, the licit and illicit trades in small arms have each been estimated to be worth between $2 billion and $10 billion per year, or only 13 per cent of the total conventional arms trade according to the Arms Control and Disarmament Agency (ACDA) (Krause, 1998: 3). Others, such as the International Action Network on Small Arms (IANSA), place the worth of the small arms trade at roughly one-quarter of the $40 to $50 billion of conventional arms sold each year (Klare, 1999: 10). In any case, the export of small arms has never been a central earner of foreign exchange or a significant generator of employment (Lumpe, 2000: 3).

Most of the human suffering in today's conflicts results from small arms such as pistols, machine guns, and grenades, not from major weapons systems such as tanks, aircraft, or artillery. In fact, an estimated 60–90 per cent of civilian fatalities in some three dozen conflicts since the end of the Cold War resulted from small arms—far more than from landmines, mortars, artillery, and major weapons systems combined (Dhanapala, 1998b: 5). In fact, 700,000 civilians are killed by small arms fire each year. The figure for firearms deaths may be doubled if worldwide firearm killings and suicides outside war zones are accounted for (Regehr, 1999a: 255). Considering that most war casualties are civilians, the small arms dilemma presents a major challenge for human security.

Even after armed conflict has subsided, civilian suffering often persists as the availability of small arms can foster a culture of violence and fuel criminal activity. A recent study of the ICRC's medical database on weapons-related casualties indicated a decrease in civilian casualties of only 20–40 per cent during the 18 months following the end of an armed conflict in a particular region (Herby, 1998: 2). In the same way, although South Africa and El Salvador are formally at peace now, both countries have experienced slayings with small arms that rival in number the people killed in former fighting. Such after-effects can also be seen with regard to international relief missions, which are being suspended more frequently as aid workers themselves have become targets of attack, and consequently, civilians often suffer increased pain and are deprived longer. In the 1990s over 40 ICRC personnel were killed in Chechnya and Rwanda alone, compared with the 15 who lost their lives in all armed conflicts between 1945 and 1990 (Boutwell and Klare, 2000: 6). Likewise, unrestricted flows of small arms frequently undermine reconciliation efforts and peacekeeping operations by making them less effective, highly hazardous, and expensive to undertake. At the same time, the availability and misuse of small arms is disrupting economic, social, and political development as the trade diverts valuable resources from development assistance. This is especially so since the world's poorest countries often spend the most on small arms.

Put differently, and ironically, the presence of small arms amounts to a major 'security dilemma' for individuals in societies experiencing violent conflict. With an abundance of weapons in society, any rise in tension and hostility means an increased chance of armed violence and casualties. For instance, the spread of small arms in Kenya from war zones in Sudan and Somalia has transformed formerly small-scale skirmishes between rival cattle owners into major violence. In turn, parties to intractable conflict often turn to the convenience of small arms for their security, which thus sustains a cycle of violence with civilians at the receiving end. This is not a problem unique to countries in the developing world trying to rebuild in the aftermath of war. For example, although the US is more stable than many other countries, high levels of gun ownership and a relaxed attitude towards them have translated into broad-scale violence. More people are killed by guns in a typical week in the US than in the whole of Western Europe in one year. This impact that small arms have on individual security has transformed the issue from one of classic arms control to a component of more broad-based humanitarian concerns. Specifically, the goal of a regime is to control small arms and to decrease, if not eliminate, human casualties associated with their availability and indiscriminate and unlawful use. Such was the goal underpinning the effort to ban anti-personnel landmines, which is thus seen as an important precedent in the realm of small arms. In the landmines case, what drove countries' activism was not any strict national interest, but a 'broadly acknowledged obligation' based on ethical and humanitarian concerns (Regehr, 1999a: 258).

As with the landmines campaign, the purpose of efforts to control small arms is to strengthen international humanitarian law and other norms, in this instance by reducing the flow of small arms to those governments and groups that violate such norms. At the same time, an effective regime of control for small arms requires a truly multilateral and multi-faceted response extending from the international arena to the national level. Such a regime must include both supply and demand measures and, most importantly, a significant commitment of resources. Since small arms are understood as expanding the security options of individual users, simple controls on small arms that do not take into account this widely and deeply held belief will likely prove inadequate. Accordingly, an effective regime will require social, political, and economic changes that create other options and decrease demand for small arms. Considering the inherent complexity of the problem, such a co-ordinated approach is imperative.

Forging a Small Arms Regime

To be sure, a wide range of organizations at the international and regional levels have begun to take the small arms issue seriously and have introduced substantive policy controls with a view to constraining the availability of small arms and their unlawful use in conflicts. A vast array of international organizations, national governments, and civil society actors have devoted substantial effort to finding ways to curb the lethal commerce in small arms. As mentioned above, the campaign to control the spread of small arms will require an integrated plan, but to date the small arms regime more resembles a loose web of initiatives and proposals focusing on the illegal trade where consensus among states is easiest. Perhaps this is the best approach considering that the small arms problem is not confined to any one area and cross-border flows of weapons lend themselves to focused efforts to tighten export controls and interdict illegal shipments. However, with the global reach of the small arms trade and the intimate relationship between its licit and illicit aspects, such an approach evokes some concerns regarding the feasibility of proposed measures and the need to co-ordinate the different initiatives. Practical efforts to address transfers of small arms have been modest, although it could be suggested that formal international organizations have had a degree of success in achieving this objective, thus lending support to the institutionalist paradigm of public good provision.

Efforts at the International Level

THE UNITED NATIONS

Although progress on the small arms issue remained elusive during the Cold War, the United Nations has come a long way in crafting a body of analysis on the small arms trade and its impact on conflict and in developing strategies for the control of such weapons. Although the issue gained salience with the Secretary-General's prominent call for 'micro-disarmament' in his Agenda for Peace in 1995, reasons for this can also be found in the expansion of UN peace and security operations and the problems that weapons flows to combatants have posed for peacekeeping and peacebuilding operations. Similarly, the focus on small arms has been driven by the work of several academics and by a significant mix of humanitarian, disarmament, religious, and violence-prevention groups—many of the same organizations active on the landmines issue.

Work on small arms has taken place within four major venues at the UN: the Special Sessions of the General Assembly on Disarmament, the UN Disarmament Commission, the ECOSOC (UN Economic and Social Council) Commission on Crime Prevention and Criminal Justice, and the Panel of Governmental Experts on Small Arms. In addition, the UN has undertaken several practical measures to stem the flow of small arms in conflict regions and has sought to oversee the effectiveness of numerous international embargoes on the transfer of weaponry into areas of conflict.

The UN's involvement in the small arms issue really began in 1988 with the Third Special Session of the General Assembly on Disarmament (SSOD III), when the proliferation of conventional arms was framed as a major area of concern with respect to international security. The forty-third session of the General Assembly saw the advancement of many of the discussions and proposals of SSOD III. Resolution 43/75 I was the first adopted on the issue, highlighting several aspects of the small arms problem and requesting that states initiate measures relevant to these concerns (UN, 1988). Perhaps most importantly, the resolution also affirmed the central role of the UN vis-à-vis the small arms issue and requested that the Secretary-General play a major part in studying ways and means of promoting transparency in international transfers of conventional arms. In response to Resolution 43/75 I, a panel of government experts began a study on transparency. Completed in 1992, the study confirmed the right of states to procure weapons for their individual and collective defence but warned that this right can have adverse effects on the security of individual states and, specifically, on their social and economic development. Responding to the study's recommendations, Colombia presented a proposal to the General Assembly regarding the illicit small arms trade, adopted as Resolution 46/36 H (UN, 1991). The proposal asserted that all UN states have a responsibility to institute an effective set of laws and administrative means for managing and monitoring their arms transfers in order to curb illicit transactions. The initiative also called on states to co-operate at the international, regional, and sub-regional levels to co-ordinate laws and regulations and to co-operate in matters of law enforcement.

The UN Disarmament Commission (UNDC) began addressing matters related to conventional arms transfers during its 1994 substantive session. It subsequently adopted guidelines for international arms transfers in 1996 in response to UN General Assembly Resolution 46/36, which had proposed the establishment of a voluntary Register of Conventional Arms covering the export and import of major weapons systems. Although the Register focused largely on the illicit trade and was restricted to major weapons systems, the guidelines served to emphasize the significance of small arms in contemporary conflict by pointing out that '[t]he use of small arms and light weapons in conflicts and war has a major bearing on regional and international peace and security and national stability' (Boutwell and Klare, 1999: 161).

Another important body working on the small arms issue has been the ECOSOC Commission on Crime Prevention and Criminal Justice. In 1997, the Commission adopted a resolution calling on the General Assembly to 'work towards the elaboration of an international instrument to combat the illicit manufacturing of and trafficking in firearms, their parts and components and ammunition within the context of a United Nations convention against transnational organized crime.' This resolution included recommendations designed to stem illicit weapons trafficking and called on Interpol, the Customs Co-operation Council, and other international bodies to establish improved methods of sharing information. Using the 1997 OAS Convention (discussed below) as a prototype, several governments—including the United States, Canada, and Mexico—pressed for the rapid negotiation by the end of 2000 of a global treaty on illicit arms trafficking. It was agreed that this Firearms Protocol[4] would be one of three protocols attached to the UN Convention against Transnational Organized Crime. The Protocol calls on all states to regulate civilian possession of small arms, but it does not prescribe any minimum regulation. Specifically, the Protocol aims to set in place common international standards for the import, export, and in-transit movement of firearms, ammunition, and other related materials. Although the Convention has been signed by more than 120 countries and is now legally binding, there is yet no consensus emerging on the Firearms Protocol. The ECOSOC Commission has since organized four regional workshops on firearms regulation aimed at developing a 'Declaration of Principles' on firearms regulation expected to be included in an international convention.

The initiatives coming out of the UNDC and ECOSOC have been given a significant push by the Panel of Governmental Experts on Small Arms, established in 1995 in response to the Japanese-sponsored General Assembly Resolution 50/70 B. The resolution posed the question of how to avert and lessen the destabilizing consequences of the excessive accumulation of small arms and served as the starting point in 1996 for the work of the Panel, commissioned by the Secretary-General to address the issue. The Panel was tasked with investigating the types of small arms being employed in conflicts in which the UN is involved, the nature of and reasons behind transfers of the weapons, and ways and means to prevent and lessen their excessive and destabilizing accumulation. The resulting 1997 report concluded that there is a definite link between the accessibility of small arms and the probability and intensity of armed conflict as well as criminal violence (see UN, 1997a). The report lists both supply and demand factors in the small arms trade and calls on UN members to 'exercise restraint' with respect to the transfer of small arms and to take all needed steps to prevent their diversion into illegitimate hands. This recommendation was endorsed by General Assembly Resolution 52/38 J, which requests member states 'to implement the relevant recommendations to the extent possible' and to promote 'international and regional cooperation among police, intelligence, customs, and border control services' (UN, 1997b). Significantly, the report also recommended that the UN convene an international conference on the Illicit Trade in Small Arms and Light Weapons in All Its Aspects, which was to be held in New York, 9–20 July 2001. The agenda of the conference has been the subject of intense negotiation, yet the conference was unlikely to result in a legally binding treaty. Although critics predict that progress will be blocked by the permanent members of the UN Security Council (which happen to be the main arms-supplying states today), it is expected that a program of action will be formulated listing initiatives at the international, regional, and national levels. At this point it looks as if the most likely outcomes will be the creation of non-binding norms relating to arms export practices and perhaps model regulations pertaining to controlling the activities of arms brokers and retransfers of imported weapons. Nonetheless, a number of states have suggested that they strongly oppose opening the agenda of the conference to include aspects of the legal trade.

Pursuant to Resolution 52/38 J, a new group of governmental experts was established in 1998 with a mandate to prepare a report on implementing the first panel's recommendations and to suggest further measures. Its recommendations, released in August 1999, again stressed the need for co-operation and promoted practical measures, such as moratoriums, designed to address the transfer and manufacture of small arms in conflict regions (see UN, 1999). In fact, the UN has undertaken such measures with a view to stemming the flow of small arms in conflict regions. For instance, in 1994 and 1995, UN advisory missions were assigned to Mali and the Sahara-Sahel region[5] to investigate national and regional implications of small arms proliferation. The missions addressed the types of incentives required to remove small arms from civilian use and how to achieve a requisite level of security. The UN has also sought to oversee the effectiveness of numerous international embargoes on the movement of weaponry into areas of conflict. However, enforcement of these embargoes has generally been weak. There are indications that the UN is getting tougher, as evidenced by the abnormally blunt March 2000 Security Council report, which pointed to complicity by several states and private actors in undermining arms, diamond, and oil embargoes levied against UNITA guerrillas in Angola.

Another practical effort is the work being undertaken by a Group of Governmental Experts appointed by the Secretary-General to carry out a study on the feasibility of restricting the manufacture and trade of small arms and light weapons. The study is also intended to investigate the brokering activities (especially illicit) relating to small arms. Headed by Canadian Ambassador Peggy Mason, the Group planned to present practical approaches to the 2001 Conference and have them incorporated into the Conference's program of action.

It is also notable that, within the UN system itself, a mechanism has been created for Co-ordinating Action on Small Arms (CASA), the purpose of which is to facilitate consultation, the sharing of information, and setting priorities among the UN departments and agencies. Since its creation in 1998, CASA has provided a basis for the UN to understand and contribute to non-UN initiatives, operates as an information centre to communicate the UN's experience in the field, and has organized resources in reply to specific requests for support by affected states (see Biggs, 2000: 31–2).

THE GROUP OF EIGHT

The issue of firearms trafficking was first added to the agenda of what was then the G-7 during the 1995 Economic Summit in Halifax and, specifically, to its roster of transnational crime issues that members sought to address. A subgroup was formed and law enforcement representatives from member states initiated a study on the firearms control situation and were asked to prepare a foundation, later developing into a set of principles, on which the small arms issue could be addressed at the intergovernmental level. At a later meeting on transnational organized crime in Lyon, firearms trafficking was identified as an area requiring further study and consultation and a group known as the G-7/P-8 Experts on Transnational Organized Crime was mandated to develop policy proposals.

At the Denver Summit in 1997 illicit weapons trafficking become a G-8 priority. There, the 1995 principles were tabled with the heads of government, but these were subsequently rejected as being too conservative. The principles were then redrafted, drawing largely from the OAS process (see below), and subsequently discussed at the 1998 Birmingham Summit. This resulted in a commitment to lend support to the 1998 resolution of the UN Commission on Crime Prevention and Criminal Justice.

In particular, the G-8 has played a leading role in accelerating progress towards the ECOSOC Firearms Protocol, laying out much of the groundwork in the course of their own negotiations in the Lyon Group. The G-8 has also encouraged the work of the UN Panel of Governmental Experts on Small Arms and its suggestion of an international instrument to combat illegal firearms trafficking. In determining the scope and purpose of such an instrument, Japan pursued a questionnaire, subsequently drafted by the US State Department with the support of Canada, that suggested that the international mechanism be based on the OAS Convention. The use of the OAS Convention as a model is seen by some critics, including European members of the G-8, as catering to US interests since it does not require changes in US legislation. Significantly, G-8 member states have agreed that the legal trade in small arms is also a concern. Nonetheless, the scope of G-8 agreement has been restricted to illicit firearms trafficking in relation to criminal activities.

Critics properly point out that the G-8 focus is narrow, but the fact that a group of countries that account for nearly 90 per cent of the world's arms exports are addressing the issue is considered a welcome first step. After all, this sends a strong signal that the unrestricted diffusion of small arms is losing legitimacy (Regehr, 1998: 11). Although at a formative stage in addressing the issue, the G-8 is seen as having the capacity to improve the prospects for developing effective international instruments to control illicit trafficking and to urge restraint in legal transfers.

LIKE-MINDED STATES

Even with the involvement of the UN and a diverse grouping of NGOs, the role of governments is key to stopping the proliferation and misuse of small arms. States make the laws, treaties, and policies, and lacking this input little can be achieved. Recognizing that the great powers are unlikely to spearhead any small arms control initiatives, cross-disciplinary coalitions of middle powers have formed to address the issue. Two groups of like-minded states have been active in small arms control efforts. The first group includes Belgium, Canada, Germany, Japan, Norway, the Netherlands, and other states with a history of activity in multilateral arms control. In effect, this group aims to further the coalition of states that collaborated effectively during the process leading up to the Ottawa Convention.

In 1998, the Norwegian and Canadian-led group of 21 like-minded states met in Oslo to consider the problem of small arms proliferation and discuss what sorts of action could be taken by concerned countries. The group agreed on a document, entitled 'An International Agenda on Small Arms and Light Weapons: Elements of a Common Understanding', that emphasizes efforts to prevent the illicit spread of small arms and greater restraint in the legal trade, and calls for improved control and destruction of surplus weapons once conflicts have ended. However, this meeting did not produce the results that the organizers were hoping for. Critics suggest that the original Norwegian text was significantly watered down during a second meeting in 1999 in its regard of NGOs as 'significant partners' and due to the failed Canadian proposal for a convention banning the transfer of weapons to non-state actors (Hubert, 2000: 51). Further, the second meeting included representatives from only 18 countries and less representation from the developing world. Consequently, although originally conceived as a core like-minded group, the Oslo meetings have not resulted in a unified government coalition reminiscent of the landmine process.

The second group, which includes such states as Colombia, Mali, Mexico, and South Africa, consists largely of states that have been directly and adversely affected by small arms proliferation and that have an interest in practical disarmament measures. Like the northern group of like-minded states, the southern group has made efforts to expand its coalition through multilateral processes such as the G-8 and the OAS.

THE BRUSSELS 'CALL FOR ACTION'

In 1998 Belgium hosted an international Conference on Sustainable Disarmament for Sustainable Development, which saw the largest gathering to date of governments and non-governmental organizations concerned about small arms proliferation. This meeting framed the issue within the context of development and post-conflict reconstruction and made calls for greater attention to human security. At the close of the two-day conference the resulting Brussels 'Call for Action' advocated a wide agenda for action and research, stressing the need for a 'security first' approach to development, effective demobilization of former combatants, the destruction of surplus arms, and regional and international co-operation to buttress the ability of police and customs services to curb illicit arms transfers. While the Call for Action was far-reaching in its identification of the various factors underpinning the proliferation of small arms, it has been criticized for falling short of acknowledging states' own role in the problem.

Civil Society

Aside from international organizations, a growing number of civil society actors have been interested in the small arms debate. These non-governmental actors come from three overlapping groups. The largest consists of disarmament and arms control groups such as the British American Security Information Council (BASIC), Saferworld, the Monterey Institute, the European Institute for Research and Information on Peace and Security (GRIP), the Norwegian Institute for International Affairs (NUPI), the Centre for European Security and Disarmament (CESD), the Center for Defense Information, the Federation of American Scientists, the Bonn International Centre for Conversion, Project Ploughshares, and the Institute for Security Studies. Such NGOs often focus on the causes of small arms proliferation at the regional and global levels. However, this view is often at odds with the interests and orientations of the development and humanitarian communities. These latter groups, which include Oxfam, Pax Christi, International Alert, the ICRC, and the World Council of Churches, have a tendency to see the issue in terms of its *impact* and promote measures of a more grassroots or community-based form. Nonetheless, civil society actors have become prominent players in applying pressure on reluctant governments to construct and implement higher standards for small arms manufacture, storage, and transfer.

One such effort has come out of the Arias Foundation in Costa Rica. Beginning in 1996, a group of Nobel Peace Prize laureates, led by former Costa Rican president Oscar Arias, has been advocating an international campaign for a Code of Conduct designed to regulate global arms transfers. The Code would require governments to uphold international standards of democracy, human rights, and peaceful international relations, and arms suppliers would have to ensure that all arms recipients meet certain criteria, such as registration in the UN Register of Conventional Arms—the idea being to enhance transparency, thereby tightening restrictions on questionable arms transfers. This effort is being supported by several national and regional campaigns undertaken by a handful of NGOs. However, by concerning itself with the entire arms trade, by invoking a number of international human rights agreements, and by placing such strict limitations on conduct, the Code has attracted modest government support. The Code is now in the process of being rewritten to make it more palatable to governments by taking existing humanitarian law into account and applying it to the arms trade.

Likewise, civil society has conducted groundbreaking research on the trade in small arms. Indeed, some of the best analysis and practical research on the topic is being done ad hoc by NGOs. Although not distributed widely, it is often 'leveraged' into effective information that serves as a framework for practical policy measures. For instance, the British American Security Information Council convened an informal network of researchers and NGO representatives in the early 1990s to address the small arms issue and produced an anthology in 1995, which has since become a primary reference point for small arms research and policy development (Regehr, 1999a: 254).

Regional Efforts

THE ORGANIZATION OF AMERICAN STATES

The Organization of American States first began considering the issue of international firearms trafficking as it related to drug trafficking and transnational crime in 1990. Two years later the OAS International Trafficking in Firearms study was initiated, largely due to long-standing Mexican and Brazilian complaints that they could not effectively control drugs flowing north so long as they were being inundated by the southward flow of small arms. By the 1990s this concern hit a peak with many Latin American countries pointing to the US flow of arms to drug cartels and guerrilla groups, and to small arms fuelling a crime wave in major cities.

The first gathering of the 'Group of Experts' took place in 1993 in Washington, DC, with 17 countries sending delegations. Although policy was not addressed, the meeting provided a foundation for a second meeting in Colombia in 1994. There, the previous link between firearms and drug trafficking was set aside and discussion converged around the actual problems member states were having with small arms. At this conference, too, a connection was made between the legal and illicit trade in firearms with Brazil's adopted suggestion that an efficient system of laws and regulations was required to control the international trade in firearms. The third meeting of the Group convened in Venezuela in 1996, where it was agreed that a uniform process of authorizations was needed to cover the legal movement of firearms in the western hemisphere.

Between May 1996 and September 1997 a number of drafting meetings culminated in the approval of the 'Model Regulations for the Movement of Firearms, their Parts and Components, and Ammunition' by the OAS Inter-American Drug Abuse Control Commission (CICAD). The Model Regulations were designed to co-ordinate and strengthen the arms export and import procedures of member states with a view to preventing illegal trafficking and diversion for clandestine uses. Although the regulations apply only to commercial transactions and not to state-to-state transfers, they make an important contribution by defining practical measures for controlling imports and exports. The Regulations, endorsed by the OAS General Assembly in June 1998, are considered key to translating political agreements into practical actions that harmonize import/export procedures.

In 1996, during the OAS's Tenth Summit of Heads of State and Government of the Mechanism for Political Consultation and Consensus (the 'Rio Group'), Mexico opened a second diplomatic track in submitting a proposal for regulating the illicit trafficking of small arms in Latin America and the Caribbean. The Rio Group subsequently agreed that, alongside the Model Regulations, a hemispheric convention against the illicit trade in firearms, ammunition, explosives, and related materials was needed. The Group presented a draft convention to the OAS in May 1997 and, after consultations lasting just over five months, a final document was adopted by the full OAS on 13 November 1997. As of February 2000, close to 30 members had signed this OAS Convention and 10 states had ratified it.

The Inter-American Convention Against the Illicit Manufacturing of and Trafficking in Firearms, Ammunition, Explosives, and Other Related Materials, as it is called, is the first such legal document to address illegal arms trafficking (see OAS, 1997). The 30-article Convention lays out a broad set of commitments, control mechanisms, legal requirements, and co-operation procedures and is an excellent regional model since it sets a precedent for agreement on minimum standards. Because of its simplicity the agreement was negotiated in less than a year, and it is hoped that similar agreements could conceivably be adapted and agreed to by other regional organizations relatively quickly. However, it may be that the level of co-operation involved in the formation of the OAS Convention resulted from the original link made to the drug trade, about which considerable political agreement and momentum already existed. The Convention has even provided inspiration at the international level, with the UN Commission on Crime Prevention and Criminal Justice of ECOSOC calling for the General Assembly to work towards an international instrument modelled after the OAS process.

Critics charge that the OAS Convention remains substantially incomplete and untested. Plainly speaking, the simplicity of the agreement is also its potential source of weakness. Based on enforcing existing import and export regulations, the agreement's focus is on co-operation, not on significant changes in attitudes or commitments to prioritize controls on small arms as a whole. Likewise, the Convention is only concerned with illicit transfers, made clear by President Clinton in his statement at the signing ceremony that the agreement 'will neither discourage nor diminish the lawful sale, ownership, or use of guns; but it will help us to fight the unlawful trade in guns that contributes to the violence associated here in America with drugs and gangs' (quoted in Dyer and O'Callaghan, 1998: 14). By effectively divorcing the legal trade from illegal trade, the Convention has been criticized for contradicting the real facts of how the trade in small arms actually works. Another major source of criticism has been the fact that, as of 1998, none of the OAS governments had committed any financial resources to implementation.

The European Union

The European Union has been comparatively slow in addressing the small arms issue. A major impediment has been Article 223 of the Treaty of Rome, which effectively confirms arms production and export as a prerogative of individual member states. In 1991 and 1992, in the aftermath of the Persian Gulf War, the EU Council of Ministers agreed on eight criteria that member states be obliged to consider when licensing the export of arms (see EU, 1998a). However, despite the adoption of these standards, export control policies continue to fluctuate widely across the EU.

In attempting to address this reality, a draft proposal for a Code of Conduct on arms exports was put forth by the United Kingdom and France. In fact, the idea of an EU Code was first offered in 1994 by a number of NGOs, including Saferworld, the British American Security Information Council, and the World Development Movement, with the objective of promoting a common understanding of the restrictive guidelines and to encourage accountability and transparency. The first Anglo-French proposal was rejected since the other 13 members considered it insufficient. A revised version was subsequently agreed to at the General Affairs Council in May 1998.

The European Code of Conduct is designed to be a more thorough, regulatory regime to replace the comparatively weak 'common export criteria' created in 1991 and 1992. The Code requires that a proposed arms transfer should not take place if it would exacerbate or prolong tensions in the recipient state or if an obvious risk exists that the arms could be used for an act of international aggression. Likewise, it prohibits transfers in situations where there is the possibility that they would be used for internal repression, and specifies significant human rights abuses as automatic grounds for the denial of an export licence.

The Code consists of two parts: (1) guidelines incorporating the eight criteria set out by the Council of Ministers alongside requirements for consultation and review; (2) operative considerations that contain procedures for notification and consultation among member states on the granting of export licences (see EU, 1998b). The Code of Conduct has subsequently been adopted as part of a legally binding joint action by EU states that includes a commitment to provide practical assistance to developing countries as they attempt to address small arms proliferation (ICRC, 1999: 17). Some EU states have already initiated such programs, for example, UK assistance to Ethiopia in training its civilian police force and the contribution of the Netherlands to the UN Development Program's activities in Mali. Nonetheless, co-ordinated and concerted action by EU states is modest overall. Critics have also pointed out that the Code fails to provide any mechanism for parliamentary or public scrutiny over arms exports and contains no reference to the need to control arms brokers, agents, licensed production of military, paramilitary, and security equipment, or the need for common EU controls governing end use.

Besides efforts at instituting a Code of Conduct, the EU has focused its attention on the illicit movements of small arms. During its presidency of the EU in 1997, the Netherlands drafted proposals and secured agreement on an 'EU Programme for Preventing and Combating Illicit Trafficking in Conventional Arms' (see EU, 1997). Although the Dutch initiative covers the illicit trade in all conventional arms, the primary focus of this program has been small arms. Different from the OAS system that addresses small arms as a law enforcement issue, the EU scheme frames small arms trafficking within the broader context of conflict prevention and long-term development. Aside from illicit trade, the program also aims to provide capacity-building to other countries and to develop measures to reduce the number of weapons in circulation. Southern Africa, where the UK sponsored a seminar in 1998 with the objective of fostering co-operation and an action plan between the EU and the Southern African Development Community, is considered a test case. However, unlike the OAS Convention, the EU program has no legally binding status since it was adopted as a 'Council Declaration' rather than as a 'Common Position'. Whereas the OAS system seeks to harmonize import/export procedures, the EU program focuses on enhanced co-operation without identifying minimum criteria. However, like the OAS, scarce financial resources have been committed to implementation.

WEST AFRICA

At a 1996 sub-regional Conference on Conflict Prevention, Disarmament, and Development in West Africa organized by the UN Department of Political Affairs in collaboration with Mali, Mali's foreign minister announced a proposed sub-regional moratorium on the import, export, and manufacture of light weapons. This was important for implementing the activities of the 1994–5 UN advisory missions and the three related UN General Assembly resolutions that were later passed. A complex and impressive Malian diplomatic effort in close conjunction with the UN and other key states was undertaken, and in October 1998 the Economic Community of West African States (ECOWAS) declared a three-year renewable Moratorium on the Importation, Exportation, and Manufacture of Small Arms and Light Weapons in ECOWAS states (see ECOWAS, 1998). Unlike the OAS Convention, the moratorium is not a legally binding agreement. In March 1999, the Program for Co-ordination and Assistance for Security and Development was developed in co-operation with the UN and, along with a code of conduct for the implementation of the moratorium, agreed upon by ECOWAS foreign ministers.

The moratorium is considered one of the more successful multilateral attempts to control the flow of small arms both prior to and following periods of civil tension and is offered as a potential model for other regions. Although its effectiveness was tempered by the continuing tensions in the region, discussions of arms control and security co-operation generated in the region by the moratorium agreement have already served to reduce tensions. At the same time, critics point to the incomplete and potentially weak quality of the text, which is made up of 'whereas' clauses with the operational part contained in one sentence (Lumpe, 1999: 162). At the same time, the success of the moratorium will require significant investment in police and customs forces, which is beyond the capacity of most governments to provide without outside assistance. Even with help, a high level of co-operation and similar moratoriums by neighbouring states will be required to make the initiative effective.

SOUTHERN AFRICA

Until recently, no institutions specifically addressed small arms proliferation in southern Africa, although the issue had been discussed in the Southern African Development Community (SADC) as it related to drug trafficking. However, in May 1998 the SADC partnered with the EU and, with technical support from several South African and European research institutes and NGOs, adopted the Southern Africa Regional Action Plan (see SADC and EU, 1998). The Plan lays out an agenda for action directed at curbing illicit small arms transfers, reinforcing the management of legal transfers, and collecting and disposing of arms in domestic circulation. Although the Plan did not initially receive a commitment of resources, it has since secured support from several governments and EU bodies.

Obstacles to Creating a Small Arms Control Regime

The greatest obstacle to a global small arms control regime is the very character of these weapons. Although the international community could unite behind a campaign to ban anti-personnel mines and seek their elimination as an obnoxious weapon of war, small arms are inherently different. Unlike AP mines, both national and many subnational actors have a recognized need for small arms for purposes of national security and self-defence. Although a body of international humanitarian law relates to the use of small arms, there are relatively few international norms against possession itself. This status has prevented small arms from being stigmatized in the same way that nuclear, chemical, and biological weapons, and most recently landmines, have been. Small arms are one of the most visible manifestations of Article 51 of the UN Charter, which confirms the right of states to use force in self-defence or in defence of sovereignty. Accordingly, a case can be made that states have a right to manufacture and acquire weapons necessary for self-defence. In other words, small arms do not lend themselves easily to arms control approaches such as a ban. Solutions will have to take into account the fundamental right of states to self-defence and likely will have to go beyond the supply side, which has dominated how the international community has dealt with the problems of weapons of mass destruction and major conventional systems.

To be sure, a confluence of factors after the Cold War, namely, the greater attention given to communal conflicts and their associated human suffering, has brought about a reassessment of small arms proliferation. Many proponents of small arms control have begun to focus on their use in certain situations, by certain groups, and particularly against civilians. As policy-makers have begun to realize the implications, a multitude of global and regional actors have been pursuing initiatives to address the pervasive flow of small arms as it relates to human suffering. At the same time, the current collection of initiatives resembles a patchwork of efforts, each dealing with a certain angle of the problem. In each case, different state and non-state actors are advocating different—possibly conflicting—initiatives. Considering this quality of the small arms campaign, it is perhaps not surprising that co-ordination of these efforts has proven difficult.

The most basic impediment to effective co-ordination is the fact that national laws governing small arms vary widely from country to country. Different states have different attitudes and regulations governing the possession, use, and transfer of small arms. In some states, such as the US and Finland, small arms are widely available and accepted as part of the national culture. In the US, there are a quarter of a million federally licensed firearm dealers—20 times the number of McDonald's restaurants (Renner, 1997: 21). However, in other states, such as Canada, Japan, Australia, and the UK, the ownership of small arms is very restricted or prohibited altogether. Likewise, there are significant differences in export policies with regard to licensing, categorization, export criteria, end use, and brokering (Benson, 1998: iv–v). Consequently, without an overriding mechanism to monitor and control domestic access to guns, it proves extremely difficult to control small arms at the international level.

Co-ordination and co-operation are also problems at the international level. As Keith Krause explains, the problem of small arms is actually being approached as several problems. Some define the issue as a human rights one, others as a public health or development issue, and still others as a problem of post-conflict disarmament, terrorism, or criminality. This disagreement over the human security dimensions of the small arms problem is reflected in the various efforts to deal with the dilemma. For instance, the OAS has interpreted the small arms problem largely as a law enforcement issue—the illicit trade of weapons (not the weapons themselves) is considered the issue. Conversely, the EU program presents the issue in the broader context of conflict prevention and long-term development and incorporates weapons collection, buy-back, and destruction programs alongside educational initiatives with a view to transforming the culture of violence that permeates societies. In contrast, the OAS Convention offers no guidelines for the destruction of collected small arms—simply, illegal weapons will be confiscated, recorded, and marked. Some observers have also pointed to a broader regional division between regime advocates in the North and South, with supporters in the South focusing largely on the role and responsibility of arms-producing countries (mainly located in the North) in contributing to the proliferation and misuse of small arms in their regions, while the North focuses largely on demand factors in countries experiencing conflict (Lumpe, 1999: 153).

A lack of co-ordination and the presence of conflicting objectives are also evident at the NGO level. At the same time, a coalition of NGOs that can publicize the humanitarian aspects of the problem is thought to be necessary to a successful global campaign for a control regime. From the start of the campaign to ban landmines, NGOs focused on the injuries to civilians caused by these weapons. No such mechanism as the International Campaign to Ban Landmines exists to co-ordinate NGO efforts on the small arms issue. As mentioned, stakeholders in the NGO community are dispersed into three different groups: disarmament and control groups, development organizations, and humanitarian and human rights groups.

Many of the NGOs that have entered the field of small arms are veterans of the debates on the arms trade, military expenditures, and other security issues that dominated the Cold War. However, they have few links with the development and humanitarian NGOs, and these groups are necessary if a campaign is to focus the world's attention on the human security aspects of the issue. Critics also point out that arms control NGOs have a tendency to favour supply-side solutions, as most of them come from industrialized states that, in the past, have been 'guilty' of fuelling conflicts in the developing world. These groups, typically, are not experienced in working in developing countries where many arms are left over from Cold War era conflicts and thus where it is often demand-side factors that need to be addressed. Further, compared with environmental and humanitarian NGOs, disarmament NGOs have little ability to influence government policy or international organizations since governments continue to have effective control over military information. At the same time, many development and human rights NGOs are reluctant to involve themselves in the small arms issues since their status and presence could be tarnished if they associate with military matters.

Another issue concerns how these various groups are to co-ordinate their efforts with those of states. Practically all of the proposed control measures described above imply strengthening the capabilities and resources of the state. Yet the humanitarian and development NGO communities view such an enterprise with concern since states are also considered to be the principal abusers of human rights and humanitarian norms. This reality will likely hinder efforts to form an NGO coalition on the small arms issue and dampen efforts to bring NGOs into a coalition of like-minded states. Indeed, this very division precluded unified NGO support behind Foreign Minister Axworthy's proposal for a convention to prohibit the access to non-state actors of small arms. However, a larger fracture in the NGO community impedes efforts to create a unified voice.

Parallel to efforts to control the trade in small arms, a burgeoning of 'pro-gun' NGOs has served as a key obstacle to small arms control. Unlike mainstream NGOs, the gun lobby has been able to coalesce around a single issue—the fear that international controls will extend into the domestic realm. The efforts of pro-gun groups began with the first meeting of the International Conference on Firearms Legislation (ICLF) held in Australia in 1993. The conference, which included representatives from groups in the US, Canada, South Africa, New Zealand, and Australia, addressed the issue of firearms laws with the stated objective of 'protecting the rights of firearms owners wherever they are threatened' (Boutwell and Klare, 1999: 111). The most co-ordinated and institutionalized effort has come from the World Forum on the Future of Sport Shooting Activities, which held its first meeting in Germany in 1997. Based in Brussels with a secretariat in Rome, the World Forum is thought to include over 20 participating organizations. Its founding members include the US-based National Rifle Association (NRA) and the Sporting Arms and Ammunition Manufacturers Institute (SAAMI), which sets standards with regard to the manufacture of sporting weapons and ammunition. Although little information is available on its activities, the World Forum's objective is believed to be 'the exchange of information, the reaching of consensus positions and actions by the member associations or the Forum itself in those situations which warrant it' (ibid., 112). Of course, the NRA has generally led the attack on proposals for small arms control. The NRA has become a UN-accredited NGO expressly to fight weapons control worldwide, maintaining that access to firearms is a fundamental freedom and that arming for self-protection is an effective anti-violence strategy (Cukier, 1998a: 13). The NRA's criticism has focused largely on the work of the UN Panel of Governmental Experts. The NRA was especially critical of the Panel's support for disposing of small arms left over in post-conflict situations, marking firearms at the time of manufacture, and studying the prospects of curbing the production and trade of small arms to manufacturers and dealers. The NRA's lobbying efforts are also thought to be behind the push in the OAS to frame the issue as one of law enforcement. In particular, the NRA worked hard to have the text in the preamble of the OAS Convention confirm the 'different cultural and historical uses of firearms' and to have it state that the agreement 'is not intended to discourage or diminish lawful leisure or recreational activities' (Dyer and O'Callaghan, 1998: 14). Essentially, the gun groups' activities have concentrated on denying the connection between domestic controls and the global small arms trade. In fact, the US has confirmed that it will not sign onto anything so long as it imposes international controls on domestic private ownership. As many commentators rightly reply, this ignores how the trade operates and, particularly, the connection between the licit and illicit markets.

Conclusion

To be sure, there has been co-operation and dialogue between several of the initiatives outlined above, as the work carried out within ECOSOC, the OAS, and the G-8 attests. However, this constellation of initiatives lacks specific mechanisms for co-ordination and formal exchange. At the same time, no significant efforts have been made to introduce proposals to other regional organizations such as the Association of Southeast Asian Nations and the Organization of African Unity. With each effort responding to a particular aspect of the small arms problem, the plethora of proposals and initiatives lacks unity. However, co-ordination is imperative at this stage to maintain momentum on the issue and avoid duplication of efforts. Ultimately, the establishment of a multi-layered regime is required to cover the global transfer of small arms, similar to the current regimes in place encompassing nuclear, chemical, and biological weapons. Specifically, a system of national, regional, and international restraints—working together—is needed to interdict illicit transfers and better manage the trade for legal ones.

In light of this imperative, it would appear that international institutions at the global and regional levels are uniquely poised to deliver a more cohesive small arms regime. Although domestic regulations, such as national codes of conduct, should be given priority, efforts should also be made to build oversight and control mechanisms at the regional and international levels. Since arms traffickers could easily work around strict regulations in one country as long as other countries have weaker regulations, there is a need to co-ordinate export regulations and develop international co-operation.

Because networks of illicit dealers, insurgents, and consenting government agencies are responsible for the small arms trade at the regional level, efforts such as the OAS Convention and EU Code of Conduct are particularly important. At the international level, the UN has been at the forefront of the issue and has played a leading role in raising awareness and understanding of the excessive and destabilizing accumulation and transfer of these weapons, as well as in laying the groundwork for international norms against their transfer. This has especially been the case through the efforts of the Panel of Governmental Experts and the ECOSOC Commission on Crime Prevention and Criminal Justice, which have encompassed both the humanitarian and legal aspects of the trade in small arms. For its part, the Panel of Governmental Experts has set the tone of the small arms proliferation debate by offering definitions of small arms and light weapons that have become mainstream, by placing small arms within a security rather than a humanitarian discourse by addressing only 'excessive and destabilizing accumulations', and by distinguishing between the licit and illicit trades (Hubert, 2000: 50). Likewise, the reports emanating from the Panel served to launch the current advocacy campaign headed by NGOs and like-minded governments, as evidenced by the 1998 meeting of 21 countries in Norway and the Brussels Call for Action.

The UN has also proved key in monitoring the effectiveness of numerous international arms embargoes and, recently, in supporting Mali's efforts to collect and destroy surplus small arms and to promote a regional moratorium. Accordingly, the activities of intergovernmental organizations suggest that these institutions are providing the main impulse for an eventual regime. This is understandable considering the stake that states have in the issue as it relates to their security and sovereignty.

At the same time, although the 'cosmopolitans' are themselves divided on the issue of small arms trafficking, pro-control civil society groups are playing an important role by helping to develop the norms that underpin the efforts of international institutions. At the local level, grassroots campaigns have sprung up to remove small arms from circulation within communities. For example, in Mozambique, the Mozambican Council of Churches has instituted a voluntary turn-in program, in which weapons, mines, and explosives are traded for other goods (Wurst, 1998: 13). Such zones of conflict have also spurred the creation of a broad range of NGOs that represent victims and remind governments of their responsibility to end the violence by dealing with small arms. Similarly, civil society has come together in Western countries such as the US, the UK, and Australia to lobby for more rigid gun control legislation. Such groups have also been key in placing the spotlight on recalcitrant governments and their role in supplying small arms to areas of conflict marked by human rights abuses. Likewise, considering civil society's aptitude for providing information, sharpening the issues, and mobilizing public opinion, such actors will bring substantial expertise to formal efforts to manage the flow of small arms.

Nonetheless, civil society actors will have to achieve a higher level of co-operation and co-ordination in their efforts if they are to be truly effective. Although in its infancy, the International NGO Action Network on Small Arms (IANSA) has created mechanisms to guide the collective work of NGOs on the small arms issue. The organizational structure of IANSA can be described as both elaborate and loose. It is made up of a large 'reference group' tasked with strategic direction, a 'facilitating committee' responsible for the day-to-day workings of the network, and a decentralized secretariat. At the same time, membership in IANSA is very loose in that organizers have prioritized breadth of membership over depth. Alongside NGOs, the network includes university departments, UN agencies, the ICRC, and groups of eminent persons. However, this breadth has come at the expense of coherence because political rivalries do exist and some critics blame the network's lack of progress on infighting.

Dedicated middle powers are also playing (and will likely continue to play) a crucial role in providing a conduit for these groups to contribute to international initiatives. The 1998 Belgian-sponsored conference, which brought together delegates from 59 countries from the North and South and 200 representatives from civil society, serves as a useful benchmark in this regard. Given the vastness of the problem, such a coalition of middle powers and NGOs will be instrumental in defining goals and bringing together an effective grouping that encompasses the major orientations on the issue. At the same time, there needs to be increased co-operation between governments and the NGOs themselves to make certain that progress in the small arms field will be steady and cumulative.

Although constructive minilateral efforts appear to be absent from this story, there do seem to be nascent efforts on the part of the US to play a more constructive role than it did during the campaigns to ban landmines and to create an International Criminal Court. In a statement made before the UN Security Council in September 1998, US Secretary of State Madeleine Albright called the 'uncontrolled flow of arms' a 'dirty business [that] fuels conflict, fortifies extremism, and destabilizes entire regions' and proposed 'full and timely disclosure of all arms shipments' to regions of conflict and a 'voluntary moratorium on arms sales that could fuel these interconnected conflicts' (ibid., 11). Still, critics have charged the US with limiting its concern to illegal arms transfers, thereby largely ignoring the role of governments in promoting the illicit trade.

Unlike the landmine treaty, often considered the standard for the small arms issue, eliminating all transfers of small arms between states will not be supported by those countries that rely on imported weapons for their basic security requirements. However, as in the campaign to ban landmines, successful efforts to control the small arms trade—especially the illicit trade—will require an array of inputs from civil society, governments, and international institutions such as the UN. Ultimately, such a coalition will be necessary to create an international instrument such as the AP mines treaty. These three streams are again present in the emerging international movement to address small arms, as is a fourth one, regional organizations such as the OAS and EU.

Given the complex nature of the problem, formal international organizations will continue to provide the driving force for change. Certainly, in the case of small arms, the UN is very involved and wants to play a much more active role compared to the minor part it played in the Ottawa Process. In fact, this is the main reason why, in December 1998, the UN decided to convene the 2001 conference. Indeed, on close analysis, it would seem that international institutions are in the forefront in achieving co-ordination as demonstrated by the efforts being made through the EU and by the G-8 and OAS in their contribution to the UN's ECOSOC Commission's Firearms Protocol.

Yet it would also seem that no one institution or set of actors is uniquely positioned to solve the small arms problem. A successful approach will require a multidimensional enterprise designed to eliminate illicit small arms transfers and to impose rigid controls on legal sales, along with efforts to foster democratic and economic development in countries divided by conflict. As the current controls on weapons of mass destruction and conventional weapon systems attest, the international community does possess the requisite knowledge to create such a regime. The real question is whether it can garner the needed political will and co-ordinate it into a solution.

Notes

1. There are many accepted definitions for small arms and light weapons. The United Nations' August 1997 'Report of Governmental Experts on Small Arms' defines *small arms* (weapons for use by individuals) as including revolvers and self-loading pistols, rifles and carbines, sub-machine guns, assault rifles, and light machine guns; *light weapons* (weapons that require a crew/team to operate) as heavy machine guns, portable anti-tank guns, recoilless rifles (sometimes mounted), portable launchers of anti-aircraft missile systems (sometimes mounted), and mortars of calibres less than 100 mm; *ammunition and explosives* include cartridges (rounds) from small arms, shells and missiles for light weapons, mobile containers with missiles or shells for single-action anti-aircraft and anti-tank systems, anti-personnel and anti-tank grenades, landmines, and explosives. For the purpose of this analysis, the term 'small arms' is used as a broad label encompassing the above-mentioned weapons and ammunition.
2. AP mines were 'loss-leaders' in arms markets—because of their low cost—and the munitions industry could profit more from demining than from continued production (Beier and Crosby, 1998: 279–81). The situation is rather different in regard to small arms.
3. According to the Stockholm International Peace Research Institute, the major conventional arms trade has contracted by a third since peaking in 1987.
4. The Draft Protocol Against the Illicit Manufacturing of and Trafficking in Firearms, Ammunition and Other Related Materials.
5. The Sahara-Sahel region includes Burkino Faso, Chad, Côte d'Ivoire, Mauritania, Niger, and Senegal.

Chapter 7

Hard Power and Human Security: Eastern Zaire and Kosovo

Nowhere does the protection of human security meet a more acute or dramatic test than in cases of coercive humanitarian intervention. The difficulties in these cases arise from two facts. First, the protection of human security is not the only global public good; it coexists with others, including the promotion of an orderly international peace and the rule of international law. The second fact—common to the provision of public goods generally—is that the costs and risks of delivering the good are rarely easy to calculate or distribute; interventions are dangerous, uncertain, expensive, and sometimes illegal, and the willing are not always the able. By examining the paired cases of eastern Zaire[1] and Kosovo, we will explore the policy implications of two kinds of problems: the conflict of norms that interventions often confront, and the practical politics of capacity and will.

The conflict of norms and the indeterminacy of law are by now familiar. On the one hand there is the public good of interstate order, underwritten by the United Nations Charter in the general prohibition against the use of force by any country against another. As a matter of treaty law, the only exceptions the Charter seems to permit are self-defence and force authorized by a resolution of the UN Security Council. On the other hand there is the public good of saving human life and rights, even when that means protecting people's security against violation by their own government. Norms and treaties of sovereignty and non-intervention are thus set against norms and treaties of human rights and tolerable standards of domestic governance.

In truth, this is not a wholly new problem. If the 1648 Treaties of Westphalia have come to stand authoritatively for norms of sovereignty and non-intervention, Stephen Krasner has reminded us that both those treaties themselves contained anti-Westphalian provisions for minority rights and external interference in a sovereign's affairs (see Chapter 2 and Krasner, 1999). International law, norms, and state practice have since then oscillated quite radically between the non-interventionist and interventionist poles; through the nineteenth and early twentieth centuries, interventionism (invariably by the strong against the weak) held sway as a matter of practice. A sort of legal stasis was reached in the 1945 UN Charter, whose preambular and governing clauses (particularly Article 2) strongly favour the rule of non-intervention as a matter of law. It is fair to add, however, that in the past decade practice has changed again: in Somalia, Haiti, Iraq, the former Yugoslavia, and elsewhere, state practice and rhetoric (much of it exhaled in the Security Council) suggest a normative transition towards humanitarian intervention at least as a moral rule, and as legal when authorized by the Security Council (DUPI, 1999: 94–5).

All of which is only to say that neither international law nor practice gives unambiguous direction in deciding or designing an actual intervention—as the cases of recent years demonstrate. It is right to protect people, and right to keep the peace against arbitrary interventions. The normative question that policy-makers must ask is never just whether or how to deliver one of these public goods, human security or interstate peace. The question is how to reconcile them.

The second category of problems goes to the practicalities of executing humanitarian interventions. Who best decides an intervention, who goes in, and with what effect? The cosmopolitan answer from Chapter 3 emphasizes non-state actors and institutions. Institutionalists turn to the UN (especially) and to other established organizations with authority enough to impart legitimacy to the project. Minilateralists expect likely action and best results from capacity-rich coalitions of strong powers—arguing that law must sometimes follow action, and that a 'just' intervention will in due course attract legitimacy. Middle-power multilateralists— often jointly with non-governmental cosmopolitans—tend to try the UN first, but if that fails to improvise coalitions of the willing and like-minded, they will try to make up in earnest ingenuity and numbers what they lack in military firepower.

The narratives to follow, the cases of eastern Zaire and Kosovo, will address the operational questions of who decides and who goes in. And they will take up the consequential issues of capacity, legitimacy, and results. What will be noticed throughout are the uncertainties and instabilities that prevail in complicated crises. These are the terrible policy puzzles created in humanitarian emergencies— puzzles of confusion and ignorance, capacity and will, law and legitimacy.

These are, to be sure, cases in contrast. The intended intervention in eastern Zaire in 1996, authorized by the Security Council, was fully endowed with legitimacy but lacked (as it turned out) needed resources. NATO's bombing of Serbia had all the resources needed, but lacked the legitimacy (and maybe the legality) that only the Security Council could have provided. In one case, a multilateral intervention led and designed largely as a middle-power enterprise faltered without superpower support. In the other, intervention was led and largely devised by the superpower itself, with support (mostly) from minilateralist allies.

In both cases, however, ambiguous and disturbing outcomes demonstrate deficiencies attaching to each approach. Those experiences point to the portfolio approach as a preferred alternative—exploiting assets and advantages of particular actors and institutions to contend with the particulars and stages of each crisis.

These short case profiles are not meant to tell the whole story of either event. Rather, they attempt only to describe who decided, who went in, and with what lasting effects. Taken together, the two cases might illuminate some of the problems inherent in the hard-power provision of human security.

Eastern Zaire

On a mid-November weekend in 1996, Canadian Prime Minister Jean Chrétien decided on a bold undertaking: Canada would attempt to form a coalition of like-minded governments and command an armed humanitarian intervention into eastern Zaire.[2] His initiative was unprecedented in the history of Canadian foreign relations; never before had Canada led a multinational force under Chapter VII of the UN Charter. Nor did the task fall naturally to Canadians. Equipped with the most modest of armies, defensive of its remaining reputation as a beneficent peace-keeper, reluctant when it came to joining in any use of force abroad, the Chrétien government also knew that it was proposing to command a military action that would have to be conducted mostly by others. In Washington and other capitals, policy voices sounded as equivocal and divided as ever. All could agree that a fear-ful evil seemed about to repeat itself in the squalor and violence of the Zairian refugee camps; none could say for certain how to stop it. In a multilateral inter-vention, the Canadian government proposed a middle power's answer.

Onset

The origins of the conflict in eastern Zaire in 1996 were rooted in the Rwandan genocide of 1994. In that slaughter, an estimated 500,000–800,000 people were killed. Nearly all the victims were minority Tutsi; the rest were generally described as 'moderate' Hutus insufficiently active in the killings or otherwise objectionable to the *génocidaires*. When Tutsi forces ultimately prevailed, more than 2 million Hutu people fled as refugees to neighbouring countries, and perhaps half as many remained internally displaced inside Rwanda.

Of the mostly Hutu refugee population, as many as 1.1 million had settled in camps in eastern Zaire (with about 144,000 refugees from Burundi). Among them lived several thousand soldiers of the Forces Armées Rwandaises, the so-called ex-FAR, the army of the defeated Hutu regime in Rwanda. In the camps as well were an uncertain number of Hutu militiamen and a still less certain number of civilian directors of the genocide. But these ex-FAR soldiers, militias, and other *génocidaires* were not simply mixed into the Hutu refugee population; they were, in effect, governing it. The United Nations High Commission for Refugees (UNHCR), following standard procedure, had facilitated aid distribution in the camps by leav-ing governance to the refugees themselves. And in practice, this meant the geno-cidal Hutu regime of 1994 was replicated in the camps in Zaire along Rwanda's border. Moreover, it did not take long after the refugee influx of 1994 before armed Rwandan Hutus were in violent conflict with indigenous Zairian Tutsis—another dimension of the crisis that erupted in 1996.

Canadian authorities by 1996 were convinced that the tragedy of 1994 in Rwanda had been preventable—that the West specifically could and should have acted to save lives, and was therefore culpable. That belief was held all the more painfully because a Canadian soldier had commanded the inadequate UN force in

Rwanda in 1994. So the moral significance of the 1994 crisis—as it was under-stood in Ottawa—imposed a normative obligation to act in 1996.

Violence in eastern Zaire had been escalating throughout 1996, though the identities and objectives of the combatants could bewilder even close observers. There was, first of all, the recurring conflict between the undisciplined Zairian army (and its kleptocratic political leadership in Kinshasa) and local Tutsi popula-tions, which had been in eastern Zaire for some 200 years. There was also rising violence between Hutu militias and ex-FAR soldiers in the refugee camps and local Zairian Tutsis—with indigenous Tutsis (some known collectively as Banyamu-lenge) retaliating with increasing force against the Hutu refugees. Finally (to simplify), there was an alliance of forces led by the career guerrilla Laurent Kabila, who enlisted the Banyamulenge in the rebellion that would ultimately overthrow the regime of President Mobutu Sese Seko in 1997.

By mid-October 1996, thousands of refugees had been forced by the fighting (and by the intimidation of Hutu gunmen) to flee the UNHCR camps. At the same time, UN and non-governmental humanitarian agencies were compelled to with-draw personnel and suspend deliveries of food, water, and medical help. By the end of October, hundreds of thousands of refugees—some in makeshift camps, some hiding in the hills—were cut off from all aid. One by one, Zairian towns (and airports useful for delivering aid) fell to the Kabila rebels. The Zairian government, fighting the uprising of the Banyamulenge and Kabila, described itself in a state of war with Rwanda, which it accused of attacking and occupying Zairian territory in fraternal support of the Tutsis. Sadako Ogata, the United Nations High Commissioner for Refugees, warned in late October of 'a catastrophe greater than the one we knew in 1994'. CARE Canada, Amnesty International, Human Rights Watch, Médecins Sans Frontières, and other NGOs active in Zaire mounted intense media-lobbying campaigns agitating for armed intervention. Television pictures grew grimmer by the day. 'Now we are confronted by a new genocide', declared Boutros Boutros-Ghali on 8 November. 'I call it a genocide by starvation', the UN Secretary-General said. 'So we must act, and we must act immediately.'

The Crisis Acknowledged

Days earlier, Boutros-Ghali had appointed, as his special envoy to Africa's Great Lakes region, Raymond Chrétien, Canadian ambassador to Washington. The Secretary-General had approached Canada and some other governments for nominees to the post—someone preferably of ministerial rank, fluent in French and English, free of any imperial associations in the area. He immediately agreed when Ottawa suggested Ambassador Chrétien (who happened also to be the Prime Minister's nephew).

In large part precisely because Canada was a middle power with little history in Africa and no geopolitical interest in the fight, the Canadian government was now, for the first time, directly involved in the Zairian conflict. But there were other and more formal pressures working on Canadian decision-makers. At 2 a.m. on Saturday, 9 November, the Security Council unanimously adopted Resolution 1078. 'Determining that . . . the present humanitarian crisis in eastern Zaire constitutes a threat to peace and security in the region,' but without expressly citing Chapter VII, the Council called on UN members 'to prepare the necessary arrangements' to allow the immediate return of humanitarian agencies and the safe delivery of aid to refugees and displaced persons. States were urged as well 'to help create the necessary conditions for the voluntary, orderly and secure repatriation of refugees'. Finally, the resolution asked the Secretary-General to 'draw up a concept of operations and framework for a humanitarian task force, with military assistance if necessary.'

Resolution 1078 bore all the marks of a compromise, which indeed it was. France (with a few others) had bargained vigorously for a Security Council authorization to deploy a multinational force; the United States refused. What was agreed, sometime after midnight, was an invitation to the willing to mount an operation if they could—and if the Security Council later approved. Canada had taken virtually no part in the argument or the outcome in New York that week.

On 6 November, however, the Prime Minister had raised the crisis in Zaire in a phone conversation with Bill Clinton, drawing the President's attention to his own concern and to Canada's role in the person of Ambassador Chrétien. The next day the subject was discussed in a phone conversation between Jim Bartleman, assistant cabinet secretary for foreign and defence policy, and Anthony Lake, Clinton's national security adviser. Lake told Bartleman during that conversation that the only country the Clinton administration 'might conceivably' allow to command its troops would be Canada; this seems to have been the first mention by anyone in authority of a Canadian leadership of a multinational force in eastern Zaire. Then, on 8 November, as the Security Council was negotiating 1078, Deputy Minister Gordon Smith at Canada's Department of Foreign Affairs and International Trade had a similar conversation with Peter Tarnoff, undersecretary of state for political affairs in Washington. 'I think this all comes back to the American reluctance to go to the party', Smith reflected afterwards. 'I think that the Americans were concluding that there was tremendous pressure on them to do something. They sure didn't want to lead it. Who could they find to lead it they could trust?' And did Smith suspect the Americans were also looking for someone they might manipulate? 'Yes, of course', Smith answered. 'Yes, exactly.' By all accounts, Lake and Tarnoff had concluded that a Canadian leadership role might allow the Clinton administration to contribute to an intervention (if ultimately necessary) without incurring the domestic controversy and opposition that US leadership would provoke.

So these were the factors evidently pressing on the Prime Minister on the decisive weekend of 9–10 November: telephone conversations with Raymond Chrétien in Africa; knowledge of the Lake and Tarnoff feelers; irresolution of the Security Council; apparent lack of international leadership to address the crisis; and the awful pictures of refugees dying in eastern Zaire. After a busy two days of telephone summitry (including calls to John Major of Britain, Jacques Chirac of France, Nelson Mandela of South Africa, and to the prime ministers of Belgium, Italy, and Japan, among others) Chrétien made up his mind to act.

On Monday, 11 November, Chrétien's cabinet formally decided after brief discussion to propose Canada as the leader of the coalition to manage an intervention in Zaire and command the multinational force (MNF) itself. The decision was communicated to the UN and to various capitals—but with conditions attached. There would have to be a satisfactory chain of command; adequate funding; a clear mandate; a finite timetable for completion of the mission; solid commitments from coalition partners to contribute 10,000–12,000 troops; and, of course, Security Council authority under Chapter VII. Beyond these provisos, however, there was little certain about the Canadian government's plan or intentions. Above all, it remained quite unclear what exactly the MNF would do when it arrived in Africa.

In Washington on 12 November a delegation of Canadian officials gathered for a meeting in the White House chaired by Lake. Representatives of the State Department and the Joint Chiefs of Staff also attended, but it was Lake who led the questioning and discussion on the US side—and who dominated what Canadian participants remember as painful hours of grilling the Canadians about their plan. In point of fact it was an uneven match: the Canadians were well aware they could claim no expertise in designing Chapter VII enforcement operations, whereas US officials came to the table with all the advantages of experience.

Nevertheless, Canadian policy-makers took the view from the start that US participation in this multilateral intervention was essential. In the first place, the United States controlled a veto on the Security Council, where permissive authority would have to be obtained. In the second place, only the United States appeared to have the military resources—including airlift, communications, and intelligence—needed to mount such a large deployment. And, finally, it was already plain that the defence departments of other powers (small, middle, and great, Canada included) were making their commitments conditional on an actual deployment of US forces.

Policy and Politics in Washington

In Washington, Bill Clinton's election in 1992 had reignited the long struggle over the definition of US policy on intervention and what was called 'multilateralism'. The intensity and acrimony of that argument were aggravated by the degeneration of the US intervention in Somalia, where four US servicemen were killed in August 1993 and 18 more in October.

In 1994 Clinton administration policy found formal expression in Presidential Decision Directive 25, a public version of which emerged as 'The Clinton Administration's Policy on Reforming Multilateral Operations'. The conditions of US support or participation ran to two full pages and will not be repeated here, except to say they included well-known US criteria: that participation 'advances US interests'; that US participation is necessary for the operation's success; that 'an endpoint for US participation can be found'; that command and control arrangements are acceptable; that 'domestic and congressional support exists or can be marshalled'; and so on.

Taken literally, PDD-25 could be understood to exclude US military participation in multilateral interventions almost entirely. But it did not stop Clinton from intervening with good effect in Haiti and in Bosnia. And it did contain this passage in justification of US intervention:

> While the President never relinquishes command of US forces, the participation of US military personnel in UN operations can, in particular circumstances, serve US interests. First, US military participation may, at times, be necessary to persuade others to participate in operations that serve US interests. Second, US participation may be one way to exercise US influence over an important UN mission, without unilaterally bearing the burden. Third, the US may be called upon and choose to provide unique capabilities to important operations that other countries cannot.

In short, although the United States held both procedural and practical vetoes over intervention in eastern Zaire, it was reasonable to believe the Clinton administration might be persuaded not to use those vetoes.

At the same time, however, the Canadians soon sensed they were witnesses throughout to the strains and bargains of interagency politics in Washington. It was Lake's apparent role from the start of this crisis to negotiate agreeable terms with the Canadian and other governments while simultaneously accommodating interdepartmental interests and objectives in his own capital. International negotiations were more than once held hostage to negotiations among the Washington bureaucracies and political factions.

As mediated through Lake, therefore, US purposes appeared to the Canadians as diverse and to some degree contradictory: invite Canada to lead an MNF, but avoid (unless necessary) a US commitment to follow with a deployment of US forces; achieve the humanitarian objective without risking US casualties; perhaps secure the removal of Mobutu without breaking Zaire apart; reassure Rwandan authorities without inciting more ethnic bloodshed in Rwanda or Zaire. But the question was, did the US government have other purposes as well—unspoken and undetected?

In any event, the leading issue for Lake and the Americans at that first White House meeting on 12 November was plainly command and control, and the recurrent US resistance to placing US troops under foreign command. As usual, this was in part a constitutional question for US authorities and in part a political/bureaucratic problem of aggregating domestic consent for US military action abroad. Canadian officials thought the issue was largely resolved that long evening by simulating the NATO-Bosnia command formula. Canadian and US officials easily agreed to the creation of a Steering Group of major troop-contributing and MNF-financing countries that would give political direction to the MNF (and in which all participants, including specifically the United States, would hold a veto on decisions). The Steering Group would oversee an MNF commanded by Canadian Lieutenant-General Maurice Baril, who would have operational control; a US deputy commander would be interposed between Baril and US forces, who would remain as always under the national command of the President. But that left other matters unsettled—rules of engagement; specifying a mandate that would not include fighting the intimidators (or anyone else); the problematic mission of opening 'safe corridors' between camps and the Rwandan border; imposing a time limit; and designs for a follow-on program of peacekeeping and a long-term regional political settlement.

In Ottawa that same day, Prime Minister Chrétien was holding his news conference to announce the Canadian initiative and his intentions. 'Canada may not be a superpower,' he said, 'but we are a nation that speaks on the international scene with a great moral authority. Now is the time to use that moral authority to stop suffering, to avert disaster.' It was the classic normative imperative justifying a humanitarian intervention.

On 13 November (after another Chrétien-Clinton phone conversation) the White House greatly encouraged the Canadians when Press Secretary Mike McCurry announced the two governments had reached 'general agreement on the mission definition, command and control arrangements, and duration of the mission'. But the agreement was contingent on securing other conditions for the deployment, including adequate rules of engagement, consent of countries in the region, and the understanding that the force 'will not separate or disarm militants, conduct forced entry, or police operations in the camps.'

Winning US participation in the intervention was now urgent. The Prime Minister himself had acknowledged in his 12 November news conference that 'the United States is vital to the success of any mission.' Indeed, military commanders in Canada and abroad were adamant that a US troop contribution was a *sine qua non* of their own deployment. Practically alone among prospective contributors, the United States commanded the aircraft, communications, intelligence production, and forces judged necessary for an intervention of 10,000 troops in eastern Zaire. More than that (and having in mind US performance in Somalia and the former Yugoslavia), other governments wanted tangible proof of a reliable US political commitment. In effect, these demands for US collaboration invested the United States with a veto over the whole project—if the United States did not go, nobody would (Smith and Hay, 1999).

Such constraints—logistic and political—shaped negotiations commencing at the UN on a Security Council resolution authorizing a Canadian-led MNF in Zaire. These negotiations—unlike those over Resolution 1078 a week earlier—found Canadian diplomats among the central players; the Canadian mission at the UN produced the first drafts (based on precedents from Haiti and Bosnia) and led the process of bargaining and agreement, with US, British, and French delegations in particular.

When members of the Permanent Five delegations met at the Canadian mission on Second Avenue, the novelty of the event was apparent to all; the great powers were unaccustomed to someone else designing a Chapter VII military operation. Canadian participants in those meetings sensed a complex set of P-5 responses to the Canadian initiative: the French skeptical of leadership by (North American) Canadians and suspicious of US motives but advocating an intervention; the British unhelpful and unforthright; the United States trying to be constructive and to push the project forward without actually committing itself; Russia and China largely passive. Indeed, it was soon apparent that the complicated dynamics of these multilateral negotiations over several weeks would affect Canadian capacity to influence US actions and lead the deployment of an MNF. As a Canadian negotiator would later remark, 'we had some fairly difficult allies.'

Among the Africans, interests clearly diverged. Rwanda's Tutsi leadership was profoundly hostile to the UN, which had failed so comprehensively to prevent or respond to the 1994 genocide; it showed an equal animosity towards the French, identified as pro-Hutu. (This alone would have disqualified the French as MNF commanders.) In Zaire, on the other hand, affinities with France were still strong. Mobutu, following prostate surgery, was resting in sumptuous convalescence on the French Riviera, where he would remain for the next several weeks. His regime for the moment welcomed any MNF that would arrest the progress of the Kabila rebellion and put a stop to Rwandan border interference. But in its corruption and decrepitude, the Mobutu government would never make a reliable diplomatic partner. Canadians officials spent considerable effort attracting the participation of other African states in the intervention, to enhance both its legitimacy and its effectiveness. But it was a difficult challenge. Ugandan President Museveni was something of a patron to the government in Rwanda, and was seen as a menace in Kinshasa. Uganda, Rwanda, and Ethiopia formed the core of what was called in Africa (and in Paris) the 'Anglophone axis'—countries aligned with Anglo–US interests. South Africa was disappointingly passive throughout the crisis, and participation by other African states was compromised by the complexity of their own interests in Zaire's wars.

Intervention Decided

US reservations about the Canadian plan were answered sufficiently at least to achieve Security Council consensus on Resolution 1080, passed unanimously on 15 November. Resolution 1080 (this time citing Chapter VII) determined again that the situation in eastern Zaire constituted 'a threat to international peace and security in the region'; welcomed members' offers to establish 'for humanitarian purposes . . . a temporary multinational force to facilitate the immediate return of humanitarian organizations and the effective delivery by civilian relief organizations of humanitarian aid . . . and to facilitate the voluntary, orderly repatriation of refugees . . . as well as the voluntary return of displaced persons'; and it authorized member states 'to conduct the operation . . . by using all necessary means'. The cost would be borne by the participating states 'and other voluntary contributions'. Participants in the operation would report through the Secretary-General at least twice monthly. The resolution specified that the operation 'shall terminate' 31 March 1997 unless the Council decided otherwise. The resolution also expressed the Council's intention to authorize 'a follow-on operation' to succeed the MNF, but no more was said of that.

Resolution 1080 was conspicuously silent on the ground-level operations of the proposed MNF, except to prescribe its double objective of facilitating the resupply of aid and the refugees' voluntary repatriation. US Ambassador Madeleine Albright left no doubt that these details remained unresolved when she spoke in the Council meeting before the vote. 'Although considerable progress has been made,' she said, 'some outstanding questions concerning the organization and operation of the mission remain to be worked out.'

Canada's UN Ambassador, Robert Fowler, was emphatic that the MNF would carry out only its two objectives, 'no more and no less'. But he was more explicit about what the MNF would not do than what it would do:

> We do not, therefore, envisage disarmament or interposition as elements of the force's mandate. Indeed, disarmament cannot be part of this mandate. If it were, we would require a much larger and more robust force and would need to engage in a war with those who most evidently do not wish to be disarmed. Such a war would bring enormous and immediate harm to the very people we are trying to save, as the elements with guns continue to find sanctuary within the refugee population that they continue to hold hostage.

As it was, Fowler said that more than 10,000 troops had already been committed by over 20 countries. 'While the main body of troops committed to date are from France, the United Kingdom, the United States and Canada, we now have firm offers from Europe, North America, Africa and Latin America, as well as expressions of interest from Asia.'

The reliability of those commitments would soon be tested. But the carefully negotiated rationale of Resolution 1080 was already being overtaken by a dramatic change of fortunes along the Zaire-Rwanda frontier. Indeed, the whole logic of the Canadian initiative was now challenged by a new confusion of facts on the ground.

Just as the Security Council was completing the terms of 1080, an astonishing migration of refugees formed on the roads out of Zaire to Rwanda. Literally within hours, hundreds of thousands of Rwandans were reported streaming towards the border. The Kabila/Tutsi forces, it seemed, had attacked refugee concentrations and successfully separated the Hutu ex-FAR and militias from the mass of the refugee population. It would later emerge that Rwandan authorities were centrally involved in designing and executing the sudden rebel offensive, partly as an attempt to forestall the deployment of an intervention force. What was clear at the time was that the refugees, no longer under the rule of their 'intimidators', suddenly were free to head home. And so, in growing numbers, they did.

The political effects were immediate and powerful. In Ottawa, as in Washington, these new developments encouraged defence officials to advocate a fast withdrawal from the intervention plan. At the UN, Rwanda (for one) quickly withdrew its previous support for the MNF, as envisaged in Resolution 1080, and argued for a redirection of resources to Rwanda to aid refugee reintegration. In eastern Zaire, Kabila himself was telling reporters he didn't 'think the international community has any reason . . . to come here. We have fulfilled the will of the international community peacefully.'

It was hardly peaceful, but Kabila was half-right. The long-standing UN objective of releasing the refugees from the Hutu gunmen to allow their repatriation did appear to be occurring. And humanitarian assistance, denied for so long, seemed likely to be accessible to most of the refugees once back inside Rwanda. But how many refugees were actually returning to safety? How many instead were walking west, deeper into the Zairian jungle? And of those, how many were in fact not so much refugees as fugitives, *génocidaires* hurrying away from the justice (or retribution) they might get in Rwanda? The future of the Canadian-led intervention was decided in some degree in bitter and inconclusive arguments over these issues.

Meanwhile, it could not have escaped notice that Canada's own military commitment to the MNF was remarkably compact for the country assuming command. By 18 November the planned Canadian deployment of 1,500–1,600 people consisted mainly of a task force headquarters, three Hercules air freighters, and a disaster response team of medical and engineering staff. It was an admittedly humble contribution for the lead government in an MNF originally conceived as requiring at least 10,000 troops, to which the United States had been contemplating a contribution of up to 4,000. Canadian officials were already asking themselves whether the small Canadian military commitment would undermine Canada's capacity to solicit and enforce the commitments of others.

An unhappy succession of negotiating sessions, in New York, at the US airbase in Stuttgart, and back again in New York, failed to achieve consensus either about events on the ground or on a military deployment. Much of the difficulty and acrimony were rooted in continuing disputes over the numbers, intentions, and whereabouts of refugees still in Zaire. Aid agencies were putting the total still in need of rescue at up to 700,000; the US government estimated 150,000–200,000. But that left unresolved the contentious issue of what to do. The United States (backed by Britain) resisted deployments of almost any kind—yet, at least. The French (with Spanish, Belgian, and Senegalese support) at one point sought a deployment directly to eastern Zaire. Airdrops of aid to refugees, if they could be located, were emerging as an intermediate option.

It was in the context of these tensions that delegates of some 25 governments, 11 UN agencies, the International Committee of the Red Cross, and the Organization of African Unity (OAU) met in New York on 26 November—and received a Canadian ultimatum. The Canadian chairman, after condemning the persisting indecision, put Ottawa's proposal to other governments: inform Canada within 36 hours of your commitment to an MNF headquarters and to participation in airdrops, and maybe later in protected convoys. Canada would then decide, within another 24 hours, whether there was enough support to proceed; if so, the envisaged Steering Group would be established.

The ultimatum bore results. On 28 November, Canadian Foreign Affairs Minister Lloyd Axworthy and Defence Minister Doug Young announced that 'more than 20 nations' had now offered support—including the United States,

France, Belgium, South Africa, Malawi, Senegal, Denmark, and Japan (offering money, not troops), among others. 'The international community has agreed to set up a multinational headquarters in the region and to put in place the capability to carry out air drops of food into eastern Zaire', their news release said. As well, a Steering Group of 'the major participating nations' would 'take responsibility for providing political direction and co-ordinating the efforts of the international community. . . . Decisions on next steps will be taken by this body. Canada will be chair, but this group will work by consensus.' By now, the news release added, more than 600 Canadian Forces personnel were assigned to the mission, including just under 300 in the Great Lakes region.

The Canadian ministers were surely putting the best possible light on things. British opposition to action remained obdurate, and the US government was expressing so many reservations in public as to make even this modest effort appear improbable.

The new Steering Group held its first meeting on 29 November in Ottawa. Besides Canada, 13 governments were represented (Belgium, Cameroon representing as well the OAU, France, Ireland for the European Union, Italy, Japan, Senegal, South Africa, Spain, Sweden, Uganda, the United Kingdom, and the United States); the Netherlands joined the Group at its second meeting. But the 29 November meeting agreed to little more than to establish an MNF headquarters and await more information from General Baril.

In Africa, circumstances were not growing easier. On 28 November, so that he could more accurately gauge the potential for aid deliveries, General Baril met the rebel leader Kabila in Goma, Zaire. Baril won Kabila's tentative approval for airdrops in rebel-held territory—but in meeting Kabila he had alienated the Zairian authorities in Kinshasa, whose hostility to airdrops became all the stronger. With every day that passed, more Zairian towns came under Kabila's control and the Zairian army retreated westward. At the same time there were distressing accounts of atrocities committed by Kabila's forces—and just as troubling, the disappearance of refugees and displaced Zairians by the hundreds and even thousands. Paradoxically, these disappearances were used by some governments as evidence that airdrops and other measures were unnecessary; when a British surveillance airplane returned from a sortie with photographs of empty roads, British military officers offered them in argument against airdrops. There was still no consensus on the population of refugees and displaced persons now in Zaire; estimates ranged from fewer than 200,000 to more than 700,000.

Standing Down

All the accumulated uncertainties served to open still wider the divisions among Steering Group governments. In Europe, and especially in France, there were continuing pressures on Canada to activate the MNF at least with airdrops. In Washington there was increasing resistance—and suggestions that perhaps the Canadians in their enthusiasm for their leadership role simply did not know when to stop.

Canadian missions in Europe and Africa were at the same time cabling Ottawa with warnings against a premature or unprepared end to the intervention that would damage Canada's reputation for dependability. At Canada's Department of Foreign Affairs, officials by early December were scripting various exit scenarios.

But inside the Canadian government itself there were divisions that complicated the multilateralist effort. Foreign Minister Axworthy remained committed to the utility and possibility of mounting an MNF operation—by willing countries even without Steering Group consensus, if consensus were unobtainable. Canadian aid officials and their NGO partners were similarly convinced that intervention was necessary and practical, with a strong preference for convoys over airdrops. The Department of National Defence (which enjoyed a long, collegial, and sympathetic rapport with the Pentagon) showed ever more open eagerness to stand down the operation.

On 10 December, in a lengthy report, General Baril made a decisive recommendation to the Canadian government to withdraw the MNF and abandon the intervention (DND, 1998). 'It is my assessment that the MNF mission has largely been accomplished and therefore the mandate should come to an end', he wrote in his covering letter—noting that his views had 'been discussed with the US and UK contingent commanders in Kampala and there is general agreement at this level on the conclusions reported.'

Baril went to some trouble in his report to analyse the problem of refugee numbers. Starting with a widely accepted estimate of 50,000 Interahamwe and other Hutu militias blamed for most of the 1994 genocide, and adding 40,000 ex-FAR soldiers and another 10,000 people who were otherwise accomplices in the killing, Baril calculated that almost 100,000 'may have a strong wish not to return to Rwanda.' That meant, 'given the average Rwandan family size', that it was 'not unreasonable to conclude that there may be as many as 250,000 refugees who would resist repatriation.' To derive the total number of refugees still in Zaire, Baril began with the UNHCR pre-November figure of 1.1 million and reduced it to 900,000 to take account 'of possible over-estimates . . . based on generous food distribution and over-registration'. Some 640,000 were known to have returned to Rwanda in recent weeks—leaving (if all this was true) about 260,000 in Zaire. If 250,000 were avoiding repatriation, that left only perhaps 10,000 refugees still in Zaire involuntarily.

These calculations have since been strenuously and angrily disputed. But the impact of Baril's recommendation was irresistible. And it was reinforced by his observations that neither Rwanda's government nor the 'new authorities' (Kabila) in eastern Zaire favoured an MNF deployment in eastern Zaire. 'It is now increasingly clear that regional support for the continued presence of the MNF is rapidly eroding. It is therefore time to cease operations and redeploy from the region.' Canada was still the only state with troops deployed (in Uganda) to the MNF. In Washington on 12 December, the Pentagon announced it had withdrawn half of the 450 US soldiers deployed (under its own command) in the crisis to Central Africa.

When the Steering Group met (for only the second time) on 13 December, Baril presented his conclusions and the Canadian chairman announced his government's new decision: Canada would end its own involvement in the MNF on 31 December, effectively ending the mission.

What followed was for the most part predictable. The French delegate argued for a continued effort, that several hundred thousand refugees (1.1 million minus 600,000 returned) might still need aid. Britain accepted Canada's recommendation, emphasizing the urgency of organizing a political settlement in the region. Belgium sided with France. South Africa was equivocal. The Dutch believed the MNF headquarters at least was still useful, and that other approaches must be found if the MNF were closed down. UNHCR and the World Food Program argued vigorously for maintaining the MNF.

The US representative, George Moose of the State Department, began by accepting the Canadian recommendation; conditions on the ground had changed and the MNF of Resolution 1080 was no longer appropriate. But Moose then surprised the Canadians by suggesting that some element of the MNF headquarters stay in place to monitor events and permit a military response if necessary. No other government took up Moose's suggestion, and the Canadians (as the only ones in the MNF at that moment) reiterated their decision to leave.

Baril departed his African headquarters for the last time on 20 December, and all the Canadians were gone in January.

On 6 January 1997 the Zairian mission at the UN wrote to the Security Council to denounce the outcome of Resolution 1080: the force was never deployed; Baril 'established contact with the aggressors and their illegal administrations'; no safe corridor had been established; the policy of providing humanitarian aid did not achieve its objective; Rwanda attacked the refugee camps to pre-empt the MNF's deployment; and the number of refugees still in Zaire 'exceeded 800,000'.

Prime Minister Chrétien, in a year-end television interview, had put it differently. 'We woke up the international community, we triggered the movement for these people to go back', he said. 'And it is the biggest movement of human beings with no violence, you know, probably for ever. . . . The goal was to give them food, medication, and help them return home. And that's exactly what happened.'

It had been, in truth, a mysterious and worrying episode—and a harsh demonstration of the limits to multilateralist intervention. How many thousands of lives had been saved by the Canadian initiative? How many thousands of people were abandoned by its outcome to suffering and death? Did multilateralism fail for want of resources, or middle-power will, or superpower support? And in the end, could any middle power initiate and manage a large-scale, hard-power humanitarian intervention?

To this last question, at least, a partial answer is offered by the later case of East Timor. Australia's successes there suggest that a middle power can lead a hard-power intervention when it enjoys advantages of proximity, local intelligence, and international acceptance as a 'natural' intervention leader. Even there, however, superpower logistic, intelligence, and political support was deemed indispensable.

Kosovo

In the muddy Balkan spring of 1999, without any express authority from the UN Security Council, the North Atlantic Treaty Organization attacked the Federal Republic of Yugoslavia. The aerial bombardment, lasting some 78 days, was aimed at stopping a familiar and dreadful evil—a methodically brutal 'ethnic cleansing' conducted by the forces of Yugoslav President Slobodan Milosevic, this time in Kosovo. NATO governments framed the action partly as a humanitarian intervention, partly as a response to an acknowledged threat to peace and security. The bombing itself was a minilateralist intervention par excellence, a small number of capacity-rich governments applying hard power to restore and protect human security. But was it right? Did it work? And did the Security Council itself, immobilized by the veto at the start, afterwards endow NATO's action with some badly needed legitimacy? These are the enduring questions defined by the course of the crisis and its unsettled outcome.

Onset

History is disputed property in Kosovo, a place divided by opposed accounts of grievance and justification. It is enough here only to summarize events that gave rise immediately to the NATO intervention of 1999—recognizing that the origins of this episode run back into deeply complex and separate communal understandings of Balkan politics and memory.

This Kosovo crisis is often and easily said to have begun in 1989, when Milosevic, then president of Serbia, abolished the relative autonomy the province had earlier exercised. Milosevic, of course, was engaging in crude ethnic politics, fostering favour among Kosovo's Serb minority as against its ethnic Albanian majority. The prompt result of that action (and other factors) was a sporadic but continual rise in Albanian Kosovar nationalist sentiment. One of those other factors was the violent disintegration of Yugoslavia elsewhere, in Slovenia, then in Croatia and Bosnia.

But if those wars did much to encourage various forms of separatism in Kosovo, the 1995 peace at Dayton may actually have done more (Judah, 2000: 125–6). Not only was Kosovo deliberately left out of the Dayton settlement, UN sanctions against Yugoslavia were lifted and the Belgrade government was formally recognized by the European Union. All of this was seized upon by the hard men of the Kosovo secessionists as evidence of abandonment by the international community and as proof that peaceable reform under Milosevic was futile. By 1997, the Kosovo Liberation Army (KLA) was becoming a significant force and was weakening the appeal of moderate politicians like the prominent Ibrahim Rugova. The KLA was furthermore strengthened in 1997 by the political collapse of neighbouring Albania; anarchy there, and an arsenal of small arms, generated a lively market in Kalashnikovs and a ready supply of guns to the KLA (ibid., 128).

Bloodshed intensified as the KLA extended its operations against Serb army, police, and paramilitary forces, which retaliated in ever more violent reprisals against

Kosovar communities. On 31 March 1998, the Security Council passed the first of its series of Kosovo resolutions. The operative gist of Resolution 1160 was to impose a new embargo against the sale or supply of arms to Yugoslavia. But it also called on Yugoslavs and Kosovars to find a political solution 'based on the territorial integrity' of Yugoslavia, taking 'into account the rights of the Kosovar Albanians and all who live in Kosovo'—while providing for Kosovo 'a substantially greater degree of autonomy and meaningful self-administration'. The resolution evenly condemned 'the use of excessive force by Serbian police forces' and 'all acts of terrorism by the Kosovo Liberation Army'. And it urged investigation in Kosovo by the prosecutor of the International Criminal Tribunal for the Former Yugoslavia in The Hague.

As conditions in Kosovo worsened, other institutional players had also become involved. Resolution 1160 itself acknowledged that the arms embargo had been proposed by an earlier Contact Group, formed by the foreign ministers of France, Germany, Italy, Russia, Britain, and the United States. The Organization for Security and Co-operation in Europe (OSCE) and the European Union also were addressing the conflict and its humanitarian costs.

By the early fall of 1998, as many as 300,000 Kosovars (of a population estimated at two million) had fled their homes; some 2,000 had been killed (Human Rights Watch, 2000). Serb security forces were by now, in the later words of NATO Secretary-General Javier Solana, 'adopting a strategy that increasingly resembled the kind of ethnic cleansing seen before in Bosnia' (Solana, 1999: 115). The human suffering was obvious, as were the potentially destabilizing political effects of a rising flow of refugees into, especially, Albania and Macedonia.

In a new resolution on 23 September 1998, the Security Council again condemned the violence on both sides and affirmed that the 'impending humanitarian catastrophe' in Kosovo constituted 'a threat to peace and security in the region'. Going further, Resolution 1199 demanded that Yugoslavia 'cease all action by the security forces affecting the civilian population and order the withdrawal of security units used for civilian repression'; enable monitoring by EU missions; facilitate the safe return of refugees and displaced persons; and proceed towards a political solution. Resolution 1199 neither provided nor expressly authorized any enforcement action. But NATO the next day itself warned Yugoslavia to stop the violence or risk air strikes (Shawcross, 2000: 362).

With Resolution 1199 in hand, the Contact Group (all but Russia members of NATO) enlisted US envoy Richard Holbrooke to broker the dispatch of unarmed OSCE observers into Kosovo to verify compliance with the Security Council's orders. In support, NATO would supply the OSCE with air surveillance and deploy an 'extraction force' in Macedonia to evacuate the observers in an emergency.

Despite Milosevic's agreement to Holbrooke's terms, the putative truce broke down almost instantly. On 24 October, in Resolution 1203, the Security Council once again condemned the violence of the Yugoslav government and KLA terrorism, lamented 'the grave humanitarian situation', and demanded full compliance from Milosevic with the OSCE/NATO terms negotiated by Holbrooke.

By now, however, control over Kosovo diplomacy had already passed from the Security Council; Canada's Lloyd Axworthy, for one, had openly regretted the fact. 'Self-appointed contact groups have little legitimacy', he declared on 22 October in the Permanent Council of the OSCE. Such contact groups 'are often counter-productive in the search for answers, and undermine the role of duly constituted institutions in advancing peace and security. In particular, we cannot allow the Security Council to be sidelined. To do so would be to run serious risks ourselves.' But the Security Council, deactivated apparently by the (untested) threat of Russia's veto against any enforcement action against Yugoslavia, was indeed sidelined.

Rambouillet

In Kosovo the killings by both sides continued into the squalid cold of winter. Murders of reprisal and revenge multiplied as entire villages were sacked and burned. More thousands of Kosovar families were displaced inside their own country or were sheltering as refugees. The KLA—not a party to the Holbrooke agreements—was launching new offensives, predictably eliciting atrocities by government forces in reaction (Judah, 2000: 190–4). Fighting on 15 January in the village of Racak reportedly left 45 dead, including a 12-year-old boy and two women; accounts then and since have differed, but the Racak 'massacre' galvanized diplomatic activity in Western capitals. On 30 January the NATO Council threatened 'whatever measures are necessary . . . to avert a humanitarian catastrophe, by compelling compliance with the demands of the international community and the achievement of a political settlement.' The NATO statement pointedly added that NATO's secretary-general 'may authorise air strikes against targets on FRY [Federal Republic of Yugoslavia] territory.'

Against that backdrop, under the sponsorship of the six-country Contact Group, negotiations opened in the château at Rambouillet, France, on 6 February 1999. Robin Cook and Hubert Védrine, the British and French foreign ministers, co-chaired the meeting; Secretary of State Albright from time to time assumed leadership in the proceedings. On one side of the negotiation was a divided and contentious Kosovo delegation representing Kosovo's various Albanian factions, including the KLA and Rugova himself. On the other was the Serbian delegation sent by Milosevic—'no one of real stature, in the main because there is only one man who makes decisions in Serbia, and he was not there' (ibid., 200).

As Tim Judah has reported in his detailed and convincing account of Rambouillet (ibid., 197–226), the Serbs participated in the ritual opening statements at the conference and then fell silent for 10 days. The Kosovars, mistrustful of each other and unsure of their popular support at home, never could bring themselves to negotiate the actual terms of a peace settlement for Kosovo.

The conference at Rambouillet wound up inconclusively on 23 February, but not without some accomplishment. The Serbs signed nothing. But Kosovar delegates, under heavy pressure especially from Albright, gave a tentative and contingent agreement in principle to a draft accord largely designed by the Contact

Group—contingent, that is, on a successful consultation with their disparate constituencies in Kosovo. That agreement was signed, some three weeks later, in Paris on 18 March, but only by the Kosovar side. Its acceptance by the Kosovars, combined with its denunciation by the Milosevic government, in effect constituted NATO's *casus belli* for its armed intervention launched the following week.

The agreement, running to 52 single-spaced pages on the US State Department Web site (www.state.gov./www/regions/eur/ksvo_rambouillet_text.html), was thick with military and political detail. But to summarize its provisions briefly, it reaffirmed the territorial integrity of Yugoslavia while asserting 'the right to self-government' for 'citizens of Kosovo'. It required that 'use of force in Kosovo shall cease immediately', along with the safe return of refugees and displaced persons. It specified powers and procedures for an elected assembly and other government bodies. Crucially, it required the withdrawal of nearly all Yugoslav security forces, leaving only 1,500 border troops with support personnel, and police to be replaced by a new Kosovar police force. It provided for OSCE/EU monitors. And perhaps most critically (for NATO and Milosevic), it provided for NATO to form and lead an occupying military force 'to help ensure compliance'. The agreement guaranteed NATO personnel 'free and unrestricted passage and unimpeded access throughout the FRY'. Finally—to attract support from Kosovars reluctant to surrender all claims to independence—the agreement called for 'an international meeting' three years hence to decide Kosovo's future 'on the basis of the will of the people'. None of this was accepted by the Yugoslav government, of course, but it remained politically pertinent as events unfolded. If nothing else, its terms became a standard by which to measure whether NATO, or Milosevic, could claim victory from the war.

To many in the NATO countries, the Rambouillet effort was a disappointing failure. The most powerful military combine on the planet—NATO in (uneasy) collaboration with Russia—had been unable to compel compliance in Belgrade. To others, however, it looked worse than failure; it was a blunder of tragic consequences. Carl Bildt, the former Swedish Prime Minister who served as the UN Secretary-General's special envoy to the Balkans through this period, faults the NATO/Contact Group reliance on the bombing threat—a misreading, he suggests, of how the Bosnian war was ended. In January-February 1999, Bildt has since argued, 'the threat of air strikes was elevated into one of the key instruments of diplomacy. When diplomacy failed, the international community was left with little choice but to fulfil its threat' (Bildt, 1999: 145).

Frustrated at the conference table, the minilateralists now turned to war with the stated objective of preventing a humanitarian catastrophe and securing regional peace. 'There seems to have been a widespread expectation', Bildt observed, 'that limited air strikes would rapidly achieve these stated objectives. Reality turned out otherwise.'

War

Whether Milosevic in March could have accepted any formulation tolerable to NATO and the Contact Group would soon become moot; he lost his chance by turning down a last appeal from Holbrooke in Belgrade on 22 March. What remained true, however, was that the NATO governments were now stuck with their own ultimatum. Having assembled a coalition around the threat of intervention, the humanitarian argument for intervention was now 'reinforced by a strategic interest in the future of the American alliance with Europe' (Nye, 1999: 34). In Kosovo, the OSCE observers had begun to evacuate; as they did, more Yugoslav troops entered from Serbia. In Brussels, the minilateralists were about to start a war.

'Good evening, ladies and gentlemen, I have just directed SACEUR, General Clark, to initiate air operations in the Federal Republic of Yugoslavia.' So began, with a certain brisk courtesy, Javier Solana's press statement of 23 March. 'Our objective is to prevent more human suffering and more repression and violence against the civilian population of Kosovo', said NATO's Secretary-General. 'We must also act to prevent instability spreading in the region.'

What then occurred (slowly at first, partly because of bad weather) was an aerial bombardment of Serbia and military targets in Kosovo. What also occurred, with shocking speed, was a near-catastrophic outflow of refugees from Kosovo, mostly into Albania and Macedonia. By NATO's own account, the numbers of Kosovar refugees more than doubled during the air campaign—finally exceeding 800,000—between the beginning of April and the end of May. Leaving aside issues of blame-placing, this seemed a painful form of humanitarianism. (UNHCR, for its part, professed itself entirely unprepared for the exodus; NATO troops were soon assigned to refugee camp construction along Kosovo's borders.)

Even after the war it was impossible to prove to what extent the flight of refugees resulted from a planned and bloody Serb strategy of expulsion, or a contagion of fear and confusion, or other causes. At NATO headquarters, as interpreted by the blustery spokesman Jamie Shea, it served as evidence of Yugoslav government malevolence and therefore the rightness of NATO's cause. But when the refugee totals were added to the numbers of Kosovars displaced inside Kosovo, NATO calculated that fully 90 per cent of the province's whole population had been forced from their homes by the end of May.

All of this—and accumulating video reports of civilian casualties and hardship under the bombing in Serbia—inevitably inspired questions about the effectiveness, and the rightness, of the NATO campaign while it was under way. Questions of effectiveness registered acutely as the campaign wore on, not least because Clinton (although he later relented) went to war insistent against using US ground troops. This reassurance may have tempted Milosevic and his generals to believe NATO's heart wasn't in the fight; it almost certainly allowed them more freedom to deploy troops against Kosovar civilians instead of for self-defence. NATO's risk-averse reliance on high-altitude flying also limited the accuracy and effectiveness of its air campaign, raising risks of 'collateral damage'.

Questions of rightness registered precisely because this was a minilateralist intervention, conducted without the legitimizing authority of the UN Security Council. It might in fact have breached international law, insofar as it carried neither Security Council authority nor the justification of self-defence offered by the UN Charter; lawyers in NATO governments, however, were ready to argue that impending humanitarian disaster, together with Yugoslavia's open violation of Resolutions 1199 and 1203, was justification enough in law.

Albright and other NATO ministers had succeeded in keeping the Kosovo question out of any Security Council vote since October. Even so, in one of those moments explicable only in the Security Council's own arcane politics, the Council did get to vote on the matter right after the war started. On 26 March, by a vote of 12-3 against, it rejected a resolution sponsored by Russia, Belarus, and India that would have demanded 'an immediate cessation of the use of force' against Yugoslavia. The result of the vote was no surprise. But it might actually have freed Russia's Boris Yeltsin, having discharged pro forma his duty to Milosevic, then to collaborate with NATO in bringing the war to an end.

And in the end, it was a collaboration. If fluid membership and hard power are minilateralist assets, they were fully exploited in the last phases of the bombing campaign. At least until the Rambouillet conference, Russia's rather passive diplomacy in the developing Kosovo crisis had been marked by nostalgia, inertia, and distraction (Levitin, 2000). But in April, Yeltsin named former Prime Minister Viktor Chernomyrdin, a man with good relationships in Washington and no fondness for Milosevic, to handle the Kosovo file. Shortly after, the US State Department advanced Finnish President Marti Ahtisaari as co-envoy—the anvil, as it was put, to Chernomyrdin's hammer (Shawcross, 2000: 376; Judah, 2000: 274–5). Together, in league with Strobe Talbott of the State Department, Chernomyrdin and Ahtisaari were to shape and finally deliver Milosevic's surrender.

The terms of that surrender were in effect prescribed on 6 May at a meeting of the G-8—the old G-7 plus Russia, therefore forming a realigned and slightly expanded version of the pre-Rambouillet Contact Group membership. Eight days later, in Resolution 1239 of 14 May, the Security Council itself endorsed those terms by emphasizing that 'the humanitarian situation will continue to deteriorate in the absence of a political solution to the crisis consistent with the principles adopted' by the G-8 foreign ministers. At this point, of the Council's five members with a veto, all but China were themselves participants in deciding the intervention's course.

The air campaign thundered on, and some NATO leaders in May spoke publicly of preparations for a ground war. Even Clinton allowed on 18 May that 'all options are on the table.' On 27 May, meanwhile, the International Tribunal for Crimes in the Former Yugoslavia publicly indicted Milosevic and others for war crimes in Kosovo. But the Chernomyrdin-Ahtisaari-Talbott diplomacy was taking effect. If he had learned nothing else in the passing weeks, Milosevic at least now understood he would get no support and little sympathy from Russia. Chernomyrdin and Ahtisaari together put the G-8–UN surrender terms personally to Milosevic, and after some tactical dodging he accepted them on 3 June. Yugoslav authorities and NATO officers concluded a 'military-technical agreement' in Macedonia on 9 June. On 10 June 1999, NATO suspended the bombing.

Occupational Hazards

More than a year after NATO (and Russian) troops established their indefinite occupation of Kosovo, the results and significance of the intervention remained as unsettled, controversial, and disturbing as ever. To some it represented a historic military success for air power—ratified, arguably, by the collapse of the Milosevic government in 2000. To others it was 'a perfect failure' of US and NATO statecraft (Mandelbaum, 1999). The object here is not to attempt any complete post-mortem, but only to address briefly two persisting issues of humanitarian intervention: legitimacy and effectiveness.

The very day that NATO commanders suspended the bombing of Serbia, the UN Security Council voted (14–0, China abstaining) to adopt Resolution 1244; what the G-8 and NATO governments had earlier decided and imposed on Yugoslavia now carried the weight of law. Indeed, the communiqué of the 6 May G-8 foreign ministers, laying down terms to Milosevic, was itself incorporated as an annex and the operative content of Resolution 1244 of 10 June. Among other things, the resolution demanded 'an immediate and verifiable end to violence and repression in Kosovo'; withdrawal of Serb security forces; 'demilitarizing' the KLA; and 'substantial autonomy' for Kosovo, while taking account of Yugoslavia's 'sovereignty and territorial integrity'. It provided for an 'international security presence with substantial North Atlantic Treaty Organization participation'—a compromise allowing Milosevic and others to describe this as an occupation by the UN, not NATO. And it created a 'civil presence', to be known as UNMIK, to administer Kosovo and arrange a transition to self-governing institutions. As for the future, the civil presence would have responsibility for 'facilitating a political process designed to determine Kosovo's future status, taking into account the Rambouillet accords'—including, presumably, Rambouillet's provision for an international meeting in three years.

It may well be that the bombing of Yugoslavia was illegal. The Milosevic authorities put that very question to the International Court of Justice; scholars, lawyers, and legislators meanwhile divide on the point. But was the bombing legitimate? Did it conform to accepted norms of humanitarian intervention sufficient to overcome—in this specific circumstance—the countervailing norms of sovereignty, non-interference, and territorial integrity? And did Resolution 1244 in some degree impart after-the-fact legitimacy to the NATO-led action?

The minilateralists will answer 'yes'. Glennon sees the emergence of a new regime—one that recognizes the state's own 'primary and initial responsibility' for domestic order, but that permits intervention as appropriate 'where the humanitarian costs of failing to intervene are too high (as in cases of genocide)' (Glennon, 1999: 5). Coalition interventions are undoubtedly preferable to unilateral action, he argues: 'The hope is that building a multinational coalition will filter out the worst forms of national self-interest' (ibid., 5). Minilateralists further propose that 'just' interventions, those that attract acceptance even from non-interveners, will eventually draw international law along behind. 'Achieving justice is the hard part;

revising international law to reflect it can come afterward' (ibid., 7; for lawyerly disagreement, see responses to Glennon from Franck, 1999; Luck, 1999b).

Still, there is something unsatisfying in the minilateralist answer. For one thing, the norm of intervention as it has so far developed adheres very closely to the procedural rules and legitimizing authority of the UN Charter and Security Council decisions. (Kofi Annan, an advocate for intervention where necessary to protect human security, scrupulously frames it in the context of the Charter and Security Council authority.) For another thing—and importantly—even NATO leaders have taken care not to describe the Kosovo case as a precedent-setting example around which new law might form. On the contrary, Secretary-General Solana has held that NATO's action was emphatically not a precedent: NATO governments understood in advance that threatening force without Security Council approval 'was the only likely solution. It was equally clear, though, that such a step would constitute the exception from the rule, not an attempt to create new international law' (Solana, 1999: 118). Norms are not laws, and legitimacy need not always signify legality. But to defend the NATO intervention by its exceptionalism suggests a weak kind of legitimacy.

Legitimacy and effectiveness interact. The precedential appeal of the NATO intervention was surely undermined by the ambiguity of the outcome. Reciprocally, its contested legitimacy might have worked against its immediate success and its long-term prospects.

The NATO air campaign and the occupation that followed were both punctuated by some horrific violence against human security. It is commonly estimated that 2,500 Kosovars were killed in the 12 months before the bombing started; in the next 11 weeks, at least 10,000 more were killed—most murdered by Serbs (Shawcross, 2000: 368). The bombing itself may have taken 500 civilian lives. Human Rights Watch and Amnesty International have both alleged (different) NATO violations of international humanitarian law in its choice of targets and in its conduct of the attacks. Nor was the aftermath peaceful. The first year of the occupation saw NATO and UNMIK unable to prevent revenge killings and the effective removal of thousands of Serb families from their Kosovo homes. By May 2000, the promised UN police force in Kosovo had reportedly attracted only 2,500 of its intended 6,500 personnel from UN member states—a measure, perhaps, of shallow commitment even among the minilateralists. (NATO's Web site in June 2000 reported the KFOR [Kosovo Force] military deployment comprised 42,500 personnel, from 30 countries, based inside Kosovo.)

To count murders and expulsions does not by itself condemn the NATO intervention. To quote James Steinberg, deputy assistant to President Clinton for national security affairs: 'The real question in judging success is not whether people are better off than they were before, but whether people are better off than they would have been if the West had not acted. The answer to that question is clearly yes' (Steinberg, 1999: 129; for other assessments, see Daalder and O'Hanlon, 2000; Ignatieff, 2000).

On the other hand, problems of effectiveness do point to troubles with mini-lateralist co-ordination—even in a practised and institutionally mature alliance like NATO. Besides the daily challenge of recruiting Russian political co-operation, there were obvious and recurring intra-alliance divisions over preparations for a ground invasion, the reach and intensity of the bombing raids, and the planned imposition of a naval blockade (Byman and Waxman, 2000: 34–5). Limiting NATO pilots to high-altitude sorties, an accommodation to political objectives within NATO constituencies, was itself an impediment to operational effectiveness.

At any rate, occupation would prove no easier than the war itself, and would last much longer, as the UN's most senior administrator in Kosovo was frank to say. 'We are not in Kosovo for 12 months or 24 months', Bernard Kouchner told the Security Council on 9 June 2000. 'We are there no doubt for a significant number of years.' Peacebuilding, the long follow-on to intervention, had only just begun.

Conclusion

The protection of human security is a global public good. So is the maintenance of a peaceful international order, in which small countries (and their people) are safe from predations of the powerful. Humanitarian intervention therefore engages two different and potentially conflicting normative orders. There are norms of intervention, evident for example in Security Council resolutions on Haiti and eastern Zaire. And there are norms, and laws, prohibiting the use of force against states, except in self-defence or as authorized by the Security Council. When human security is grossly abused, and when the Security Council is prevented by a veto from authorizing intervention, which norms should prevail? Who decides? That is one kind of problem with intervention.

The other kind has to do with capacity and result. Who goes in? With what sort of force? And with what effect? But as we have seen, norms and consequences affect each other. The rightness of what is done can sometimes hang on later inter-pretations of success or failure. And as we have also seen, outcomes defy such simple definitions when they are ambiguous, unexpected, and complicated.

Both kinds of problems—normative and practical—are seen to have beset conduct and analysis of interventions in eastern Zaire and Kosovo. The Zaire inter-vention, though conceived as a coalition enterprise, was understood from the start to require the military resources and political support of the superpower. The support was given tentatively, the resources not at all. In the end, an intervention wholly authorized by the Security Council never got the military capacity, or the threshold political consensus among coalition members, to deploy as first intended.

The Zaire case illustrates the real constraints operating against the multilater-alist answer to human security interventions—constraints of military power, of coalition co-ordination and decision-making, and of bargaining with the multiple power centres of government in Washington. The Zaire case also exhibits the powerful effects of muddle and surprise and murky outcomes. Tens of thousands of deaths (hypothetically) are better than hundreds of thousands of deaths. But is that what distinguished success from failure in eastern Zaire in 1996?

The institutionalists have a familiar answer to the troubling questions raised by the Zaire case: enhance the UN's own capacity to detect and especially to respond with timely force to crises of human security. Improving institutional capacities would better arm middle powers with forces for intervention and reduce their reliance on the superpower.

Another answer is to engage the superpower itself more dependably in these international projects—if only to attract the co-operation of others. The United States 'has to recognize', Joseph Nye has argued, 'a basic proposition of public goods theory: if the largest beneficiary of a public good (such as international order) does not provide disproportionate resources toward its maintenance, the smaller beneficiaries are unlikely to do so' (Nye, 1999: 27).

Kosovo, by contrast, was conceived as a minilateralist intervention, explicitly justified by the immobilization of the Security Council at a moment of desperate human need. And its central military objective was by and large accomplished: Yugoslav security forces were removed from Kosovo and regional interstate peace restored. But the legitimacy of NATO's assault was at best defective, lacking both Security Council approval and the excuse of self-defence. Neither, say some, was its legitimacy much repaired by the war's conduct or its aftermath. Hundreds of thousands of refugees, undetermined numbers of civilian bombing casualties, and a peacebuilding process scarcely in place all undermine a definition of the Kosovo war as an unambiguous success.

Both cases demonstrate the logic and the opportunity of the portfolio approach to using hard power for human security. Middle powers, particularly in concert, can sometimes do what great powers cannot; in central Africa, Canadian diplomats were welcomed where others were spurned. Sometimes, however, middle and smaller powers lack the capacity that only a superpower can bring to bear. Every intervention is probably strengthened by the legitimacy that only the UN and Security Council can confer. But for all its power to legitimize, the UN remains capacity-poor. (The later case of Sierra Leone gives further evidence of the UN's incapacity, and of the prevailing reluctance of able states, notwithstanding Britain's singular contribution, to intervene in the bloodiest African conflicts.)

The Kosovo intervention shows the portfolio approach in sequenced stages. The Security Council presided to October 1998, setting general outlines for Kosovo's autonomy and authorizing international monitors; the six-government Contact Group, including Russia, took over in the January-March Rambouillet phase; the 19-member NATO alliance executed the bombing from March through May; the G-8, including Russia again, decided terms for Milosevic's capitulation; and in June his surrender was certified by the Security Council.

Nonetheless, the Kosovo war endures as a troubling case of vigilante intervention—conducted outside the law, and maybe against it. The danger in such interventions (even if for worthy purposes) is that they will discredit not only the self-appointed posse, but the laws and institutions it purports to uphold. NATO's results, moreover, are not so completely beneficial as to dispel all misgivings about faulty process.

There is another argument for the portfolio approach, and it is this. From the viewpoint of the policy-maker, the universe hardly ever unfolds as it should. Surprises, confusions, and mistakes abound. So there is an evolutionary advantage to providing for the unforeseen—creating capacity not just to do, but to adapt. To prepare and deploy hard power for human security requires continuous and adaptive realignments of governments and others in the international community. Responding to new threats, and new opportunities, will demand agility and wisdom. Success will be judged not by formulaic resort to procedure, institution, or self-interest, but by standards of legitimacy—and good effect.

Notes

1. Zaire is now called the Democratic Republic of Congo.
2. Unless otherwise cited or widely reported at the time, facts and interpretations in this case are based on 31 open-ended interviews conducted in 1997–8 with 27 present and former officials of the Canadian and US governments, the UN Secretariat, and CARE Canada. All but one submitted to interviews on the condition of anonymity. The exception was Gordon Smith, former deputy minister in the Canadian Department of Foreign Affairs and International Trade. UN and NATO documents and statements cited in this chapter are from their Web sites: www.un.org and www.nato.int/home.htm.

Chapter 8

Human Security and the Global Development Agenda

In June 2000, the World Bank held a major conference on development prospects in Latin America. Its theme was 'Economic Insecurity', and a report called *Securing Our Future in a Global Economy* was its *pièce de résistance*. A quick look between its covers reveals that its authors are mainly preoccupied with economic 'volatility', which they treat in pretty traditional terms. Yet their ultimate point of reference is not regional or national economies, as one could have expected, but workers, households, and their concern about future living standards (de Ferranti et al., 2000: 11).

This particular event is one more indication of a significant movement within development circles towards increasing references to security and a growing preoccupation, beyond broad economic indicators and state-level issues, with people and their concerns. 'Human security' is becoming a key component of the vocabulary, thinking, and practice of international development. The word 'security' is now to be found in most statements and studies that touch on international development. A case in point is the latest *World Development Report* on poverty, one part of which is devoted to security (World Bank, 2001a: 135–79). In the broad development debate, security has thus joined the slightly older emphasis on individuals brought to the fore by the United Nations Development Program's 'human development' outlook. As the morphing of 'insecurity' into 'volatility' in the above-mentioned document testifies, the process is slow and not without contradictions. Yet 'freedom from fear and want' for people as an underlying motif and 'security' as a slogan have penetrated the development discourse and practice to a significant and possibly irreversible extent.

This chapter shows how and to what extent new preoccupations and a new outlook have recently penetrated the thinking, operations, and structure of the three dominant institutions of international development: the World Bank, the United Nations Development Program (UNDP), and the Development Assistance Committee (DAC) of the Organization for Economic Co-operation and Development (OECD). Although these three institutions are in varying degrees now engaged in providing for human security, thus lending support to the institutionalist thesis (discussed in Chapter 3) that international organizations can indeed be providers of human security public goods, the depth of this support and commitment is limited. On the one hand, these organizations are restrained, by internal bureaucratic differences of opinion or organizational inertia, about how far they should move in the direction of being human security providers. These problems are compounded by conflicts of interest among their own (state) donors as well as continuing financing and resource problems.

On the other hand, given the obvious complexities about the different meanings of human security—'safety of peoples' versus rights/rule of law versus sustainable human development—these organizations have tended to adopt those elements among the different conceptions of human security that are most compatible with *existing* organizational mandates and prevailing institutional and ideological philosophies. This has meant that while some aspects of the new human security agenda have been adopted by these organizations, in particular, the narrower conception of human security, which is anchored in the rights/rule-of-law and 'safety of peoples' conceptions, other aspects, notably the broader sustainable human development conception of human security, have not received widespread support or any kind of institutional endorsement—except perhaps rhetorically.

It is important to recognize that the human security enterprise as it is evolving in the three development organizations discussed in this chapter is very much a work-in-progress. Even so, the ensuing discussion sounds a cautionary note not only about the obvious limitations of institutional reform in support of human security objectives among key donor and development bodies, but also in regard to resistance to the philosophical premises behind the broader, 'social justice' conception of human security, which stresses the importance of 'market' as opposed to 'political' failures in the human security deficit.

Human Security and Development

To a significant extent, as Chapter 2 showed, there is much overlap between traditional development views and the human security outlook. Development as a policy field effectively emerged from security concerns, first as reconstruction in post-World War II Europe, and then as a means to resist and counteract the potential alignment of the poor countries of the South with the Soviet bloc in the context of the Cold War. Over time, new considerations emerged, such as trade opportunities and basic humane concerns, but the security agenda has never fully disappeared from the broad motives that underlay development aid. 'Fear of the poor', as Cranford Pratt (1999: 316) explains, remained an important impetus of global efforts to quell poverty, economic stagnation, lack of infrastructure, social disparities, health and education deficits, and institutional deficiencies in the South.

In the last decade, however, conflict within countries has become a major preoccupation for development agencies. The first reason is rather straightforward: the economic impact of civil wars is massive and it has been borne disproportionately by the poorest countries. In 1998, relief operations engulfed more than 10 per cent of official development assistance, up from 2 per cent at the turn of the decade; billions are spent in peacekeeping; and in many countries communications and transportation infrastructure, built over decades, has been destroyed in a few months. Moreover, 'although conflict has touched both rich and poor societies, its effect on low-income countries has been most severe. Fifteen of the 20 poorest countries in the world have had a major conflict in the past 15 years' (World Bank, 1998b: 2, 15). Helping the poorest countries and people, in other words, has come to mean dealing with civil war, conflict prevention, or post-conflict reconstruction.

This invasion of the development arena by conflict was compounded by the analysis brought in to make sense of civil wars in development circles. Previously quoted statements by Kofi Annan and Boutros Boutros-Ghali (see Chapter 2 and Annan, 1999: 4, 7) clearly indicate that senior UN officials believe that there is a clear link between poverty, socio-economic inequality, and violent conflict. As argued below, this view also has wide currency among the major development agencies. The continuing prominence of the 'poverty causes conflict' paradigm helps explain why fair and sustainable development is seen as a major tool of long-term peacemaking. As a result, not only is conflict now perceived as a major impediment to development, but, in turn, development itself, when fair and sustainable, appears to offer the best hope for the long-term containment of violence and war. Conflict reduction (or prevention) and development are thus seen as two sides of the same coin.

As we saw in Chapters 2 and 3, however, the concept of human security encompasses a wider understanding of the kinds of public goods necessary to sustain human survival and existence—an understanding that clearly goes beyond public goods of the more traditional 'law-and-order' or peace variety. In fact, in its broadest understanding the concept calls for the inclusion of a wide range of domains, including the economy and the environment, on the grounds that disparities in wealth and barriers to access to renewable resources (e.g., clean air, clean water) jeopardize human survival. This broader conception of human security, most closely associated with the UNDP, emerged intellectually from the fusing of two broad concepts that define the contemporary development agenda: sustainable development and human development. The first one, introduced by the Brundtland Commission, established environmental protection as a necessary condition for the long-term survival of humanity and ipso facto as the basic parameter of any long-term development strategy (World Commission on Environment and Development, 1987). This notion crystallized with the growing preoccupation with the risks involved in the dominant growth model and rapidly became a core preoccupation of development agencies. As discussed in Chapter 2, the linkage with traditional notions of security was also drawn as governments of the South and of the North contemplated the dangers that global warming, natural resource depletion, and ultraviolet-ray penetration posed to their populations and to their countries' economic activities. Some also tried to draw a link between environmental degradation and conflict (Kaplan, 1994; Homer-Dixon, 1999), arguing that sustainable development was the key to conflict prevention in the South.

The next ingredient was provided by the UNDP in the first *Human Development Report*, published in 1990, which argued that 'people must be at the centre of all development [and] . . . that while growth in national production (GDP) is absolutely necessary to meet all essential human objectives, what is important is to study how this growth translates—or fails to translate—into human development' (UNDP, 1990: iii). Naturally, with that as background, the UNDP went on to produce the seminal work on human security as its fifth *Human Development Report* (UNDP, 1994), fusing human development with the now much broadened security agenda. If the broad outlines of this new outlook have been defined, the extent to which it has effectively penetrated development action and thinking, even at the UNDP, is far from clear.

The World Bank, the UNDP, and the Development Assistance Committee of the OECD are without a doubt the most influential development entities in the world. Together, they concentrate much of the resources, financial and intellectual, of the global development field. Specifically, their influence has three main sources. The first is the sheer magnitude of financial resources that they, or their member countries, control directly. OECD countries essentially provide all of the bilateral aid that flows to developing countries; they are the main funders of all the development banks, at the global (the World Bank) and regional (the Asian, African, and Inter-American Development Banks) levels. The World Bank Group, for instance, is the biggest single source of multilateral development financing. The second source of their influence is their intellectual role as a generator and clearing house for theoretical and, more importantly, practical ideas that touch on development. Third, these organizations are also a kind of rating agency for countries. For example, the World Bank's assessment of a country's creditworthiness plays a substantial role in influencing the flows of private capital that now dwarf the amount of direct aid. For all these reasons, the ultimate impact of the human security agenda will be significantly shaped by these three institutions and the level of their involvement in the provision of human security.

We now turn to the degree of penetration of the human security paradigm in the discourse and actions of these major players in international development, first looking at the specific type of human security (rights-based, humanitarian, comprehensive) and then considering the ways in which the sources of human insecurity are understood and how human security as a public good is to be produced. The discussion is based on a systematic review of the major statements of these organizations since 1993, as well as the direction of their programming, primarily, but not exclusively, on the basis of the evolution of their spending priorities. In addition, some of the recent secondary literature on the three organizations will be examined to assess the direction in which they appear to be moving.

The World Bank

What we usually call the World Bank is in fact made up of two institutions, the International Bank for Reconstruction and Development, which assists 'creditworthy' poorer or middle-income countries through loans and technical assistance, and the International Development Agency (IDA), which focuses on the poorest countries and whose loans are interest-free. There are three other organizations in the 'World Bank Group'—the International Finance Corporation (IFC), the Multilateral Investment Guarantee Agency (MIGA), and the International Centre for Settlement of Investment Disputes (ICSID)—but their functions are highly specialized and they play little role in development policy.

The World Bank was established in 1944 at Bretton Woods, New Hampshire, as part of a set of institutions designed to provide for economic governance in what would soon become the West side in the Cold War. While the International Monetary Fund (IMF) was to help stabilize the international system of payments, the Bank was meant to provide aid to the countries of Europe to help them in a difficult process of reconstruction. Once Europe was dealt with, the Bank increasingly moved towards developing countries as most of them emerged from colonialism. Since the 1960s, it has become the most important development agency in the world (Kapur et al., 1997, vol. 1).

The Bank wields that influence in two main ways. The first is the raw size of its lending program, which oscillates between $15 billion and $30 billion a year (US) and gives it important leverage in the discussion of policy options for its mostly poor state clients. That size also enables it to influence how other private, bilateral, and multilateral institutions act: for a donor's bilateral aid program to be at odds with Bank policy reduces its impact, whereas leverage is greatly enhanced by working with the Bank. Through its almost unique capacity to provide 'policy-based' loans, i.e., conditional financing, the Bank has had a major impact on multilateral donor efforts (Culpeper, 1997: 56). More broadly, the Bank's incomparable institutional capacity has enabled it to steer global lending along its preferred lines: 'The Bank family's major influences on the lending side may indeed reside in its role as a rating agency for others, both by its data collection and country analysis efforts and, more importantly, by way of its example as a lender' (Ranis, 1997: 73).

A massive research capacity is the second source of influence for the Bank. It 'employs around 800 professional economists and has a research budget of around $25 million (US) a year. These resources dwarf those of any university department or research institution working on development economics' (Stern, 1997: 524). In addition, it has proven nimble at taking over ideas generated elsewhere and making them, literally overnight, mainstays of development thinking and practice (Ranis, 1997: 74). The combination of these factors makes the World Bank a pivotal influence on human security and is likely to continue to determine the depth and scope of its penetration on the global development scene.

Since 'development' replaced 'reconstruction' as its main role, and the World Bank focus moved to the South, the Bank's thinking has gone through four broad phases, with emphasis on industrialization and investment in physical capital in the 1950s and 1960s; poverty, income redistribution, and basic needs in the 1970s; budget and balance-of-payments deficits, public-sector efficiency through cuts, credit restraints, and elimination of subsidies in the 1980s; and finally, a return to a more people-centred outlook in the 1990s (Elson, 1997: 50; Wolfensohn, 1999). At a deeper level, the original emphasis on planning was replaced by a fondness for market-based mechanisms in the 1980s. Acknowledging the central role played by the public sector in the 'Asian Miracle' and then the various large-scale financial crises of the 1990s, the importance of the state but especially of 'institutions' was reaffirmed without the primacy of the market, however, being challenged (World Bank, 1997, 1998b).

This recent intellectual evolution is reflected in the Bank's lending trends between 1985–9 and 1995–9. The four sectors that have increased most—in order of the fastest growing—are the environment; social protection; public-sector management; and population, health, and nutrition. The four sectors that have witnessed the greatest decline are industry, oil and gas, telecommunications, and agriculture (World Bank, 1990, 2000). The trend is unmistakable: although transportation, finance, agriculture, and electric power and energy remained the four sectors that received the most financing in 1995–9, their share of total lending declined from 61 to 44 per cent.

Recent years have also seen an increasing preoccupation with the relationship between violent conflict and development. This interest was, in part, imposed on the World Bank, as civil wars became all too common among the poorest of its clients; willy-nilly, the Bank found itself thrown back in many cases to its original 'reconstruction' mandate. In the mid-1990s, '24 percent of IDA commitments (excluding those for China and India) went to countries that had been under or were in the process of emerging from significant periods of intrastate conflict' (World Bank, 1998a: 23). Soon a full-fledged 'Framework for World Bank Involvement in Post-Conflict Reconstructions' was developed, and at the time of writing operational procedures are being finalized, following a broad and public process of consultation.

The Framework contemplates specific Bank inputs depending on the position of the country in a stylized 'conflict cycle' (see Figure 8.1), with distinct policies when the country is at risk, in violent conflict, and in the post-conflict stage. In addition, conflict prevention is meant to be 'mainstreamed', i.e., the Bank is to devise policies that are likely to lessen social and political tensions and to make sure that its 'interventions do not exacerbate conflict' (ibid., 59).

The main focus remains post-conflict reconstruction, which is seen as a way not only to repair the damage done but also to consolidate the peace process. For that reason, the Bank considers that special programs might be needed: 'Because sustainable development depends heavily on peace building and visible "peace dividends," especially during the fragile early period, physical reconstruction and transitional initiatives may need to be undertaken before the larger economic reform program gets fully under way' (World Bank, 1998b: 26). Similarly, the Bank wants to move into new areas that are not part of the more narrowly defined traditional development agenda, with programs on demobilization and reintegration of ex-combatants, reintegration of displaced populations, and demining (ibid., 33, 35; World Bank, 1998c). To ensure that these goals are effectively turned into policy, a special Post-Conflict Unit, has been created as part of the Social Development Department of the Bank and undertakes research, information, lobbying, and policy development functions.

In a more provisional way an attempt is also being made to bring conflict prevention into the picture. Implicit in the various initiatives being contemplated is a theory of conflict that stresses the role of grievances, vertical and horizontal inequalities, and political closure in generating conflict. Correspondingly, the main foci are measures that favour inclusiveness and that 'address inequities in distributive policies [and] excluded groups' (World Bank, 1998a: 59).

Figure 8.1 World Bank Framework: Breaking the Cycle of Conflict and Resuming the Path of Development

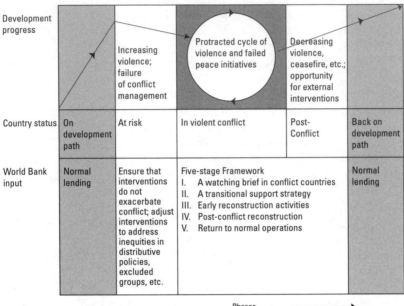

Phases ———————————————→

Source: World Bank (1998a: 59).

The Framework notes that Bank operations in conflict situations are still guided by its operational policies on 'emergency recovery assistance', which put civil wars in the same category as natural disasters such as typhoons and earthquakes. It states that 'emergency lending procedures need to be specifically designed for the special circumstances of post-conflict countries—in particular, the diminished government capacity and the uncertain dynamics of reconciliation and unification' (ibid., 50). New procedures were drafted and submitted to a broad Internet-based consultation process that ended on 28 May 2000. The procedures on 'Development Assistance and Conflict' essentially build on the Framework but adopt a broader perspective that gives prevention and intervention in conflict areas as much importance as reconstruction in its objectives. In addition, the Bank's preoccupation with 'doing no harm' is much more explicit: 'The Bank aims to support inclusive development strategies that reflect a sensitivity to potential sources of conflict, and to avoid interventions that may exacerbate existing tensions.' The Framework, in conjunction with the new procedures, clearly demonstrates an interest within the Bank to 'mainstream' conflict in its operation, as does the Bank's presence in a long list of countries emerging from conflict.

All these initiatives, however, stop short of a commitment to the broadest understanding of human security, i.e., one that fuses 'safety of peoples' with sustainable human development. The human security preoccupation evident in the above measures and initiatives remains essentially humanitarian (Wolfensohn, 1999) and falls short of merging 'freedom from fear' with 'freedom from want' as contemplated by supporters of the comprehensive, i.e., sustainable human development view of human security. Beyond factoring conflict as a cause of disruption in the development process and as a possible consequence of unequal development, World Bank documents and reports do not conceive of unequal distribution or global inequities in wealth and income as a security issue per se.

An illustration of those limits is provided by a recent report prepared by the Bank's Latin American division. *Securing Our Future in a Global Economy* (de Ferranti et al., 2000) focuses on the 'economic insecurity' of workers and households, which it understands as a consequence of 'volatility'. The report first examines 'aggregate volatility', i.e., 'the extent and frequency with which [it] tends to depart from its central trend' (ibid., 14), and then looks at its impact on private consumption and on labour market instability. Aside from the word 'insecurity', in other words, one sees little that is new here when compared, for instance, with the kind of analysis the Inter-American Development Bank produced in 1995 in a report entitled *Overcoming Volatility* (Inter-American Development Bank, 1995: 13).

Critics contend that the Bank has a recurring tendency to retrofit heterodox concepts within an orthodox framework. Diane Elson, for example, asserts that the Bank's growing emphasis on people has not led it to adopt the UNDP's human development outlook, a stand that she attributes to the Bank's continuing adherence to 'the paradigm of orthodox neoclassical welfare economics' (Elson, 1997: 51). In fact, now that the Bank's Development Research Group has come up with an analysis of conflict that challenges the primacy given normally, for instance in the Bank's own post-conflict policy framework on inequality, lack of democracy, and inclusiveness, as well as on ethnic and religious divisions, it may further retreat to neo-classical principles. The Research Group's new 'economic theory of conflict' argues that the motivation of conflict is unimportant: 'what matters is whether the organization can sustain itself financially' (Collier, 2000: 4).

Recent instances of civil war, in Sierra Leone, Angola, and the Democratic Republic of Congo, in particular, appear easy enough to understand on those terms and the research on which the broader proposals are based also seems to have a very strong empirical basis. Be that as it may, it is clear that the outlook on this 'greed' school of conflict (Berdal and Malone, 2000) is a better fit with the Bank's traditional outlook than the very general and tentative propositions that one finds even in its own earlier documents on the relationship between poverty and conflict.

The World Bank appears to adopt an approach to human security that stresses the importance of 'political' as opposed to 'market' failures to explain why human security is an underprovided public good. The conception implicit in the post-conflict Framework and the 'conflict and development' operational procedures essentially target political and institutional failures and not distributive ones, i.e., those arising out of the failure of local and international markets to redistribute wealth and income. To the extent that distributive problems are identified or discussed, they are related less to market failures per se than to the inability of state institutions to manage, among other things, the tensions generated by development and economic liberalization. The type of policy options contemplated by the recent 'greed' school of conflict are even more narrowly focused, emphasizing dependence on primary commodity exports, low average income, and slow growth.

Interestingly, the way in which the provision of human security is contemplated in these same reports could hardly be broader, stressing the need to involve international institutions, from the UN to military alliances to the IMF donor states individually or as groups, as well as NGOs. However, to the extent that conflict prevention and post-conflict reconstruction are considered by the Bank, they are treated in a technical manner, and no significant reforms of international institutions or global governance structures (as urged by proponents of the sustainable human development school) are considered.

Recent events, such as the resignation of Ravi Kanbur, who was responsible for preparing the Bank's *World Development Report* (*Financial Times*, 2000), as well as the harsh criticisms of its former chief economist, Joe Stigliz (*The New Republic*, 2000), suggest that the Bank remains primarily committed to a narrow free-market philosophy. The preoccupation with the causes of violent conflict in some of the Bank's current research does represent a significant departure from is previous unwillingness even to consider these kinds of problems. However, the findings and direction of this research, which emphasize poverty per se instead of distribution, do not challenge the Bank's traditional free-market outlook, and there is little evidence that a broader concern for social justice, which underlies the sustainable human development conception of human security, has gathered a major constituency in World Bank circles.

The UNDP

The United Nations Development Program was formally established in 1967 by merging two previously existing technical co-operation funds of the United Nations. The program is part of the UN's Economic and Social Council (ECOSOC), along with UNICEF, the Food and Agriculture Organization, the World Food Program, the World Health Organization, and many other organizations devoted, mostly or exclusively, to development in its broadest possible conception in the North and the South. For obvious reasons, ECOSOC organizations are primarily oriented to lesser-developed countries, and for that core part of their mission, the UNDP is formally meant to be the chief co-ordinator of their activities. That position was given further impetus with the formation, as part of Kofi Annan's *Agenda for Change*, of the UN Development Group, whose oversight, predictably, fell to the UNDP. The Program, in sum, is best seen as the conductor of the UN's development orchestra.

Co-ordination is only part of its mission, however, for while New York-based, the UNDP also has a massive field presence enabling it to work closely with the governments of developing countries. Together, these characteristics make it the biggest and most broadly based technical co-operation organization in the world.

In the South, particularly in the poorest countries, the UNDP is often the most visible bearer of the UN's blue flag. Traditionally lesser known in the North, it has gained much visibility since the launching in 1990 of its 'Human Development Index', which ranks countries on the basis of their performance in areas, such as education and life expectancy, that do not always go hand in hand with GDP levels. This broader gauge of the quality of life makes front-page news when the annual ranking is announced. Fittingly, human development has become the UNDP's trademark, along with poverty eradication, which also defines the organization.

The UNDP brings sizable assets, in theory at least, to these tasks. In spite of significant budget and personnel cuts in recent years, it still has more than 6,000 employees and an annual budget of $700 million (US). As mentioned above, it also occupies a critical location within the UN system, as official co-ordinator of the UN's development effort. That prominence is mirrored in the field, where UN agencies' work is overseen through a 'resident co-ordinator' system, which the UNDP funds and manages. The program is also involved in joint initiatives that reach beyond the UN system; it co-manages, for instance, the Global Environment Facility with the UN Environment Program and the World Bank.

What is perhaps unique among the UNDP's assets is its close association with developing countries' governments. Its offices in essentially all developing countries work in close collaboration with the local governments, who are often called upon to co-finance projects. To its own staff, moreover, it adds a significant pool of local consultants, who together often end up constituting, especially in the poorest countries, a powerful policy player.

The UNDP also has a sizable research capacity, with 140 policy professionals at headquarters, some of whom are involved in the preparation of the *Human Development Report*. The Program's policy staff is multidisciplinary and their interests and outlook range broadly, which certainly underlies the 'heterodox' orientation of much of their work and, perhaps most clearly, the significant ability of the UNDP to 'mainstream' issues such as gender to its development thinking, especially when compared with the World Bank. A reform process currently under way intends to reinforce that capability, moving 'upstream' towards policy development both at headquarters and in the field, while downsizing implementation work, where the Program is not felt to have much of a comparative advantage.

As noted in Chapter 2, the concept of human security was, to a large extent, put on the global stage by the UNDP's 1994 *Human Development Report*. Its central idea involves 'a transition from the narrow concept of national security to [an] all-encompassing' one (UNDP, 1994: 24), a shift and redefinition that moves the concept of security away from conflicts between states and widens it to include a broad array of threats to people's daily lives (ibid., 2). It 'means, first, safety from such chronic threats as hunger, disease and repression. And second, it means protection from sudden and hurtful disruptions in the patterns of daily life—whether in homes, in jobs or in communities' (ibid., 23). A listing of 'main' sub-areas shows how broadly the new idea reaches: economic security (from basic income to employment), food security, health security, environmental security, personal security, community security, and political security (ibid., 24–35). Global security, in sum, 'no longer means carefully constructed safeguards against the threat of a nuclear holocaust [but] instead . . . responding to the threat of global poverty travelling across international borders in the form of HIV/AIDS, climate change, illegal migration and terrorism' (ibid., 24).

Given the emphasis that the UNDP had been putting on 'human development' since 1990, the new concept looks like a natural extension of that thinking in the security field. The catalyst for that extension in the 1994 *Report* was the upcoming 1995 Copenhagen Social Summit, which the UNDP saw as a perfect occasion to take advantage of the expected 'peace dividend' and to bring to the development field many of the resources that had gone into military expenditures during the Cold War. That intention is explicit in the *Report*, which stands openly as 'An agenda for the Social Summit' (ibid., 1–13) and devotes a full chapter to 'Capturing the peace dividend' (ibid., 47–61).

While the breadth of the concept is certainly its main characteristic, it also makes human security somewhat difficult to distinguish from human development per se. The *Report* acknowledges this difficulty and tries to resolve it:

> It is important that human security not be equated with human development. Human development is a broader concept—defined in previous Human Development Reports as a process of widening the range of people's choices. Human security means that people can exercise these choices safely and freely—and that they can be relatively confident that the opportunities they have today are not totally lost tomorrow. (Ibid., 23)

This rhetoric is only half-convincing, however, especially as one tries to contemplate its actualization beyond policies and programs that were not already on the sustainable human development agenda.

The merging of these two agendas, however, points to a central characteristic of human security as conceived by the UNDP. The causes of insecurity—and of underdevelopment—are conceived in the broadest possible sense as a combination of market and political failures, especially at the global level. At the core of UNDP thinking, and reflected in its treatment of all important development issues, from the environment to poverty and gender, one finds a critique of the inability of the market to ensure sustainable development. The 1996 *Report*, the theme of which is 'Growth for Human Development?', puts this objection in the starkest possible way: 'there is no automatic link between economic growth and human development. . . . We now know . . . the limits of trickle-down economics' (UNDP, 1996: iii). That stance, moreover, is not limited to a technical/economic reading of the development field, but, in a later *Report*, is expanded to include its political implications, especially at the global level: 'the international economic environment has seen a surge of activity and new initiatives, especially in trade, capital flows and financial liberalization. Many changes are positive—but are driven overwhelmingly by the economic interests of the rich and powerful countries. Less attention is being given to the needs of the poorer and weaker countries. Their interests have become even more marginalized. Global inequalities have grown even more extreme' (UNDP, 1998a: 99; see also UNDP, 1999a: 44–5).

The comprehensiveness of the UNDP outlook is clear from this merging of global market and political failures. The discussion of global political failures explicitly targets the 'global political system' (UNDP, 1998a: 85) and criticizes, for instance, 'the mechanisms of global governance [that] are inadequate for managing . . . critical environmental issues' (ibid., 97).

Significantly, the delivery of human security/human development is also conceived by the UNDP as a comprehensive, system-wide endeavour involving change and action at all levels: individuals and households, community organizations and NGOs, the private sector, governments—local, regional, and national—and international institutions (ibid., 100–1). It must be noted, however, that while the diagnosis of market and political failures touches on a wide range of issues, it is most specific regarding international mechanisms. That emphasis on global institutions is striking, especially when contrasted with the World Bank's primary preoccupation with national-level governance and institutions.

The conceptual merging of human security and human development, as they are understood by the UNDP, makes it difficult to assess the role of the new concept in the implementation of programs that would be specific and presumably unique to the human security agenda. One must note, however, that, as with the World Bank, the UNDP's activities in the poorest countries forced it into the conflict/post-conflict field. The growing importance of these issues was recognized with the establishment in 1994 of an Emergency Response Division. An internal report noted in 1999, however, that 'the unit has never been adequately staffed or properly used. Instead of being used to improve UNDP's work in CPC (Crisis/post-conflict) ERD has served mainly as an accounting office for a series of CPC projects that often lacked coherence and focus' (UNDP, 1999b: 53).

In spite of these problems, it must be noted that the ways in which the UNDP looks at conflict are strictly in keeping with its comprehensive understanding of security issues. In the plan developed in response to the just-quoted report, crisis and conflict issues are framed as 'special development situations' and the measures to deal with them as mainstream policy orientations (UNDP, 2000: 12).

Given this outlook and the means at its disposal, the UNDP should have become the standard-bearer of the human security agenda and the latter a key point of reference for development policy the world over. This has not yet happened, however, and even in the UNDP's own work, human security has not gained much space.

A variety of factors appear to have contributed to this state of affairs. The first is no doubt the inability of the UNDP to operationalize the concept it introduced in the 1994 *Report*: human security remains underdeveloped conceptually and as a policy tool. That *Report*, for instance, calls for the development of 'a set of indicators to identify global threats to human security' (UNDP, 1994: 38), yet neither in that year's edition nor in subsequent ones was any attempt made to provide such information. Admittedly, the *Report* was designed as a call for the Copenhagen

Social Summit, which it was assumed (wrongly) at the time would adopt specific measures to ensure the operationalization of the idea.

Still, one cannot help but compare this situation with the success of the UNDP's effort to mainstream gender issues, providing not only broad policy orientations but also data and developing 'gender equality' and 'gender empowerment' indexes that have facilitated the operationalization of UNDP policies. In fact, only in the 1998 *Report* on globalization does one find a significant discussion of the human security concept, most of it taken directly from the 1994 *Report*. Human security, in fact, never even made it into the glossary of the annual *Human Development Report*.

In practical terms and in spite of the emphasis given to human security in the 1994 and 1998 reports, no institutional change or innovation has ever been dedicated to human security research or activities. This is less surprising if one considers that the annual *Human Development Report* (HDR) is in fact *not* meant to be the 'motor' of UNDP action. As noted by a specially mandated internal review team, to make it so 'would certainly enhance UNDP's policy credibility and capacity, but it would also change the nature of the HDR and possibly its value to the broader development community as an independent vehicle able to rove across a wide policy terrain' (UNDP, 1999b: 24). Accordingly, the HDR team is structurally independent from the rest of the organization. This position is certainly defensible from an institutional standpoint, but for the human security agenda it means that not even its chief advocate has necessarily meant to put the concept into practice.

Nevertheless, the very close identification of the human security and human development agendas could in effect mean that human security is being implemented, incognito, both through the broader policy work of the UNDP and through the work of its global staff. It appears, however, that even from this perspective the reach of human security is likely to be limited by the many problems that plague the UNDP. For every asset of the Program, there appears to exist a liability that limits the potential impact of its policy innovations. The UNDP has a relatively small, multidisciplinary policy staff whose interests range from gender to the environment and who have to cover almost every conceivable development problem there is. On the operational side, the UNDP has 7,000 projects in 120 countries, while its outlays represent barely 3 per cent of total overseas development assistance (UNDP, 2000), which is about as close to being overextended as one can get. In addition, the UNDP has suffered from a massive financial crunch in recent years, with spending in program countries diminishing some 40 per cent between 1992 and 1999. Finally, its co-ordination role in the UN and in the field has met with fierce resistance from the notoriously independent fiefs that make up the UN system, all of which also had to confront massive budget cuts in recent years.

It is difficult to see which of the many potential assets of the UNDP could have made human security a serious point of reference for development thinking or practice. In the end, the concept looks a lot like a tactical weapon used by a nimble think-tank to wrestle defence dollars from developed countries that were suddenly at peace but did not appear willing to spend it on the poor. When the Copenhagen Social Summit proved unwilling to 'buy' into the new agenda, the concept was put back into its box, if not buried.

At a more fundamental level, however, one must recognize that the basic diagnosis of the comprehensive human security agenda is alive and well: the UNDP has been steadfast in its 'strategic' identification of global political and market failures as the chief obstacles to the production of freedom from fear and want. Its insistence on the global character of this failure, already noted, can perhaps be linked to the profound 'rooting' of the Program within developing countries, resulting from the UNDP's close work with the governments of the South. This very partial reading of the neo-institutionalist critique is in fact the mirror image of the typical World Bank view, which focuses almost exclusively on the problems with domestic institutions (largely under the rubric of 'good governance'). This is reflected in the somewhat surprising refusal of the UNDP to formally adopt 'governance' as a priority and in the open admission by the Program's administrator that the label 'had provoked concerns' (UNDP, 2000). Although the UNDP has decided to reinforce its involvement in the development of 'appropriate policies and institutions, often around sensitive issues intimately wound up with national and local circumstances', its refusal to frame those activities explicitly under the 'good governance' label suggests that the 'reverse' institutionalism of the UNDP could to a large extent be an emanation of its South-centred nature. Its special slant on human security should therefore probably be understood as an expression of the views of its primary constituency. As we will now see, the same holds for the DAC.

The OECD's Development Assistance Committee

The Development Assistance Committee (DAC) is a consultation forum on development co-operation set up as one of the many committees of the Organization for Economic Co-operation and Development (OECD). Development co-operation is a 'founding' issue of the OECD, which grew out of the 'Organization for European Economic Co-operation (OEEC) established in April 1948 by a convention signed by the recipients of the Marshall Plan. The OEEC formally became the OECD in September 1961 and has since consolidated its place as the main club of developed countries (Führer, 1996). With a membership of 29 states plus the European Union (EU), it is openly devoted to the consolidation of the liberal economic order through achieving 'the highest sustainable economic growth and employment and a rising standard of living in Member countries, while maintaining financial stability, and thus [aims] to contribute to the development of the world economy . . . sound economic expansion in Member as well as non-member countries . . . [and] the expansion of world trade on a multilateral, non-discriminatory basis' (OECD/DAC, 2000: 2).

Twenty-two OECD members are also members of the DAC, which is charged specifically 'to consult on the methods for making national resources available for assisting countries and areas in the process of economic development and for expanding and improving the flow of long-term funds and other development assistance to them' (Führer, 1996: 10). The DAC is directed by the development co-operation ministers and by the heads of aid agencies of its member countries, who meet twice a year. It has a secretariat and a research unit that produce, in addition to an annual report on development co-operation, a number of studies on all possible aspects of development. DAC countries now provide $60 billion (US) per year in development assistance, which represents more than 90 per cent of global bilateral aid. Although a small portion (.24 per cent) of OECD countries' GDP (OECD/DAC, 2000: 182), this is larger than the total GDP in the majority of the countries in the world. The members of the EU, the G-7, and basically all the significant groups of developed countries are members of the DAC, and they also provide the vast majority of funds to the UN system, the World Bank, and the regional development banks. Over the years, moreover, the DAC has developed a remarkable capacity to generate documents that provide clear guidance to member countries' development agencies on both policy and operations, with neat assessments of 'lessons learned' and comprehensive 'guidelines' such as those developed for conflict (OECD/DAC, 1998). DAC priorities, such as those outlined in its 1996 report, *Shaping the 21st Century* (OECD/DAC, 1996b), quickly find their way into most multilateral and bilateral programs and, to the extent that they reflect a clear outlook, the orientations developed by the DAC powerfully shape the development agenda.

DAC documents certainly present the crispest treatment of human security of all the institutions covered here. That understanding is strategic and does not involve a rethinking of the nature of security. Instead, it recognizes that threats are now much more multi-faceted and that the collaboration of the South is critical to tackling them. While it would be ridiculous to dismiss the moral rationale behind the OECD aid program, the DAC's concept of human security is best summarized as 'freedom from fear of the poor'.

Development thinking at the OECD has always been structured around the basic liberal precepts of trade liberalization and the free circulation of capital. For a period, however, with the consolidation of the welfare state and the prominence of social democracy in Western Europe, the ultimate application of those parameters left considerable room for state intervention and nationalist policies. Since the 1980s, however, an increasingly narrow concept of economic development has held sway that puts quick market liberalization and export-led development at the core of a universal recipe book to be used by all. The key parameters of development have thus become integration with the global market, access to private capital and technology, and institutional reforms that facilitate the smooth functioning of market mechanisms within a country but also 'open, participatory economic and political systems . . . including high standards of accountability, and a strong civil society' (OECD/DAC, 1996c: 18).

In the 1990s, the DAC also joined the UNDP and the World Bank on the human development bandwagon, but in a characteristically pragmatic way, insisting that 'efforts that are people-centred . . . tend to be more credible and popular [and are] also likely to be the most effective' (OECD/DAC, 1995: 7). With the end of the Cold War, similarly, the DAC has shown a growing preoccupation with conflict, focusing at first on the impact of conflict on development (OECD/DAC, 1993), but quickly moving on to an exploration of the complex interaction between development and conflict that has laid the ground for its work on human security.

As introduced in its 1993 and 1994 annual reports (OECD/DAC, 1994, 1995), the DAC human security concept is quite distinct from that proposed by the UNDP. Instead of weaving it with the sustainable development agenda primarily as a *condition* of sustainable development, the DAC presents it as an *effect* of the latter: sustainable development is critical to tackling a broad range of problems that threaten the whole world. This view of human security flows out of the Palme (Independent Commission on International Development Issues, 1982) and Brundtland (World Commission on Environment and Development, 1987) reports on 'common security' and sustainable development, but while it broadens the range of threats it does not fuse the security and development agenda as the UNDP concept does by radically redefining security in the process. The DAC outlook is thus more 'security for humanity' than 'security for people': the global nature of the new threats determine the new object of security, not the way in which we understand security. The concept, in other words, plays on the same kind of fears as the 'old' security agenda. Its primary public is not humanity as a whole but the people of the OECD who now happen to be threatened by problems that are global in reach and that can only be tackled globally. Epidemics, for instance, were not seen as a security problem before, but a sense of moral duty vis-à-vis the sad reality of the poor meant an effort had to be made to help them. The main reason why they suddenly become security issues, along with environmental degradation, clearly is because they now also threaten the North: 'citizens and political leaders in the industrialized countries should care about . . . sustainable development because without it many interests of the industrialised countries will suffer and their own people will be less secure' (OECD/DAC, 1995: 2).

With the new concept, the DAC attempts to rekindle the traditional security rationale for development aid and its political motivation. The chair of the Committee, James H. Michel, could hardly have been more explicit on the problem he confronts, and on its solution:

> In the 1994 Report I expressed concern that the end of the Cold War had removed a traditional and well understood security rationale for development co-operation, while also creating new and largely unanticipated demands. As a result, increased opportunities for productive collaboration were threatened by a diminished commitment of both political will and related financial resources. . . . The stakes for future generations throughout the world in increased human security through sustainable development would become the new focal point of political motivation. (OECD/DAC, 1997a: 1, 2)

It would be wrong, however, to be cynical about such statements, finding in them little more than a bureaucratic preoccupation with work areas and sources of funding. Just as the older security rationale for development aid was accepted by a broad section of mainstream political opinion, the new security agenda is also gaining ground in the same milieu. It is, in fact, clear from DAC documents that the Committee has internalized the diagnosis that led the Brundtland Commission to coin the concept of 'sustainable development'. A new understanding of security also flows from a deeper appreciation of the dangers inherent in current global tendencies. The problem the DAC confronts, however, is that this view is not yet shared broadly within the OECD, either at the level of governments or among the broader public.

This tension is graphically conveyed by the increasingly desperate tone of the reports regarding the declining amount of aid flowing from DAC members to developing countries:

> The shared objective of human security, combined with a respectful concern for others, clearly has not yet brought sustainable development to a place of central importance on the international agenda. Governments and public opinion in 1995 often failed to make the connection between sustainable development and their concerns about regional conflict, unemployment, societal divisions, international migration and the global environment. There did not yet exist a widespread aware- ness of the need to apply at the international level the logic that has caused social disintegration and exclusion to gain recognition as serious problems within national societies. (OECD/DAC, 1996a: 2)

The DAC has confronted this problem by working on three fronts. First, it has repeatedly called on OECD members to reverse the decline in aid flows, which fell from 0.33 per cent of OECD GDP in 1992 to 'an unprecedented low of 0.22 per cent in 1997' (OECD/DAC, 1999: 2), only increasing slightly in 1998 to 0.24 per cent (OECD/DAC, 2000: 182). The DAC has also tried to increase the effectiveness of aid in order to maximize the impact of what little is made available. As a result, exten- sive evaluations of a broad variety of donor experiences have been undertaken by the DAC, and guidelines and 'best practice' compendiums have been developed. Finally, the DAC has become a champion of 'policy coherence', stressing the need for consistency between the formal aid objectives of its members and the broader universe of their policies that have a bearing on developing countries, especially regarding trade liberalization (OECD/DAC, 1995: 9–10). As stated in the DAC's major policy statement of 1996, *Shaping the 21st Century*: 'The ramifications and opportu- nities of policy coherence for development now need to be much more carefully traced and followed through than in the past. We should aim for nothing less than to assure that the entire range of relevant industrialised country policies are consis- tent with and do not undermine development objectives' (OECD/DAC, 1996b: 20).

The tension between growing needs and declining resources was made even worse in the 1990s by the massive investment that followed the explosion of acute conflicts in developing countries, especially in Africa:

> Emergency assistance and distress relief, which had constituted less than 3 per cent of bilateral aid until 1990, had come to exceed 8 per cent of the total by 1993. Expressed in current dollars, what had been a $300 million item in the early 1980s had become a $3.2 billion claim on bilateral aid budgets in 1993. Multilateral insti- tutions have been similarly affected. The United Nations saw the shares of its assis-

tance going to help refugees and assist in humanitarian emergencies increase massively. In addition, UN expenditures on peacekeeping escalated to new levels in 1993. (OECD/DAC, 1995: 2)

This massive effort has threatened to make matters worse because it is often driven by very short-term objectives. In particular, it has not typically considered the impact, often negative, of donor assistance on the conflicts themselves or on the capacity of the receiving society to build the viable political and economic arrangements that would lessen future possibilities of conflict (OECD/DAC, 1997b).

The DAC is at the forefront of the initiative to situate humanitarian efforts within a longer-term development process that tackles the 'root causes' of conflict and humanitarian disasters: 'ongoing humanitarian emergencies involving civil conflict, dislocation and suffering—all these immediate challenges demand attention. But they should not distract us from what must be done now to build effective development partnerships for human security and well-being over the long term' (OECD/DAC, 1996a: 16). In examining the impact of the humanitarian effort on the conflict itself, the DAC has drawn attention to the consequences of development programs for the social and political tensions that feed or lead to conflict, as well as the political and institutional conditions that lessen conflict potentials. Policy coherence as a principle has also been a new focus because '[d]iplomatic, humanitarian and economic strategies must be closely integrated in the phases of preparation for and assistance to post-conflict rehabilitation and reconstruction. Impartially helping to restore human and social capital is every bit as important as traditional work in the reconstruction of physical infrastructure' (ibid., 32).

The consistency that the DAC brings to its work on sustainable development, conflict, and now human security reflects the clarity of the OECD's reading of the fundamental conditions of growth, peace, and security. Ever since the Marshall Plan, in fact, the OEEC/OECD has embodied the conviction that free markets, prosperity, democracy, and peace all go hand in hand, a conviction faithfully applied by the DAC to the developing world. The inability to produce these sought-after public goods is never attributed to market failures, particularly at the global level. Instead, in keeping with the neo-institutional orientation of the World Bank, the DAC has tended to focus on institutional deficiencies at the national level.

Explanations for development or its failure are put squarely in the lap of developing countries, particularly their institutions: the 'key elements of integrated development strategies' are 'the primary responsibility (including financial responsibility) of governments, institutions and people of the developing countries', with external actors expected 'to support the strengthening of local capacities, provide needed complementary resources, and carry out co-ordinated and coherent policies supportive of development in a true spirit of partnership' (OECD/DAC, 1997a: 2). Until very recently, supranational institutional arrangements were not considered worthy of critical examination. The treatment of the 1994–5 Mexican crisis is a case in point, being described alternatively as an 'unfortunate surprise' (OECD/DAC, 1996a: 60) or as a good example of the institutional requirements of the new economy: 'the volatility of private capital flows . . . [was] demonstrated in the market response early in 1995 to Mexico's devaluation. As the developing countries are becoming more active participants in a global economy the forces of globalisation are holding them to ever higher standards of performance' (ibid., 5). In sum, the problem lay strictly in Mexico's own front yard.

The 1997 Asian crisis, however, prompted a sober second look at the role of globalization in human security. Financial instability in the South suddenly became a global problem. Predictably, however, it was not framed by the OECD—or the World Bank—as a market failure, but, instead, as an institutional one. This time, however, the crisis was seen as reaching to the core of global financial and economic governance arrangements. For the DAC, it led to a further broadening of the reach of its co-ordination activities, as it worked actively with bilateral donors, multilateral development institutions, the UN system, and the private sector. The DAC's new agenda includes such issues as the international financial architecture, corporate governance, and especially 'partnership and the "governance" of aid' (OECD/DAC, 2000: 17–19). To a significant extent, the OECD is a primary player in the development of this joint agenda, and a powerful one. However, the directions this new partnership appears to be taking suggest that the traditional outlook of the OECD is unchanged and that any new agendas will not challenge the philosophy that market liberalization must serve as the basis for sustainable development. Moreover, it is remarkable that the political dimensions of global arrangements, so central to the UNDP's analysis, do not appear problematic in those policy statements focused on organizational issues.

Human insecurity, for the DAC, is a consequence of poverty and the lack of sustainable development in the South. The latter, in turn, is seen to result primarily from institutional deficiencies at the national level, but problems such as environmental degradation and financial instability are proving impossible to confine to the South. Hence the DAC perceives an urgent need to provide sufficient and effective aid, and to pursue economic policies consistent with the needs of developing countries in order to ensure that they adequately deal with their own problems, which now happen to be those of the industrialized North, too. This change in outlook, however, implies neither a challenge to the basic economic principles of liberalism nor a significant change in current international governance arrangements.

Human Security, Development, and the New Interventionism

In June 2000, a joint statement on development, with targets similar to the priorities identified in the OECD's *Shaping the 21st Century* (1996), was issued by the IMF, the OECD, the UN, and the World Bank. Probably the first concrete statement of the new global aid strategy and philosophy (OECD/DAC, 2000: 19), *A Better World for All* (IMF et al., 2000) focuses on poverty reduction and identifies a series of targets that build on seven social goals identified by the UN summits of the 1990s.

To the extent that it expresses and reflects a new consensus, this document is probably depressing news for the advocates of a comprehensive view of human security. Its discussion of conflict is a throwback to pre-1994 statements about the relationship between conflict and development. Its diagnosis is narrowly focused on the institutional deficiencies of developing countries: 'What are the obstacles [to overcoming poverty]? Weak governance. Bad policies. Human rights abuses. Conflicts, natural disasters and other external shocks. The spread of HIV/AIDS. The failure to address inequities in income, education and access to health care, and the inequalities between men and women.' The corresponding responsibilities of the rich countries follow the usual OECD/DAC line: 'Limits on developing countries' access to global markets, the burden of debt, the decline in development aid and, sometimes, inconsistencies in donor policies also hinder faster progress' (IMF et al., 2000: 2–3). Not surprisingly, the alignment of the UN with the more liberal financial and development institutions was criticized by many NGOs who felt that the joint report leaned 'too far in the direction of market-oriented policies'(*Financial Times*, 2000).

The original attempt of the UNDP to redefine security by questioning the ability of the market and of the current 'global political system' to provide 'freedom from fear and want' thus appears to have come to nought. If human security remains an issue, it is as defined by the OECD: a global public good whose production is to take place within existing global economic and political arrangements. It depends fundamentally, in other words, on the development of institutional capacity in the South, a process that the North is expected to help through increased foreign aid and by eliminating barriers to exports from developing countries. Instead of contemplating the possibility of fundamental market and political failures at the global level (i.e., framing the problem of human security in the broadest possible terms) and the consequent need to reform these institutions, the debate has been largely framed in terms of the problems surrounding the institutional capacity of less-developed countries and the requisite need for improved systems of governance at the national or even subnational levels. The logic of human security, as the North's development establishment understands it, is thus interventionist when it comes to the policies and practices of states in the South, but essentially *laissez-faire* and status quo regarding the role of the market and global governance arrangements.

The preceding discussion also suggests that there may be an emerging consensus within these institutions on narrower concepts of human security that revolve around the safety of peoples and human rights/the rule of law. There is little institutional or bureaucratic support beyond the level of rhetoric for the broader concept of human security, which stresses the distributive aspects of development and views the human security *problématique* as arising from deep-rooted socioeconomic inequalities and a lack of social justice not just at the national level but also at the global level. This should come as no surprise. The broader conception of human security is not only incompatible with how these institutions conceive of their organizational mandates and missions, but it also challenges prevailing free-market orthodoxies.

Chapter 9

Portfolio Diversification and Human Security

We began by stipulating that there are several different meanings of human security: the human rights/rule-of-law conception, the 'safety of peoples' conception, and the much broader, sustainable human development conception. Although these three different views of human security share certain elements in common, in particular, their focus on the individual as the object of security and the elevation of the individual (and by extension, human needs) over and above those of the state or other actors and institutions in the international system, they also differ in terms of their understanding about the kinds of market and political failures that contribute to the human security deficit in international relations. Whereas the two somewhat narrower conceptions of human security (human rights/rule-of-law, 'safety of peoples') tend to focus on political failures, largely at the subsystemic or state level, to explain why human security is an underprovided public good, the broader, sustainable human development view has tended to focus on market failures at the global level and the failure of the world's political economy to provide for greater levels of equity and social justice that would raise the living standards, reduce the vulnerability of the world's neediest citizens, and also raise income levels in the world's poorest societies, which are more conflict-prone than those with higher per capita incomes.

There is obviously a continuing tension between these different conceptions of human security. On the one hand, exponents of sustainable human development focus on the need to develop correctives (institutional and otherwise) to the forces set in motion by globalization and the world's changing political economy. On the other hand, those who couch the human security challenge in terms of strengthening and promoting human rights and the rule of law while simultaneously addressing the needs of peoples in conflict situations (i.e., enhancing the safety of peoples) typically stress the importance of promoting (exporting) democracy and the rule of law and strengthening international institutions (governmental and non-governmental) that can provide for these human security public goods.

To the extent that any consensus exists at the international level (including among key donor agencies) about which conception of human security should prevail, such a consensus would appear to endorse the narrower conception of human security with its corresponding emphasis on promoting human rights, the rule of law, and the safety of peoples. This is reflected in the sorts of undertakings that have come to characterize the human security 'enterprise', e.g., the landmines campaign and treaty, the creation of the International Criminal Court, efforts to control small arms. As argued in Chapter 8, the world's principal donor agencies are also more comfortable with human security initiatives that focus on fostering democracy and the rule of law, reducing corruption, and tackling greed, as opposed to human security initiatives directed at promoting a redistribution of wealth and income or changing governance structures in the international political economy. In some respects, the human security enterprise as it has evolved in recent years is a rather traditional liberal undertaking. It is an enterprise that for the most part has tended to focus on reforming states, not markets. But unlike traditional liberalism it is highly interventionist when it comes to reforming failed or failing states.

But even to the extent that there is an emerging consensus that human rights/rule of law and safety of peoples are legitimate global public goods, this consensus is not universally shared. There continue to be important differences in the way states view particular human security initiatives and the implications of these initiatives for national security and state sovereignty. Negotiations leading to the Ottawa Convention to ban anti-personnel landmines were marked by the defection of the United States from the Ottawa Process as well as by opposition from a number of other key countries, such as Russia and China. The same is true of the International Criminal Court, where the United States, a chief supporter of the idea in early years, balked about signing onto the treaty that emerged from the negotiations in Rome. Although President Clinton did eventually sign the treaty as one of his last acts in office, most observers give it little chance of being ratified by the Senate of the United States any time soon. Much of the opposition to these two initiatives in the United States has come from the Pentagon, which is reluctant to endorse the creation of new international institutions that will compromise its missions and purported US national security interests. The campaign to ban small arms is also notable for the lack of consensus, even among supporters of the idea to control international trade in light weapons, because of continuing differences about the modalities and scope of a control regime.

On the matter of whether force should be used in support of human security objectives, the recent history of military interventions in Kosovo and eastern Zaire (the two cases discussed in this volume) also shows that the consensus is weak: Western liberal democratic states have found themselves at odds not just with developing countries, but also with great powers like Russia and China, about whether international institutions should sanction the use of force in humanitarian interventions. Human security values have tended to sit somewhat uneasily alongside more traditional international norms like sovereignty and the principle of non-intervention in the internal affairs of states. Though it would be wrong to suggest that sovereignty and non-intervention are hard and fast norms in international politics—we have provided much evidence that sovereignty is conditional and borders are not sacrosanct (see also Krasner, 1999)—it would also be incorrect to say that human security values have somehow replaced these traditional Westphalian norms in international politics. What we do see is an uneasy coexistence between these two normative systems where conflicting interpretations as to which norms should guide international behaviour and state practice have all too often polarized the international community.

The norms, values, and assumptions that inform the human security paradigm are in a state of flux and tension—a tension reflected not just in the different meanings of human security, but also between the concept of human security and other norms, values, and principles that have traditionally informed and shaped state behaviour and served as guide to action (or inaction). However, the qualified success of a number of human security initiatives and undertakings, such as the anti-personnel landmines treaty and the successful conclusion of negotiations for the International Criminal Court, suggests that new norms and principles are taking root and slowly reshaping the international landscape. These gestures are not just theoretical exercises in norm creation, but are deliberate efforts to improve the security situation and welfare of ordinary people around the globe. How have these human security public goods come about? And can we make any sort of meaningful generalizations about the production function that characterizes the delivery of these new public goods? It is to these questions we now turn.

Producing Human Security Public Goods

International relations scholars, particularly in the United States, have generally tended to stress the importance of great powers, usually hegemonic actors, in the direct creation and provision of international public goods (Waltz, 1979; Walt, 1987; Snidal, 1985). This perspective is by no means confined to scholars of a realist or neo-realist persuasion but also characterizes much of the work by liberal scholars who, while acknowledging the importance of international institutions in *maintaining and sustaining* the provision of public goods (Katzenstein et al. 1998), nonetheless continue to stress the role of hegemonic leaders—or occasionally minilateral 'clubs' or coalitions of great powers—in the actual *creation* of those goods (Keohane, 1984). There is growing recognition, of course, that hegemonic influence and leadership can take a variety of forms; it need not depend on military power (or prowess), but can also be projected through economic control over markets or a variety of what Joseph Nye calls 'soft power' resources and capabilities such as information technologies, cultural industries, and even civil society (Nye, 1991, 1999).

Even so, there is considerable reluctance in realist/neo-realist and even in liberal quarters to acknowledge that small powers (i.e., middle-power multilateralists) or even non-governmental, civil society actors (cosmopolitan forces) have much to contribute to the generation and maintenance of global public goods, including those concerning human security, except perhaps at the margins of the production function curve. Typical reasons given for this are, first, that the provision of global public goods, particularly public goods that maintain international order (especially economic or military security order), is an extremely costly undertaking. Only great powers or hegemonic leaders have the kind of resources to provide these goods or, as argued by Ruggie, the beneficence to do so because the returns to them tend to fall short of their initial investment (Ruggie, 1983, 1996). These costs are usually very high in the early stages of international regime formation, as are the risks of failure, though they may level off and even decline once the regime is in place and other states accept the normative foundation and rules on which the regime is based.

Second, it is argued that in the provision of any global public good, international co-operation is likely to be thwarted by defectors (those who, for their own gains, seek to exploit or flaunt the rules under which the good is provided) or by free riders (those who want to take advantage of the good being provided but are not prepared to pay their fair share of the price of membership) (Grieco, 1990). Realists/neo-realists argue that only great powers or hegemonic leaders possess the resources, capacity, and political will to discipline defectors and sanction free riders (Waltz, 1974; Walt, 1987). In a somewhat different vein, liberals argue that international institutions, by lowering transaction costs and promoting greater levels of transparency through the monitoring of the behaviours of different actors, can increase the costs of defection and free riding (Keohane, 1984). But those institutions backed up by hegemonic leadership tend to be the most durable because there will always be incentives to defect even in a transparent environment.

As discussed in Chapter 3, other schools of thought stress the role of epistemic communities, social groups, and learning for changing state preferences and promoting co-operation though a process of cognitive convergence and the generation of knowledge-based public goods (E. Haas, 1990; P. Haas, 1989). But again, these communities of knowledge are generally seen as working through the state; they are considered incapable of providing public goods (other than knowledge, itself a public good) on their own, particularly when it comes to global public goods requiring co-operative solutions that are extremely costly to obtain and maintain, though others take issue with this view (see Cusimano, 2000; Hewson and Sinclair, 1999; Lipschutz and Mayer, 1996). Others argue that international organizations and intergovernmental institutions generally have greater levels of political legitimacy than non-governmental organizations and are therefore able to wrest resources from states, get them to act, and ensure compliance, which are important when global public goods are involved (see Young, 1999).

Although the findings from the case studies presented in this volume should be viewed cautiously, because the number of instances of human security public goods provision is small and there continues to be some debate as to whether some of them, in fact, are genuine reflections of human security (we have argued that most of them are), they do point to a somewhat different understanding from realist/neo-realist and liberal traditions about which actors/institutions in international politics are public goods providers, especially when human security values are at stake. As we said in Chapter 3, there are four schools of thought about human security public goods providers: the *minilateralist*, the *middle-power multilateralist*, the *cosmopolitan*, and the *institutionalist*. Human security minilateralist and institutionalist conceptions, as also noted earlier, tend to mirror the realist/neo-realist and liberal/neo-liberal arguments about international public good providers. Minilateralists, like realists/neo-realists, stress the importance of great powers, or what is sometimes referred to as the sheriff's posse, in defending and promoting human security values. Institutionalists, on the other hand, stress the importance of formal international organizations, like the UN, in providing for human security because these institutions possess the critical quality of global legitimacy that comes from their near-universal membership that minilateral coalitions, when they choose to act on their own, typically lack.

The newest of these four schools of thought about international public good providers are the middle-power multilateralist and cosmopolitan schools. Middle-power multilateralists argue that middle powers, when allied with non-governmental organizations and elements of civil society, can mobilize international coalitions to promote human security. The traditional middle-power argument suggests that this kind of influence is best wielded in the negotiating and institutional arenas of formal international organizations where decision-making procedures and voting rules tend to favour smaller and middle powers, especially if they can assemble the requisite majority (Hampson, 1995). The newer middle-power multilateralist position is that formal international organizations are too often hamstrung or paralysed by the veto power exercised by great powers (especially the United Nations Security Council) and that it is sometimes necessary to create new institutions and negotiating fora that bypass or circumvent the logjam within existing institutions. The legitimacy of these efforts is also enhanced and strengthened by supportive elements in civil society who can work with middle powers to promote the creation of new international institutions. New communications technologies, such as the Internet, are essential to the projection of influence and the mobilization of public opinion around human security concerns.

Cosmopolitans consider civil society and the vast network of non-governmental organizations that span the globe as the real movers and shakers behind the human security agenda. Cosmopolitans believe that not only do civil society actors have the potential to mobilize public opinion and thus change the preferences of state (i.e., governmental) actors in ways that foster co-operative solutions to human security problems, but they also have a comparative advantage in mobilizing resources (through public fund-raising campaigns) and engaging in the delivery of human security public goods themselves. Part of this advantage comes from their presence on the ground in many conflict regions and their long-standing involvement in and commitment to human development and assistance. As observed earlier, cosmopolitans also favour the creation of new, international governance structures that not only confer greater legitimacy to their efforts, but give them a greater voice and role in the provision of global goods than they now have within existing international institutions and organizational arrangements.

In assessing the claims of each one of these schools, the case studies in this volume highlight the deficiencies of the various actors and institutions characterized by each school of thought. First, with regard to the minilateralist position, it is by no means self-evident that great powers are necessarily effective or, for that matter, deeply committed to providing human security public goods. Although it can be argued that the United States has been a long-standing champion of human security values, on closer inspection it is evident that the United States has on more than one occasion sought to thwart the creation of institutions, such as the landmines treaty and the

International Criminal Court, that others have erected in the name of human security. Much of the US government's ambivalence with the human security agenda has stemmed from internal divisions pitting the Pentagon against other elements of the bureaucracy that have supported various human security initiatives. This ambivalence extends to the public and the US Congress, which is also divided on these matters. But it is also the case that the United States has not had the power or ability to block human security undertakings that it opposes, suggesting that there are real limits to the exercise of minilateral or hegemonic power and influence.

When hegemonic actors, like the United States, decide to act in the name of human security and to assemble coalitions to support their missions, as the US did in Kosovo, it is not clear that these initiatives can stand on their own. As Chapter 7 shows, the minilateralist argument that 'just' interventions taken in the name of human security will drag international law behind them has raised too many red flags. Although norms are not law, and legality and perceived legitimacy are not always coterminous, the precedent-setting appeal of the NATO intervention was tarnished by the ambiguity of the outcome and the absence of a clear UN mandate. The NATO bombing campaign and the occupation that followed have seen violence against human security. Such results do not necessarily condemn the NATO intervention, but they do raise some sober second thoughts about military actions taken in the name of human security.

If there are limits to minilateralism there are also observable limits to middle-power multilateralism. Although middle powers are increasingly vocal and recognizable in international politics, and have undeniably advanced and promoted human security causes across a wide range of issues—the landmines campaign being the most notable—they also have their own deficiencies and limitations, not the least of which are their lack of resources and capabilities, especially when 'hard', i.e., military, power has to be used in the name of human security. The discussion in Chapter 7 of the failed mission in 1996 in eastern Zaire illustrates the constraints against the multilateralist answer to human security interventions. This does not diminish the importance of middle-power multilateralism to the human security enterprise, but it does suggest that the comparative advantage of middle powers may be confined to issue areas where 'soft', i.e., negotiating, power is required as opposed to hard power.

Institutionalists, like some of the earlier students of international regimes, believe that formal international organizations are critical to the provision of human security public goods. Although international institutions are generally viewed by all schools as essential to the human security enterprise insofar as they embody human security norms and values (e.g., the International Criminal Court) and are also human security public good providers, there are sharp disagreements about which particular institutions and organizations are most effective and whether genuine reform of organizational mandates is possible in the current political environment or whether new institutions can or should be created to serve human security objectives. On the other hand, institutional reformers say that real reform is possible and has occurred. They point to the landmines treaty and the International Criminal Court statute as firm evidence that the international institutional landscape is changing in a positive direction. Institutionalists also like to point out that many of these groundbreaking human security initiatives were the inspiration of individuals working within international organizations, e.g., the important role played by the International Committee of the Red Cross (an intergovernmental body) and its president, Cornelio Sommaruga, in the landmines campaign; the key roles of A.N.R. Robinson and Cherif Bassiouni in promoting the idea of an International Criminal Court. On the other hand, the situation is less reassuring when one considers the kinds of obstacles that human security proponents have encountered in bodies like the UN Security Council and the sorts of bureaucratic resistance even among professed organizational champions of human security like the UNDP, as discussed in Chapter 8. Further, to the extent that bureaucratic entrepreneurs have been successful in rallying international organizations around human security concerns, they have done so by mobilizing constituencies outside the formal setting of international organizations.

The cosmopolitan argument that civil society actors are independently capable of providing human security public goods is not borne out in the examples discussed in this volume. First, although civil society actors are generally capable of focusing public attention on a particular issue and have been successful in mobilizing political support (e.g., the landmines campaign), they are not necessarily able to project their influence in those international arenas that are dominated by states without the assistance of governmental allies within those fora. It must also be recognized that on certain issues (e.g., small arms) different elements of civil society may not necessarily be marching to the same drummer. This is because nongovernmental organizations often have different if not competing views on the best way to frame human security issues and to deliver what they consider to be a legitimate public good. The problems of collective action among the vast array of civil society actors are compounded by different institutional mandates, different institutional capacities and resources, and different sources of financial and donor support.

Portfolio Diversification in the Pursuit of Human Security

As is demonstrated by the various case studies in this volume, which reflect upon the experience of different kinds of human security undertakings, most, when they have succeeded, have combined the efforts over time of great powers, middle powers, various elements of civil society, and international organizations. Such coalitions, especially if they enjoy strong leadership and have gathered sufficient political momentum, can also withstand defections during the negotiating process, even if those defections come from some of the most powerful actors in the international system. Where human security initiatives have failed, or only partially succeeded, this is because a sizable subset of the above portfolio has decided that it does not wish to provide the public good in question or considers that the public good being provided threatens the national interest or some other core value(s). The more successful human security undertakings, therefore, involve a diverse portfolio of institutions and actors, all of which have different capabilities, resources, levels of political legitimacy, sources of leverage, and track records of success and failure.

In the classical theory of portfolio diversification, investors will split their capital into different assets in order to maintain their overall expected return while reducing the risk of their portfolio (Markowitz, 1952, 1959). In the mean-variance approach to portfolio diversification, investors select assets that differ in regard to their expected return and risk, i.e., they do not place all of their eggs in the same basket. The operational theory of portfolio selection under uncertainty demonstrates that under certain conditions, an investor's portfolio choice can be reduced to balancing two dimensions, namely, the expected return on the portfolio and its variance. Due to the possibility of reducing risk through diversification, the risks of the portfolio, measured by its variance, will depend not only on the individual variance of the return on the different assets, but also on the pairwise covariances of all assets (i.e., investors want to choose investments that are negatively correlated so that when the value of some stocks in the portfolio drops, others will rise). The essential aspect pertaining to the risk of an asset is not the risk of each asset in isolation, but the contribution of each asset to the aggregate of the portfolio even though the risk cannot be completely eliminated because the returns on different assets are typically correlated.[1]

Although the theory of portfolio diversification is a sophisticated branch of financial economics (Dobbins, 1994; Elton, 1995; Frankfurter, 1995; Levy, 1995), the basic concept is helpful in understanding why institutional diversity is preferable when it comes to the provision of human security public goods. In a temporal context, the perceived political 'stock' or value of different actors and institutions tends to fluctuate over time depending on their record of success or failure when it comes to intervention in defence of human security public goods. Witness, for example, the declining political stock of the UN following its disastrous interventions in Somalia and Bosnia in the early 1990s vis-à-vis NATO, whose stock rose appreciably with the IFOR (Implementation Force) intervention in Bosnia and then began to fluctuate with the intervention in Kosovo, particularly as the crisis wore on. The same is true of humanitarian NGOs and the various specialized agencies of the UN, such as the UNHCR and the Office of the High Commissioner for Human Rights, whose records of intervention and corresponding political stock have also fluctuated over time. By analogy with portfolio theory, the instruments of human security should reflect a range of institutional assets whose political capital and record of successes and failures are negatively correlated in order to maximize 'mean' human security returns while constraining the risk exposure measured by the 'variance' of portfolio returns. But there are other reasons of an organizational and normative nature that go beyond portfolio theory and speak for a diversification strategy in the provision of human security public goods.

Acquiring Legitimacy through Strength in Numbers and Diversity

The provision of most human security public goods in a fundamental way depends on the creation and promotion of new international norms that inform the rules, principles of behaviour, and institutions that deliver these goods (Katzenstein, 1996; Finnemore and Sikkink, 1998). The creation of new norms in international politics, especially norms that are *voluntarily* subscribed to and are not the result of having been imposed or forced on the members in the international system, essentially involves a numbers game. The larger the size of the coalition that subscribes to a new set of norms, principles, and institutions the greater the sense of legitimacy that is accorded to those norms and the institutions on which they are based. In addition to size, the diversity of the coalition's membership is also critical to its perceived legitimacy. International coalitions that have memberships spanning the North-South, East-West divide and that also have members perceived to be leaders (in the functional, institutional, or regional sense) typically enjoy greater levels of political legitimacy and credibility than coalitions with a narrower membership that are formed along more partisan (i.e., North-South or East-West) lines.

It is also the case that international coalitions supported by a wide array of civil society actors (especially NGOs with transnational memberships) carry an aura of democratic legitimacy because they are perceived (rightly or wrongly) as being in some sense more accountable than state-based coalitions. In a world in which a growing number of states subscribe to democratic principles of government, public officials want to be seen as acting on and responding to the interests of their domestic constituents even in the realm of foreign policy. Thus, the diversity of international coalitions in both the horizontal (state-to-state) and vertical (state-civil society) senses is absolutely critical to the human security enterprise. To the extent that the provision of any human security public good depends on fostering new norms, the success of any given venture may ultimately depend more on the size, depth (in the civil society sense), and diversity of the international coalition that supports these new norms. The 'naming and shaming' exercises frequently associated with the advancement of human rights and rule of law also have greater force and legitimacy if a broad-based coalition in the international community is seen to be expressing the values and principles of the majority of democratic states in the international system.

In both the landmines treaty and the movement to establish an International Criminal Court, the numbers game was played to great effect by those states and non-governmental organizations that supported the creation of these two institutions. As the size and diversity of the international coalition in both cases grew, there was practically a stampede to join the coalition in the final stages of negotiations as former holdout states or states that were deeply ambivalent about these institutions decided that it was better for a country's reputation (and a politician's reputation, too) to be seen supporting norms and values that a growing majority in the world shared. Some scholars have referred to this process as the cascade effect, referring to the way new international norms can suddenly overwhelm the international system (Finnemore and Sikkink, 1998). But this process also has important implications for the way we view the provision of human security public goods because it suggests that a large and diversified portfolio of institutions and actors in the international system is critical to the legitimacy of these goods and the norms upon which they are based.

Acquiring Legitimacy from International Institutions

If legitimacy through numbers and representational diversity are important aspects of human security public goods, the other is the legitimacy acquired from international institutions. Nowhere is this dimension more important than in the exercise of force to promote human security when lives are threatened or when force is used in support of humanitarian objectives. When force is used by a minilateralist coalition, as was the case in Kosovo, there is something inherently unsatisfying in the minilateralist answer that 'just' interventions will eventually attract the support of the broader international community as it comes to appreciate the precedent-setting nature of interventions that defend and protect human security.[2] However, the norm of intervention as it has developed up to now is very much driven by the procedural rules and legitimizing authority of the United Nations Security Council, which itself has been an advocate for human security. Human security interventions in Haiti, Somalia, northern Iraq, and even the former Yugoslavia were framed in the context of the UN Charter and under a Security Council mandate. When minilateralists in effect say that the United Nations no longer matters, they undermine the institutional and normative precedents for their own actions. Other states will rightly contest the legitimacy of minilateralist interventions that do not have the blessing and support of the Security Council on the grounds that they flout the norms and rules of international law and established state practices. Contested legitimacy is no substitute for genuine legitimacy that comes with actions taken under the authority of international institutions, in general, and the UN Security Council, in particular. As Kofi Annan states in his millennium report, 'the essential role that formal governance structures must continue to play is normative: defining objectives, setting standards and monitoring compliance' (Annan, 2000: 15).

Doubtless, the UN Security Council and UN system as a whole have their faults (Claude, 1996; Fomerand, 1996; Gallarotti, 1991). But institutional reform, difficult though it is, will not come about if UN institutions themselves are undermined by vigilante interventions. Furthermore, to the extent that the resort to measures of force in support of humanitarian objectives is part of a larger human security undertaking involving the creation of new international institutions and regimes, like the International Criminal Court or the Landmines Convention, disregarding the very institutions and organizations that are required to support the creation of these new human security mechanisms and public goods will wreak havoc on the entire enterprise. Human security minilateralists have to recognize that ad hoc coalitions of the like-minded have to work with international institutions, not against them, in the promulgation of new international norms and the provision of human security public goods.

Sharing Costs, Reducing Risks, and Isolating Spoilers

The provision of human security, as noted in Chapter 3, also depends on the ability of international actors and institutions to share the costs and risks of delivery of public goods, especially when the costs and risks (domestically and internationally) are potentially quite high. Broad-based coalitions of actors and institutions (intergovernmental as well as non-governmental) provide a mechanism for sharing costs and risks in the delivery and provision of human security and also for multiplying sources of leverage and access. As discussed in Chapters 4 and 5, a wide array of non-governmental actors and institutions helped promote the idea of an international criminal court and a comprehensive landmines treaty by lobbying governments in different regions around the globe. In many respects, these efforts were more critical to building support for these human security institutions than direct state-to-state diplomatic lobbying efforts. The delivery of development assistance in support of human security objectives by leading international donor agencies, as discussed in Chapter 8, has depended heavily (and increasingly so) on a vast array of non-governmental organizations and agencies that have the requisite knowledge, expertise, and institutional capacity to tailor program delivery to those people who are most in need.

Portfolio approaches to human security also make it easier to isolate potential or would-be 'spoilers' and to bring pressure on them. There is obvious leverage that comes when the international community is seen to be working together in pursuit of common objectives. But different actors within a given coalition may also possess unique resources or sources of credibility that are essential to shaming 'spoilers' or raising the profile of human security concerns that others want to bury. The special role played by South Africa, which had just shed the last vestiges of apartheid, was critical in bringing other developing countries—and not just those in Africa—into the international mine ban coalition. So, too, was the media visibility given to the landmines problem as a result of the highly publicized meetings of Britain's Princess Diana with mine victims. In the case of the International Criminal Court, the Canadian chairman, Philippe Kirsch, played a critical leadership role and was able to do so partly because of Canada's perceived neutrality and integrity as a middle power and because of Canada's close ties with the United States.

When the use of force is involved in the provision or pursuit of human security objectives, as discussed in Chapter 7 in the cases of Kosovo and eastern Zaire, there may be an even greater need to resort to multilateral instruments to share the political risks, if not the actual military costs, of intervention. This is because publics and legislative constituencies in most democracies, but especially the United States, are not willing to sanction the use of force in countries and/or regions where the purported 'national interest' is not directly involved or threatened and the corresponding risk of loss of life of military personnel is high. A military undertaking that has the active support and engagement of key allies is easier to justify domestically than one where a country is being asked to shoulder the burden alone. Thus, although the United States was responsible for carrying out almost 85 per cent of the air strikes in the aerial bombardment of Kosovo and Serbia, it was enormously important domestically that President Clinton was able to justify the operation as part of a larger, NATO-led operation that had the direct support of 18 other allies. Even so, the veneer of multilateralism may not be enough in some instances to justify military intervention, particularly to the US public. The eastern Zaire operation is a case in point where the US turned to some of its Western allies to lead and conduct the operation because President Clinton feared that in the aftermath of the fiasco in Somalia the US public and Congress would not tolerate the deployment of US troops in another humanitarian operation in Africa even if it was carried out with others. Further, as mentioned above, minilateralism is a poor substitute for genuine multilateralism; actions taken by coalitions of the willing (or like-minded) will have greater political legitimacy if they are taken under the authority of the United Nations.

To the extent that non-governmental organizations and actors are part of this portfolio mix, it may also be easier to deliver human security public goods without offending the sovereignty sensibilities of states, particularly if such a delivery were instead to be undertaken by a great power(s) or formal intergovernmental body. This is especially true in the provision and delivery of humanitarian assistance where the International Committee of the Red Cross is clearly a more acceptable deliverer of medical aid than, say, the United States government. Diversity is also helpful in other kinds of interventions where negotiating authority that does not raise stakes and the threshold of the dispute is required. A fairly benign middle power may mediate more effectively in certain kinds of disputes than a great power or a superpower, as the negotiations that preceded the imminent deployment of peacekeeping forces in eastern Zaire attest.

Even so, efforts of like-minded NGOs and states to develop agreements that some big powers are unwilling to ratify raise concerns about the self-selecting nature of such coalitions. The reputation of international law and institutions will suffer if there is a perceived (and growing) gap between what is negotiated and what can be effectively implemented, especially if the depth and durability of support for the resulting agreements and arrangements prove inadequate (or politically unsustainable) over time. In such cases, coalitions of the like-minded should perhaps direct their efforts towards national capitals in holdout states in order to change policies and political attitudes rather than seek to bypass all-too-real domestic political obstacles.[3]

Obstacles and Limits to Portfolio Diversification in the Pursuit of Human Security

If diversity in the mix of actors and institutions is desirable for the promotion and advancement of human security public goods for the reasons just mentioned, it must also be recognized that there are actual limits, if not major obstacles, to successful portfolio diversification and the assembly of the appropriate mix of actors and institutions.

Minilateral Obstructionism

One of the main obstacles to the provision of human security public goods is mini-lateral obstructionism. As we have seen in the cases of landmines and the International Criminal Court, the United States played a critical role in the gestation of these ventures. Many of the ideas that led to these initiatives originated in American-based civil society and some even had the backing of the US government. But as negotiations directed at creating new international institutions to promote these human security initiatives gained momentum, official US policies changed as domestic groups opposed to these initiatives brought pressure to bear on the US government. The US thus went from sponsor to spoiler and in the case of both the landmines treaty and the International Criminal Court actively tried to thwart the creation of the institutions in question.

Clearly, the issue of bureaucratic/political strife in the United States helps to explain President Clinton's ambivalent and inconsistent approach in the Ottawa Process and the ICC. As a consequence, other great powers, such as Russia and China, who also opposed these initiatives, were able to hide behind the US position, although the rather unseemly group of states that actively opposed the landmines treaty, which included Iraq and North Korea, cast the US in a rather bad light. However, considering the rather substantial financial support the US government has given to the landmines action campaign, it is really only a partial spoiler. With respect to the International Criminal Court, US failure to ratify the treaty (even though Clinton signed it) will create difficulties once the requisite number of states ratify the treaty and the Court begins operations. In the end, the US role as a participant-provider in any human security enterprise can only be explained or predicted with an account of domestic politics.

Passing the Buck and Avoiding Blame

A second obstacle to successful portfolio diversification is weaknesses of will characteristic of any collective enterprise where more than one set of actors are responsible for delivering or providing public goods. There is always the risk, especially in those human security interventions requiring a commitment of real resources, that various states and organizations will duck the tough issues and try to pass responsibility and blame others when the costs/risks are deemed to be too great or things start to go wrong. There are also incentives for actors to distance themselves from the most problematic cases and from failures, particularly if failure seems imminent. The eastern Zaire crisis of 1996 (see Chapter 7) illustrates this problem. The Clinton administration, unwilling to engage in a humanitarian mission, asked Canada to take the lead in assembling a multinational humanitarian intervention. Although the impending deployment of a multinational force led by Canada provoked local actors into a series of military moves of their own and prompted the sudden return of thousands of refugees to their homeland, it was apparent as the crisis unfolded that Canada had neither the influence to orchestrate the diplomacy of the multilateral intervention nor the military capability to deploy forces to the areas where they were most needed.

Organizational and Bureaucratic Selection Bias

A third set of problems in the provision of human security concerns organizational and bureaucratic selection bias. As the discussion of the three global donor agencies in Chapter 8 shows, the human security agenda has been grafted onto the organizational mandates and functions of these organizations. Similar is the case of the United Nations Security Council, which originally was conceived to be an instrument of collective security and not of human security. As a consequence of this grafting process, international organizations and institutions have adopted those elements of the human security agenda most compatible with existing organizational mandates and functions, while rejecting those that are incompatible with these mandates or that cast the ideological and normative premises of these institutions in a bad light. In the case of the OECD's Development Assistance Committee, for example, although the DAC's new agenda has come to embrace certain human security themes such as the need to tackle the 'root causes' of conflict and humanitarian disasters and to examine the consequences of development programs for the social and political tensions that feed conflict, the DAC is unwilling to embrace human security agendas that challenge the philosophy of market liberalization, which the OECD considers critical to long-term sustainable (human) development. For some this may be good news, but to those who believe in the broader concept of human security and the need to reform global governance structures in order to humanize the forces of globalization, such resistance means that these international institutions are part of the problem rather than the solution.

Portfolio Diversification and the Role of Leadership

The diversity of actors and institutions in the provision of human security public goods places a special premium on leadership and coalition-building skills and acumen. Leadership in a co-operative venture, as Young reminds us, may involve three different kinds of leadership roles: structural leadership relating to the use of strategic leverage; entrepreneurial leadership relating to skill in presenting issues so as to bring parties together for a common purpose; and intellectual leadership relating to the use of ideas to shape perceptions and attitudes about policy questions (Young, 1991). However, other aspects of leadership are also important to the complexities of human security. First, there is the kind of *constituency-building* leadership that is essential to building supportive coalitions within and across societies that will support new international human security norms. Transnational groupings and social movements are essential to shaping and mobilizing public opinion and bringing pressure to bear on governments that will change policies and political preferences.

Second, there is leadership of the *coalition-building* and *coalition-maintaining* variety once a political constituency has developed or rallied around a particular set of concerns or issues. Keeping the parties to a coalition together so that they work and operate according to a common script requires special brokering and negotiating skills:

> Leaders . . . need to find means of including people, sharing credit, borrowing leverage, learning how to help other third-party players to save or maintain face, and identifying their work at every step with a widely shared agenda . . . [but it] is not simply a question of good manners and learning the diplomatic graces. It is a question of building relationship with the other [coalition] members . . . so that it hangs together and remains firmly goal oriented. (Crocker et al., 1999: 696).

In some situations, it may also be necessary to offer a combination of symbolic and actual rewards (or side payments) to keep the coalition intact.

The third aspect of leadership that is essential to the multi-party nature of most human security endeavours has a hortatory or didactic quality to it that goes beyond constituency- or even coalition-building. *Didactic leadership* in the best sense involves not just bringing others into the coalition, but also imparting a sense of moral urgency and vision to the human security enterprise at hand, particularly if those involved in helping to deliver the public good are being asked to incur substantial costs or risks and have to be persuaded that what they are being asked to do is morally and ethically the right thing. Needless to say, there is a fine line between exercising moral leadership and lecturing (or hectoring) from the pulpit. The didactic qualities and hortatory skills required to promote a morally 'just' cause may not sit well with constituency-building and coalition leadership skills, where the leader sometimes has to sit with the audience and allow others to take the spotlight.

Those human security undertakings that succeed are those where all three kinds of leadership are available. For example, constituency-building qualities were evident in the role played by the International Committee of the Red Cross, which helped to galvanize and focus domestic and international opinion on the landmines problem through its educational campaigns and subsequent lobbying efforts. The ICRC also worked closely with the more visible and vocal leaders of the International Campaign to Ban Landmines, who also demonstrated the didactic qualities for building a large base of public support for the goals of the campaign. Coalition-building qualities were clearly important to the landmines campaign and were demonstrated by Norway and Canada in building an international coalition of states (and NGOs) that were supportive of the treaty. Such qualities were also reflected in the work of the like-minded states coalition and the civil society Coalition for the International Criminal Court (CICC), both of which were important in conquering the North-South divide through regional co-ordination and outreach. But we must also recognize that leadership by others, both hortatory and coalition-building, requires politicking among Washington constituencies. And any show of leadership by a US administration must include effective political action domestically as well as sensitivity to the enormous asymmetries in power among nations that have bred real ambivalence towards Washington in regard to how and when the US exercises its leadership and influence.

Conclusion

Although we have tried to suggest that there is a degree of intellectual coherence and consistency to the meaning and concept of human security, we have also shown that human security means different things in different institutional contexts. The obvious tensions between the narrower and broader definitions of human security are plainly evident and ultimately are based on rather different understandings about the sorts of problems and threats that are responsible for the human security deficit in today's world. It would be a mistake to suggest that the ideas of human security have greater coherence and logical consistency in theory than they do in practice. But the potentially large number of diverse elements that fall within the definition of human security poses a problem for collective undertakings that will necessarily engage a wide variety of institutions and actors (state and non-state) in the international community. To the extent that these actors share fundamentally different understandings about the meaning of human security, its goals, and what the human security enterprise is all about, it will be difficult to lay the foundations for effective collective action. Those human security undertakings that succeed will do so because the normative foundations have been laid beforehand and because there is genuine international consensus about the kinds of public goods that have to be provided to address very specific market or political failures. Creating this consensus and forging coalitions, however, will clearly require real leadership of the kind discussed above, if not from minilateral coalitions, then from middle powers and their civil society partners. With such leadership, the human security enterprise is likely to move forward.

Notes

1. With formulation of the Capital Asset Pricing Model (CAPM), Markowitz's model was developed further from microanalysis to market analysis of price formation for financial assets. The basis of the CAPM is that an individual investor can choose exposure to risk through a combination of lending-borrowing and a suitably composed (optimal) portfolio of risky securities. The composition of this portfolio depends on the investor's assessment of the future prospects of different securities, and not on the investor's own attitudes towards risk (Sharpe, 1970).
2. We should be careful not to impute to NATO any intention to make Kosovo a legal precedent. NATO Secretary-General Javier Solana, at least, expressly said it was to be the exception, not the rule. However, those of the minilateralist school discussed in Chapter 3, of course, propose otherwise.
3. I am grateful to Edward Luck for making this observation.

Bibliography

Abel, Pete. 2000. 'Manufacturing Trends: Going to the Source', in Lumpe (2000).

Almond, Gabriel A., and Sidney Verba. 1963. *The Civic Culture: Political Attitudes and Democracy in Five Nations.* Princeton, NJ: Princeton University Press.

Alston, Philip, ed. 1992. *The United Nations and Human Rights: A Critical Appraisal.* Oxford: Oxford University Press.

Amnesty International. 2000. 'NATO/Federal Republic of Yugoslavia: "Collateral Damage" or Unlawful Killings? Violations of the Laws of War by NATO During Operation Allied Force'. Available at: www.amnesty.org (accessed June 2000).

Anderson, John B. 1991. 'An International Criminal Court—An Emerging Idea', *Nova Law Review* 15: 433–47.

Anderson, Mary B. 1996. 'Humanitarian NGOs in Conflict Intervention', in Crocker et al. (1996: 34–54).

———— and Peter J. Woodrow. 1989. *Rising from the Ashes: Development Strategies in Times of Disaster.* Boulder, Colo. and Paris: Westview Press and UNESCO.

Andrews, David M. 1994. 'Capital Mobility and State Autonomy: Toward a Structural Theory of International Monetary Relations', *International Studies Quarterly* 38, 2: 193–218.

Annan, Kofi A. 1999. 'Two Concepts of Sovereignty', *The Economist,* 18 Sept. Available at: http://www.un.org/Overview/SG/kaecon.htm

————. 1999. *Facing the Humanitarian Challenge: Towards a Culture of Prevention.* New York: UN Department of Public Information, Sept.

————. 1999. *Towards a Culture of Prevention.* Statements by the Secretary-General of the United Nations, Carnegie Commission on Preventing Deadly Conflict. New York: Carnegie Corporation, Dec.

————. 2000. *We the Peoples: The Role of the United Nations in the 21st Century.* New York: UN Department of Public Information.

'Arms and the minister'. 1999. *National Post,* 8 Oct., A19.

Arsanjani, Mahnoush. 1999. 'The Rome Statute of the International Criminal Court', *American Journal of International Law* 93, 1: 22–43.

Atwood, David C. 1999. 'Tackling the Problem of Anti-Personnel Landmines: Issues and Developments', in David C. Atwood, Shahram Chubin, Pál Dunay, Jozef Goldblat, Martin Schütz, and Heiner Staub, *Arms Control and Disarmament*. Papers presented at the 3rd International Security Forum, Zurich, 19–21 Oct.

Axelrod, Robert, and Robert O. Keohane. 1993. 'Achieving Cooperation Under Anarchy: Strategies and Institutions', in David A. Baldwin, ed., *Neorealism and Neoliberalism: The Contemporary Debate*. New York: Columbia University Press, 85–115.

Axworthy, Lloyd. 1997. 'Canada and Human Security: The Need for Leadership', *International Journal* 52, 2: 183–96.

―――― and Sarah Taylor. 1998. 'A Ban for All Seasons', *International Journal* 53, 2: 189–204.

'Axworthy to urge small arms control'. 1998. *Toronto Star*, 19 Aug., A11.

Ball, Nicole, with Timothy Halevy. 1996a. *Making Peace Work: The Role of the International Development Community*. Baltimore: Johns Hopkins University Press.

―――― . 1996b. 'The Challenge of Rebuilding War-torn Societies', in Crocker et al. (1996: 607–22).

Bass, Gary Jonathan. 2000. *Stay the Hand of Vengeance: The Politics of War Crimes Tribunals*. Princeton, NJ: Princeton University Press.

Bassiouni, M. Cherif. 1992. *Crimes Against Humanity in International Law*. Dordrecht: Martinus Nijhoff.

―――― . 1997. 'From Versailles to Rwanda in Seventy-Five Years: The Need to Establish a Permanent International Criminal Court', *Harvard Human Rights Law Journal* 10: 11–62.

―――― and Christopher L. Blakesley. 1992. 'The Need for an International Criminal Court in the New International World Order', *Vanderbilt Journal of Transnational Law* 25, 9: 151–82.

Beier, J. Marshall, and Ann Denholm Crosby. 1998. 'Harnessing Change for Continuity: The Play of Political and Economic Factors Behind the Ottawa Process', in Cameron et al. (1998: 269–91).

Benson, William. 1998. 'Light Weapons Control and Security Assistance: A Review of Current Practice', *International Alert/Saferworld* (Sept.).

Berdal, Mats, and David M. Malone, eds. 2000. *Greed and Grievance: Economic Agendas in Civil Wars*. Boulder, Colo. and Ottawa: Lynne Rienner and International Development Research Centre, 91–113.

Best, Geoffery. 1999. 'Peace Conferences and the Century of Total War', *International Affairs* 75, 3: 619–34.

Betts, Richard K. 1996. 'The Delusion of Impartial Intervention', in Crocker et al. (1996: 333–42).

Biggs, David. 2000. 'United Nations Contributions to the Process', *Disarmament Forum*, 25–37. Available at: http://www.unog.ch/unidir/2-00-ebiggs.pdf

Bildt, Carl. 2000. 'Force and Diplomacy', *Survival* 42, 1: 141–8.

Bonner, Raymond. 1998. 'Truth of arms trade stranger than fiction', *Globe and Mail*, 15 July, A13.

Boutros-Ghali, Boutros. 1992. *An Agenda for Peace—Preventive Diplomacy, Peacemaking and Peace-keeping: Report of the Secretary-General*. UN GAOR/SCOR, 47th Sess., Preliminary List Item 10, at 55, UN Docs. A/47/277 & S/2411.

———. 1995. *Supplement to an Agenda for Peace: Position Paper of the Secretary-General on the Occasion of the Fiftieth Anniversary of the United Nations*. UN GAOR/SCOR, 50th Sess., at 55, UN Docs. A/50/60 & S/1955/1.

Boutwell, Jeffrey, and Michael T. Klare. 1998. 'Small Arms and Light Weapons: Controlling the Real Instruments of War', *Arms Control Today* 28 (Aug.–Sept.): 15–23. Available at: www.armscontrol.org/ACT/augsep98/mkas98.htm

——— and ———. 1999. *Light Weapons and Civil Conflict: Controlling the Tools of Violence*. New York: Rowman and Littlefield.

——— and ———. 2000. 'A Scourge of Small Arms', *Scientific American* (June). Available at: www.sciam.com/2000/0600issue/0600boutwell.html

Buckley, Peter, and Mark Casson. 1976. *The Future of Multinational Enterprise*. London: Macmillan.

——— and ———. 1988. 'A Theory of Cooperation in International Business', in Farok Contractor and Peter Lorange, eds, *Cooperative Strategies in International Business*. Lexington, Mass.: Lexington Books, 31–53.

Buzan, Barry, Ole Waever, and Jaap de Wilder. 1998. *Security: A New Framework for Analysis*. Boulder, Colo.: Lynne Rienner.

Calhoun, Herbert L. 2000. 'Small Arms and Light Weapons: Can They Be Controlled?', Federation of American Scientists Arms Sales Monitoring Project, 53–60. Available at: http://www.fas.org/asmp/campaigns/smallarms/smallarms21.pdf

Cameron, Maxwell A., Robert J. Lawson, and Brian W. Tomlin, eds. 1998. *To Walk Without Fear: The Global Movement to Ban Landmines*. Toronto: Oxford University Press.

Campbell, Menzies. 1999. 'The International Arms Trade', *CDS Bulletin of Arms Control* 33 (Mar.): 1–8.

Carnegie Commission on Preventing Deadly Conflict. 1997. *Preventing Deadly Conflict: Final Report*. New York: Carnegie Corporation of New York, Dec.

Casson, Mark. 1982. 'Transaction Costs and the Theory of Multinational Enterprise', in Alan Rugman, ed., *New Theories of Multinational Enterprise*. London: Croom Helm, 24–43.

Chairman's Agenda for Action on Anti-Personnel (AP) Mines. 1996. 'Towards a Global Ban on Anti-Personnel Mines', International Strategy Conference, Ottawa, 3–5 Oct. Final Version, 5 Oct.

Claude, Inis L., Jr. 1996. 'Peace and Security: Prospective Roles for the Two United Nations', *Global Governance* 2: 289–98.

Coalition for the International Criminal Court (CICC). 1998. *Terraviva: The Rome Conference Newspaper*. 15 June–17 July.

Coflin, James. 1999a. 'Marking Small Arms: An Examination of Methodologies', DFAIT, Feb.

————. 1999b. 'State Authorization and Inter-State Information Sharing Concerning Small Arms Manufacturers, Dealers and Brokers', DFAIT, Feb.

Collier, Paul. 2000. 'Doing Well out of War: An Economic Perspective', in Berdal and Malone (2000: 91–113).

Commission on Global Governance. 1995. *Our Global Neighborhood.* New York: Oxford University Press.

'Controlling Small Arms: International Action Network Established'. 1998. *Ploughshares Monitor* 19, 3 (Sept.): 18–22.

'Convention on Prohibitions or Restrictions on the Use of Certain Conventional Weapons Which May Be Deemed to Be Excessively Injurious Or to Have Indiscriminate Effects: Protocol on Prohibitions or Restrictions on the Use of Mines, Booby-Traps and Other Devices' (Protocol II), (CUSHIE), Geneva, 10 Oct. 1980. Amended 3 May 1996.

'Convention on the Prohibition of Anti-Personnel Mines', Austrian Draft Treaty, n.d.

'Convention on the Prohibition of the Use, Stockpiling, Production and Transfer of Anti-Personnel Mines and On Their Destruction' (Ottawa Convention), 18 Sept. 1997.

Cowhey, Peter F. 1990. 'The International Telecommunications Regime: The Political Economy of Regimes for High Technology', *International Organization* 44, 2: 169–200.

Crawford, James. 1994. 'The ILC's Draft Statute for an International Criminal Tribunal', *American Journal of International Law* 88: 140–52.

Crocker, Chester A., Fen Osler Hampson, and Pamela Aall, eds. 1996. *Managing Global Chaos: Sources of and Responses to International Conflict.* Washington: United States Institute of Peace Press.

————, ————, and ————. 1999. 'Rising to the Challenge of Multiparty Mediation', in Crocker, Hampson, and Aall, eds, *Herding Cats: Multiparty Mediation in a Complex World.* Washington: United States Institute of Peace Press, 665–700.

Cukier, Wendy. 1998a. 'Firearms and Small Arms Control: In the Aftermath of the Victory over Landmines, A New Objective is Coming', *Peace Magazine* 14, 2 (Mar.–Apr.): 12–13, 23.

————. 1998b 'International Fire/Small Arms Control', *Canadian Foreign Policy* 6, 1 (Fall): 73–89.

Culpeper, Roy. 1997. *Titans or Behemoths.* Boulder, Colo.: Lynne Rienner for the North-South Institute.

Curtis, John, and Robert Wolfe. 2000. 'The WTO in the Aftermyth of the Battles of Seattle', in Fen Osler Hampson and Maureen Appel Molot, eds, *Canada Among Nations 2000: Vanishing Borders.* Toronto: Oxford University Press, 321–41.

Cusimano, Maryann K. 2000. *Beyond Sovereignty: Issue for a Global Agenda.* New York: St Martin's Press.

Czempiel, Ernst-Otto, and James N. Rosenau. 1992. *Governance without Government: Order and Change in World Politics.* Cambridge: Cambridge University Press.

Daalder, Ivo H., and Michael E. O'Hanlon. 2000. *Winning Ugly: NATO's War to Save Kosovo.* Washington: Brookings Institution.

Danish Institute of International Affairs (DUPI). 1999. 'Humanitarian Intervention: Legal and Political Aspects'. Available at: www.dupi.dk (accessed May 2000).

'Declaration of the Brussels Conference on Anti-Personnel Landmines', 27 June 1997.

de Ferranti, David, Guillermo E. Perry, Indermit S. Gill, and Luis Servén. 2000. *Securing Our Future in a Global Economy*. Washington: Latin American Division of the World Bank.

Department of Foreign Affairs and International Trade (DFAIT). 1996. 'The Closing Session of the International Strategy Conference Towards a Global Ban on Anti-Personnel Mines: Notes for an Address by the Honourable Lloyd Axworthy, Minister of Foreign Affairs', 5 Oct.

———. 1997a. *Mine Ban: Progress Report* no. 1 (Feb.).

———. 1997b. *Mine Ban: Progress Report* no. 2 (Apr.).

———. 1997c. *Mine Ban: Progress Report* no. 3 (June).

———. 1997d. *Mine Ban: Progress Report* no. 4 (Sept.).

———. 1997e. *Mine Ban: Progress Report* no. 5 (Nov.).

———. 1998a. *Mine Ban: Progress Report* no. 6 (Mar.).

———. 1998b. *Mine Ban: Progress Report* no. 7 (Sept.).

———. 1998c. 'Notes for an Address by the Honourable Lloyd Axworthy, Minister of Foreign Affairs, to the International NGO Consultations on Small Arms', 19 Aug.

———. 1999. *Human Security: Safety for People in a Changing World*. Ottawa: DFAIT, Apr.

———. 2000. 'Notes for an Address by the Honourable Lloyd Axworthy, Minister of Foreign Affairs, on Human Rights and Humanitarian Intervention', Washington, 16 June, 29.

Department of National Defence (DND). 1998. Documents relating to the operation in eastern Zaire and released by DND in January 1998 under the Access to Information Act, as Case (A) 96–1168.

Dhanapala, Jayantha. 1998a. 'Mali Urges World Drive to Curb Small Arms Trade', Reuters, 10 Apr.

———. 1998b. 'Achieving Sustainable Disarmament: The Small Arms Issue', *Ploughshares Monitor* 19, 4 (Dec.): 3–5.

Dobbins, Richard. 1994. *Portfolio Theory and Investment Management*, 2nd edn. Oxford: Blackwell Business.

Dolan, Michael, and Chris Hunt. 1998. 'Negotiating in the Ottawa Process: The New Multilateralism', in Cameron et al. (1998: 392–423).

Donnelly, Jack. 1986. 'International Human Rights: A Regime Analysis', *International Organization* 40, 3 (Summer): 599–642.

———. 1993. *International Human Rights*. Boulder, Colo.: Westview Press.

Downs, George W., David M. Rocke, and Randolph M. Siverson. 1986. 'Arms Races and Cooperation', in Kenneth A. Oye, ed., *Cooperation Under Anarchy*. Princeton, NJ: Princeton University Press, 118–46.

Doxey, Margaret P. 1996. *International Sanctions in Contemporary Perspective*, 2nd edn. London: Macmillan.

Doyle, Michael. 1997. *Ways of War and Peace*. New York: W.W. Norton.

Dyer, Susannah L., and Geraldine O'Callaghan. 1998. 'Combating Illicit Light Weapons Trafficking: Developments and Opportunities'. Washington: British American Security Information Council, Jan. Available at: www.basicint.org/

———— and ————. 1999. 'One Size Fits All? Prospects for a Global Convention On Illicit Trafficking by 2000', British American Security Information Council Research Report 99.2, Apr. Available at: www.basicint.org/onesize.htm

Dymond, William A. 1999. 'The MAI: A Sad and Melancholy Tale', in Fen Osler Hampson, Michael Hart, and Martin Rudner, eds, *Canada Among Nations 1999: A Big League Player?* Toronto: Oxford University Press, 25–54.

Economic Community of West Africa States (ECOWAS). 1998. Declaration of a Moratorium on the Importation, Exportation, and Manufacture of Small Arms and Light Weapons, 30–1 Oct. Available at: http://www.ib.be/grip/bdg/g1649.html

Eden, Lorraine, and Fen Osler Hampson. 1997. 'Clubs Are Trump: The Formation of International Regimes in the Absence of a Hegemon', in J. Rogers Hollingsworth and Robert Boyer, eds, *Contemporary Capitalism: The Embeddedness of Institutions*. Cambridge: Cambridge University Press, 361–94.

Edwards, Michael, David Hulme, and Tina Wallace. 1999. 'NGOs in a Global Future: Marrying Local Delivery to Worldwide Leverage', *Public Administration and Development* 19, 2: 117–36.

Egeland, Jan, and Ole-Petter Sunde. 1998. 'Norway Debates Small Arms', *Peace Magazine* 14, 2 (Mar.–Apr.): 14–15.

Elson, Diane. 1999. 'Economic Paradigms in Old and New: The Case of Human Development', in Roy Culpeper, Albert Berry, and Frances Stewart, eds, *Global Development Fifty Years After Bretton Woods*. London: Macmillan, 50–72.

Elton, Edwin J. 1995. *Modern Portfolio Theory and Investment Analysis*, 5th edn. New York: Wiley.

English, John. 1998. 'The Ottawa Process: Paths Followed, Paths Ahead', *Australian Journal of International Affairs* 52, 2: 121–32.

European Union (EU). 1997. *EU Programme for Preventing and Combating Illicit Trafficking in Conventional Arms*. Available at: http://www.iansa.org/documents/regional/reg6.htm

————. 1998a. *European Code of Conduct on Arms Transfers*, 24–5 Apr. Available at: http://www.iansa.org/documents/regional/reg4.htm

————. 1998b. *European Union Code of Conduct for Arms Exports*, 8-9 June. Available at: http://www.basicint.org/eucode.htm

Evans, Gareth. 1993. *Cooperating for Peace: The Global Agenda for the 1990s and Beyond*. London: Allen & Unwin.

Falk, Richard A. 1995. *On Human Governance*. University Park: Pennsylvania State University Press.

Farer, Thomas J., and Felice Gaer. 1994. 'The UN and Human Rights: At the End of the Beginning', in Adam Roberts and Benedict Kingsbury, eds, *United Nations, Divided World*. Oxford: Oxford University Press.

Faulkner, Frank, and Lloyd Pettiford. 1998. 'Complexity and Simplicity: Landmines, Peace and Security in Central America', *Third World Quarterly* 19, 1: 45–61.

Ferencz, Benjamin B. 1992. 'An International Criminal Code and Court: Where They Stand and Where They Are Going', *Columbia Journal of Transnational Law* 30: 375–99.

'Final Communiqué', Ashgabat, Central Asian Regional Conference on a Global Ban on Anti-Personnel Mines, 12 June 1997.

Financial Times. 2000. 15 June, 67.

Finnemore, Martha, and Kathryn Sikkink. 1998. 'International Norm Dynamic and Political Change', *International Organization* 45, 4: 887–918.

Fisher, William F. 1997. 'Doing Good? The Politics and Antipolitics of NGO Practices', *Annual Review of Anthropology* 26: 440-64.

Fomerand, Jacques. 1996. 'UN Conferences: Media Events or Genuine Diplomacy', *Global Governance* 2: 361–75.

Forsythe, David P. 1993. *Human Rights and Peace: International and National Dimensions*. Lincoln: University of Nebraska Press.

Franck, Thomas M. 1999. 'Break It, Don't Fake It', *Foreign Affairs* 78, 4: 116–18.

Frankfurter, George M. 1995. *Forty Years of Normative Portfolio Theory: Issues, Controversies, and Misconceptions*. Greenwich, Conn.: JAI Press.

Fredenburg, Major Paul W. 1997. 'The Banning of Anti-Personnel Landmines', *Canadian Defence Quarterly* 27, 2: 5–9.

Führer, Helmut. 1996. *The Story of Official Development Assistance: A History of the Development Assistance Committee and the Development Co-operation Directorate in Dates, Names and Figures*. Paris: OECD.

Ghai, Dharam. 1997. *Economic Globalization, Institutional Change, and Human Security*. Geneva: United Nations Research Institute for Social Development (UNRISD), 12 Nov.

Gallarotti, Giulio M. 1991. 'The Limits of International Organization: Systematic Failure in the Management of International Relations', *International Organization* 45: 183–220.

George, Alexander L., Philip J. Farley, and Alexander Dallin. 1988. *Soviet Security Cooperation: Achievement, Lessons, Failures*. New York: Oxford University Press.

Gilbert, Alan. 1999. *Must Global Politics Constrain Democracy? Great-Power Realism, Democratic Peace, and Democratic Internationalism*. Princeton, NJ: Princeton University Press.

Gilmore, William C. 1995. 'The Proposed International Criminal Court: Recent Developments', *Transnational Law and Contemporary Problems* 5: 264–85.

Gilpin, Robert. 1987. *The Political Economy of International Relations*. Princeton, NJ: Princeton University Press.

Gleditsch, Nils Petter. Forthcoming. 'Environmental Change, Security, and Conflict', in Chester A. Crocker, Fen Osler Hampson, and Pamela Aall, eds, *Turbulent Peace: The Challenges of Managing International Conflict*. Washington: United States Institute of Peace Press.

Glennon, Michael J. 1999. 'The New Interventionism', *Foreign Affairs* 78, 3: 2–7.

Goodman, John. 1992. *Monetary Sovereignty: The Politics of Central Banking in Western Europe*. Ithaca, NY: Cornell University Press.

———— and Louis Pauly. 1993. 'The Obsolescence of Capital Controls? Economic Management in an Age of Capital Markets', *World Politics* 46, 1: 50–82.

Grieco, Joseph M. 1990. *Cooperation Among Nations: Europe, North America, and Non-tariff Barriers to Trade*. Ithaca, NY: Cornell University Press.

Gurr, Ted Robert. 2000. *Peoples Versus States: Minorities at Risk in the New Century*. Washington: United States Institute of Peace Press.

————, Monty G. Marshall, and Deep Khosla. 2000. *Peace and Conflict 2001: A Global Survey of Armed Conflicts, Self-Determination Movements and Democracy*. College Park: University of Maryland, Center for International Development and Conflict Management.

Haas, Ernst B. 1990. *When Knowledge Is Power: Three Models of Change in International Organizations*. Berkeley: University of California Press.

Haas, Peter. 1989. 'Do Regimes Matter? Epistemic Communities and Mediterranean Pollution Control', *International Organization* 43, 3: 377–404.

————, ed. 1996. *Knowledge, Power, and International Policy Coordination*. Columbia: University of South Carolina Press.

Haass, Richard N. 1996. 'Using Force: Lesson and Choices for U.S. Foreign Policy', in Crocker et al. (1996: 197–208).

Hall, Christopher Keith. 1997. 'The First Two Sessions of the UN Preparatory Committee on the Establishment of an International Criminal Court', *American Journal of International Law* 91, 1: 177–87.

————. 1998. 'The Third and Fourth Session of the UN Preparatory Committee on the Establishment of an International Criminal Court'; 'The Fifth Session of the UN Preparatory Committee on the Establishment of an International Criminal Court'; 'The Sixth Session of the UN Preparatory Committee on the Establishment of an International Criminal Court', *American Journal of International Law* 92, 2: 124–33, 331–9; 92, 3: 548–56.

Hampson, Fen Osler. 1995. *Multilateral Negotiations: Lessons from Arms Control, Trade, and the Environment*. Baltimore: Johns Hopkins University Press.

————. 1996. *Nurturing Peace: Why Peace Settlements Succeed or Fail*. Washington: United States Institute of Peace Press.

———— and Judith V. Reppy. 1996. *Earthly Goods: Environmental Change and Social Justice*. Ithaca, NY: Cornell University Press.

Handicap International, Human Rights Watch, Medico International, Mines Advisory Group, Physicians for Human Rights, and Vietnam Veterans of America Foundation. n.d. 'A Joint Call to Ban Antipersonnel Landmines'.

Havel, Václav. 1999. 'Address to a Special Joint Session of the House of Commons and Senate'. 30 Apr. Available at: http://www.parl.gc.ca/36/1/parlbus/chambus...e/debates/218_1999-04-29/han218_1045-e.htm

Held, David, Anthony McGrew, David Goldblatt, and Jonathan Perraton. 1999. *Global Transformations: Politics, Economics, and Culture*. Stanford, Calif.: Stanford University Press.

Herby, Peter. 1998. 'Arms Transfers, Humanitarian Assistance and International Humanitarian Law', *International Review of the Red Cross* 325 (31 Dec.). Available at: http://www.icrc.org/icrceng.nsf

Hewson, Martin, and Timothy J. Sinclair, eds. 1999. *Approaches to Global Governance Theory*. Albany: State University Press of New York.

'Hey, anybody want a gun?'. 1998. *The Economist* 347, 8068 (16 May): 47–8.

Higgott, Richard A., and Andrew Fenton Cooper. 1990. 'Middle Power Leadership and Coalition Building: Australia, the Cairns Group, and the Uruguay Round of Trade Negotiation', *International Organization* 45, 3.

Hobbes, Thomas. 1968 [1651]. *Leviathan*, ed. C.B. MacPherson. Harmondsworth: Penguin.

Hoffmann, Stanley. 1998. *World Disorders: Troubled Peace in the Post-Cold War Era*. Lanham, Md: Rowman and Littlefield.

Homer-Dixon, Thomas F. 1999. *Environment, Scarcity, and Violence*. Princeton, NJ: Princeton University Press.

Hubert, Don. 2000. 'The Landmine Ban: A Case Study in Humanitarian Advocacy', Thomas J. Watson Jr. Institute for International Studies Occasional Paper #42. Providence, RI: Thomas J. Watson Jr. Institute for International Studies.

Human Rights Watch. 2000. *World Report*. Available at: www.hrw.org (accessed May 2000).

Ignatieff, Michael. 2000. *Virtual War: Kosovo and Beyond*. New York: Metropolitan Books.

Independent Commission on Disarmament and Security Issues (Palme Commission). 1982. *Common Security: A Programme for Disarmament*. London: Pan Books.

Independent Commission on International Development Issues (Brandt Commission). 1980. *A Programme for Survival: Report of the Independent Commission on International Development*. Cambridge, Mass.: MIT Press.

Inter-American Development Bank. 1995. *Overcoming Volatility: Economic and Social Progress in Latin America*. Washington: Inter-American Development Bank, Oct.

International Campaign to Ban Landmines. 1995. 'The "Good List": Nations Calling for a Comprehensive Ban on Anti-Personnel Landmines', *Report on Activities: Review Conference of the CCW*, Vienna, 25 Sept.–13 Oct.

———. 1996. 'The "Good List": Nations Calling for a Comprehensive Ban on Anti-Personnel Landmines', *Report on Activities: Review Conference of the CCW, 2nd Resumed Session*, Geneva, 22 Apr. –3 May.

International Committee of the Red Cross (ICRC). 1999. 'Arms Availability and the Situation of Civilians in Armed Conflict', 1 June. Available at: http://www.icrc.org/icrceng.nsf/4dc394db5b54f3fa4125673900241f2f/10805a47444523884125680f0034a72c?OpenDocument

International Monetary Fund, Organization for Economic Co-operation and Development, United Nations, and World Bank Group. 2000. *2000 A Better World for All: Progress towards International Development Goals*. June.

Isaac, Jeffrey. 1998. 'Reclaiming the Wasteland: Thinking About Land Mines and Their Eradication', *Dissent* (Fall): 67–72.

Jervis, Robert. 1978. 'Cooperation Under the Security Dilemma', *World Politics* 30, 2: 167–214.

———. 1983. *Perception and Misperception in International Politics*. Princeton, NJ: Princeton University Press.

Judah, Tim. 2000. *Kosovo: War and Revenge*. New Haven: Yale University Press.

Kahler, Miles. 1993. 'Multilateralism with Small and Large Numbers', in John Gerard Ruggie, ed., *Multilateralism Matters: The Theory and Praxis of an Institutional Form*. New York: Columbia University Press, 295–326.

Kamarotos, Alexandre S. 1995–6. 'Building Peace, Democracy and Human Rights: International Civilian Missions at the End of the Millennium', *International Peacekeeping* 2, 4: 483–509.

Kant, Immanuel. 1992. *Political Writings*, trans. H.B. Nisbet. Cambridge: Cambridge University Press.

Kaplan, Robert D. 1994. 'The Coming Anarchy', *The Atlantic* (Feb.): 45–76.

———. 2000a. *The Coming Anarchy: Shattering the Dreams of the Post-Cold War World*. New York: Random House.

———. 2000b. 'Peace in Our Time? Not Likely', *Globe and Mail*, 11 Mar., D8–9.

Kapur, Devesh, John P. Lewis, and Richard Webb, eds. 1997. *The World Bank, Its First Half Century*, 2 vols. Washington: Brookings Institution Press.

Katzenstein, Peter J., ed. 1996. *The Culture of National Security: Norms and Identity in World Politics*. New York: Columbia University Press.

———, Robert O. Keohane, and Stephen D. Krasner. 1998. 'International Organization and the Study of World Politics', *International Organization* 52, 4: 645–86.

Kaufmann, Chaim. 1996. 'Possible and Impossible Solutions to Ethnic Wars', *International Security* 20, 4: 136–75.

Kaul, Hans-Peter. 1997. 'Towards a Permanent International Criminal Tribunal, Some Observations of Negotiator', *Human Rights Law Journal* 18: 169–74.

Kaul, Inge, Isabelle Grunberg, and Marc A. Stern, eds. 1999a. *Global Public Goods: International Cooperation in the 21st Century*. New York: Oxford University Press.

———, ———, and ———. 1999b. 'Introduction', in Kaul et al. (1999a: xix–xxxviii).

———, ———, and ———. 1999c 'Defining Global Public Goods', in Kaul et al. (1999a: 2–19).

Keohane, Robert O. 1983. 'The Demand for International Regimes', in Krasner (1983a: 141–72).

———. 1984. *After Hegemony: Cooperation and Discord in the World Political Economy*. Princeton, NJ: Princeton University Press.

————. 1995. 'The Analysis of International Regimes: Towards a European-American Research Program', in Volker A. Rittberger, ed., *Regime Theory and International Relations*. Oxford: Oxford University Press, 23–48.

———— and Lisa L. Martin. 1995. 'The Promise of Institutionalist Theory', *International Security* 20, 1: 39–51.

———— and Joseph S. Nye, Jr. 2000. 'Globalization: What's New, What's Not (And So What?)', *Foreign Policy* 118: 104–19.

Kirsch, Philippe, and J.T. Holmes. 1999. 'The Rome Conference on an International Criminal Court: The Negotiation Process', *American Journal of International Law* 93, 1: 2–12

Klare, Michael. 1999. 'Small Arms Proliferation and its Impact on Security and Development', United Nations Symposium on Disarmament and Development, 20 July. Available at: http://www.ecaar.org/library16.pdf

Korey, William. 1998. *NGOs and the Universal Declaration of Human Rights*. New York: St Martin's Press.

Krasner, Stephen, ed. 1983a. *International Regimes*. Ithaca, NY: Cornell University Press.

————. 1983b. 'Structural Causes and Regime Consequences: Regimes as Intervening Variables', in Krasner (1983a: 1–21).

———— 1991. 'Global Communications and National Power', *World Politics* 47, 3: 226–366.

————. 1995. 'Sovereignty, Regimes, and Human Rights', in Volker A. Rittberger, ed., *Regime Theory and International Relations*. Oxford: Oxford University Press, 139–67.

————. 1999. *Sovereignty: Organized Hypocrisy*. Princeton, NJ: Princeton University Press.

Krause, Keith. 1998. 'The Challenge of Small Arms and Light Weapons', paper presented at the Third International Security Forum, Zurich, 19-21 Oct. Available at: www.isn.ethz.ch/securityforum/Online_Publications/WS5/WS_5D/Krause.htm

Kritz, Neil J., ed. 1995. *Transitional Justice: How Emerging Democracies Reckon with Former Regimes*, vol. 1. Washington: United States Institute of Peace Press.

Kupchan, Charles A., and Clifford A. Kupchan. 1991. 'Concerts, Collective Security, and the Future of Europe', *International Security* 16, 1: 114–61.

Kymlicka, Will. 1996. *Multicultural Citizenship: A Liberal Theory of Minority Rights*. Oxford: Oxford University Press.

————. 2000. *Politics in the Vernacular: Nationalism, Multiculturalism, and Citizenship*. New York: Oxford University Press.

LaRose-Edwards, Paul. 1996. *UN Human Rights Operations: Principles and Practice in United Nations Field Operations*. Ottawa: Human Rights and Justice Division, DFAIT.

Laurance, Edward J. 1997a. 'The Light Weapons Problem: The Way Ahead', Working Paper for the Canadian Council for International Peace and Security. Ottawa: Canadian Centre for Foreign Policy Development, 24 Oct.

————. 1997b. 'Small Arms and Light Weapons as a Development and Disarmament Issue', *BICC* conference on 'Converting Defense Resources to Human Development', 9–11 Nov. Available at: http://www.bicc.de/general/events/devcon/laurance.html

———. 1999. 'At Long Last, Action to Address the Plague of Small Arms and Light Weapons', *BICC Bulletin* no. 11 (1 Apr.). Available at: http://www.bicc.de/general/bulletin/bull0499.pdf

Lauren, Paul Gordon. 1998. *The Evolution of Human International Rights: Visions Seen.* University Park: Pennsylvania State University Press.

Layne, Christopher. 1994. 'Kant or Cant: The Myth of the Democratic Peace', *International Security* 19, 2: 5–49.

Leahy, Senator Patrick. 1997. 'Banning Landmines: The United States After Ottawa', statement, 2 Dec.

Lee, Roy S., ed. 1999. *The International Criminal Court: The Making of the Rome Statute: Issues, Negotiations, Results.* The Hague: Kluwer Law International.

Levitin, Oleg. 2000. 'Inside Moscow's Kosovo Muddle', *Survival* 42, 1: 130–40.

Levy, Azriel. 1995. *The Gains from Diversification Reconsidered: Transactions Costs and Superior Information.* Cambridge, Mass.: Blackwell.

Lipschutz, Ronnie D. 1992. 'Reconstructing World Politics: The Emergence of Global Civil Society', *Millennium: Journal of International Studies* 21, 3.

——— and Judith Mayer. 1996. *Global Civil Society and Global Economic Governance: The Politics of Nature from Place to Planet.* Albany: State University of New York Press.

Little, David W. 1996. 'Religious Militancy', in Crocker et al. (1996: 79–92).

Locke, John. 1952 [1690]. *Second Treatise on Government.* Indianapolis: Bobbs-Merrill.

Long, David, and Laird Hindle. 1998. 'Europe and the Ottawa Process', in Cameron et al. (1998: 248–68).

Luck, Edward C. 1999a. *Mixed Messages: American Politics and International Organization, 1919–1999.* Washington: Brookings Institution Press.

———. 1999b. 'A Road to Nowhere', *Foreign Affairs* 78, 4: 118–19.

Lumpe, Lora. 1999. 'Curbing the Proliferation of Small Arms and Light Weapons', *Security Dialogue* 30, 2 (June): 151–64.

———. 2000. *Running Guns: The Global Black Market in Small Arms.* London: Zed Books.

Lund, Michael S. 1996. *Preventing Violent Conflict.* Washington: United States Institute of Peace Press.

Luttwak, Edward N. 1999. 'Give War a Chance', *Foreign Affairs* 78, 4 (July–Aug.): 36–44.

MacPherson, Bryan F. 1998. 'Building an International Criminal Court for the 21st Century', *Connecticut Journal of International Law* 13, 1: 1–60.

Mandelbaum, Michael. 1999. 'A Perfect Failure', *Foreign Affairs* 78, 5: 2–8.

Mansfield, Edward D., and Jack Snyder. 1995. 'Democratization and the Danger of War', *International Security* 20, 1: 5–38.

Markowitz, Harry. 1952. 'Portfolio Selection', *Journal of Finance* 7, 1 (Mar.): 77–91.

————. 1991. *Portfolio Selection: Efficient Diversification of Investments*, 2nd edn. Cambridge, Mass.: Blackwell.

Martin, Lisa L. 1999. 'The Political Economy of International Cooperation', in Kaul et al. (1999a: 51–64).

Matthew, Richard, and Ken R. Rutherford. 1999. 'Banning Landmines in the American Century', *International Journal on World Peace* 16, 2: 23–6.

Mearsheimer, John J. 1994. 'The False Promise of International Institutions', *International Security* 19, 3: 5–49.

————. 1995. 'A Realist Reply', *International Security* 20, 1: 82–93.

Mendez, Ruben P. 1999. 'Peace as a Global Public Good', in Kaul et al. (1999a: 382–416).

Mill, John Stuart. 1939 [1859]. 'On Liberty', in Edwin A Burtt, ed., *The English Philosophers From Bacon to Mill*. New York: Random House, 949–1041.

Miller, Ian. 1998. 'Small Arms and Light Weapons: An Annotated Bibliography, Update 1996–1998', DFAIT, Sept.

Milner, Helen. 1993. 'The Assumption of Anarchy in International Relations Theory: A Critique', in David A. Baldwin, ed., *Neorealism and Neoliberalism: The Contemporary Debate*. New York: Columbia University Press, 143–69.

Mine Action Coordination Group. 1998. 'Years Not Decades: Proceedings from the Mine Action Coordination Workshop', Ottawa, 23–4 Mar.

Mitterand, François. 1993. 'Excerpts from an Address by M. François Mitterand, President of the French Republic at the Royal Palace, Phnom Penh, Cambodia', 11 Feb.

Moisy, Claude. 1997. 'Myths of the Global Information Village', *Foreign Policy* 107: 78–87.

'Momentum Grows to Address Problem of Small Arms'. 1999. *NGLS Roundup* 45 (Nov.). Available at: ngls.tad.ch

Moore, Jonathan. 1996. *The UN and Complex Emergencies: Rehabilitation in Third World Transitions*. Geneva: UNRISD.

Moravcik, Andrew. 1995. 'Explaining International Human Rights Regimes: Liberal Theory and Western Europe', *European Journal of International Affairs* 1, 1 (June): 157–89.

Morsink, Johannes. 1998. *The Universal Declaration of Human Rights: Origins, Drafting and Intent*. University Park: University of Pennsylvania Press.

Morton, Jeffrey S. 1997. 'The ILC of the UN: Legal Vacuum or Microcosm of World Politics', *International Interactions* 23, 1: 37–54.

Moynihan, Daniel Patrick. 1993. *Pandaemonium: Ethnicity in International Politics*. New York: Oxford University Press.

Nef, Jorge. 1995. *Human Security and Mutual Vulnerability: An Exploration into the Global Political Economy of Development and Underdevelopment*. Ottawa: International Development Research Centre.

Neier, Arey. 1998. 'Waiting for Justice: The United States and the International Court', *World Policy Journal* 15, 3: 33–7.

Nowak, Manfred, ed. 1994. *World Conference on Human Rights, Vienna June 1993: The Contributions of NGOs: Reports and Documents.* Wien, Austria: Manzche Verlags.

Nye, Joseph S., Jr. 1991. *Bound to Lead: The Changing Nature of American Power.* New York: Basic Books.

———. 1999. 'Redefining the National Interest', *Foreign Affairs* 78, 4: 22–35.

Olson, Mancur. 1971. *The Logic of Collective Action: Public Goods and the Theory of Groups,* 2nd edn. Cambridge, Mass.: Harvard University Press.

Organization for Economic Co-operation and Development (OECD)/Development Assistance Committee (DAC). 1993. *Orientations on Participatory Development and Good Governance.* Endorsed by the DAC at its High Level Meeting on 13–14 Dec. Paris: Development Assistance Committee of the OECD.

———. 1995. *Development Co-operation 1994 Report.* Paris: Development Assistance Committee of the OECD.

———. 1996a. *Development Co-operation 1995 Report.* Paris: Development Assistance Committee of the OECD.

———. 1996b. *Shaping the 21st Century: The Contribution of Development Cooperation.* Paris: Development Assistance Committee of the OECD.

———. 1996c. 'Development Partnerships in the New Global Context', statement of orientation agreed on at the 3–4 May 1995 meeting of the Development Co-operation Ministers and Heads of Aid Agencies, in OECD/DAC, *Report 1995.* Paris: Development Assistance Committee of the OECD, 18–21.

———. 1997a. *Development Co-operation 1996 Report.* Paris: Development Assistance Committee of the OECD.

———. 1997b. *DAC Guidelines on Conflict, Peace and Development Co-operation.* Paris: Development Assistance Committee of the OECD.

———. 1998a. *Development Co-operation 1997 Report.* Paris: Development Assistance Committee of the OECD.

———. 1998b. *Civilian and Military Means of Providing and Supporting Humanitarian Assistance During Conflict: Comparative Advantages and Costs.* Paris: Development Assistance Committee of the OECD.

———. 1999. *Development Co-operation 1998 Report.* Paris: Development Assistance Committee of the OECD.

———. 2000. *Development Co-operation 1999 Report.* Paris: Development Assistance Committee of the OECD.

Organization of American States (OAS). 1997. Inter-American Convention Against the Illicit Manufacturing of and Trafficking in Firearms, Ammunition, Explosives, and Other Related Materials, OAS Document: AG/RES.1 (XXIV-E/97), 13 Nov. Available at: http://www.iansa.org/documents/regional/reg5.htm

Ostrom, Elinor. 1990. *Governing the Commons: The Evolution of Institutions for Collective Action.* Cambridge: Cambridge University Press.

Owen, John M. 1995. 'How Liberalism Produces Democratic Peace', *International Security* 19, 2: 87–125.

Pahor, Borut. 1998. 'Drawing Up a European Code of Conduct on Arms Sales', Council of Europe Parliamentary Assembly Doc. 8188, 10 Sept.

'Plan of Action: First Continental Conference of African Experts on Landmines', 21 May 1997.

Posen, Barry R. 1993. 'Nationalism, the Mass Army, and Military Power', *International Security* 18, 2: 80–124.

Pratt, Cranford. 1999. 'Competing Rationales for Canadian Development Assistance: Reducing Global Poverty, Enhancing Canadian Prosperity and Security, or Advancing Global Human Security', *International Journal* 54, 2: 306–24.

Price, Richard. 1995. 'A Genealogy of the Chemical Weapons Taboo', *International Organization* 29, 1: 73–104.

———. 1998. 'Reversing the Gun Sights: Transnational Civil Society Targets Land Mines', *International Organization* 52, 3: 613–44.

Puley, Greg. 1999. 'Codes of Conduct and the Legal Trade in Light Weapons', *Peace Magazine* 15, 4 (Summer): 8-12.

Putnam, Robert D. 1993. *Making Democracy Work: Civic Traditions in Modern Italy*. Princeton, NJ: Princeton University Press.

Rao, J. Mohan. 1999. 'Equity in a Global Public Goods Framework', in Kaul et al. (1999a: 28–87).

Regehr, Ernie. 1998. 'Getting Started: The G8 and Small Arms', *Ploughshares Monitor* 19, 2 (June): 10–14.

———. 1999a. 'Small Arms: Testing the Peacebuilding Paradigm', in Fen Osler Hampson et al., eds, *Canada Among Nations 1999: A Big League Player?* Toronto: Oxford University Press, 253–73.

———. 1999b. 'The UN and an Emerging Small Arms Agenda', *Ploughshares Monitor* 20, 3 (Sept.): 2–4.

Regional Seminar for Asian Military and Strategic Studies Experts. 1997. 'Anti-Personnel Mines: What Future for Asia?' Sponsored by the International Committee of the Red Cross in Co-operation with the Government of the Republic of the Philippines and the Philippine National Red Cross Society, Manila, 20–3 July.

Regional Seminar for the States of the Southern African Development Community (SADC). 1997. 'Final Declaration of Participants, Anti-Personnel Mines: What Future for Southern Africa?' Sponsored by the International Committee of the Red Cross in Co-operation with the Organization of African Unity and the Republic of Zimbabwe, Harare, 21–3 Apr.

Renner, Michael. 1997. 'Small Arms, Big Impact: The Next Challenge of Disarmament', *World Watch Paper* 137, World Watch Institute, Oct. Available at: http://www.worldwatch.org/pubs/paper/137.html

Roderick, Dani. 1997. 'Sense and Nonsense in the Globalization Debate', *Foreign Policy* 107: 19–37.

Rosenau, James N. 1990. *Turbulence in World Politics: A Theory of Change and Continuity*. Princeton, NJ: Princeton University Press.

———. 1997. 'The Person, the Household, the Community, and the Globe: Notes for a Theory of Multilateralism in a Turbulent World', in Robert W. Cox, ed., *The New Realism: Perspectives on Multilateralism and World Order*. Tokyo: United Nations Press, 57–82.

Rothschild, Emma. 1995. 'What is Security?', *Daedalus* 124, 3 (Summer): 53–98.

Ruggie, John Gerard. 1983. 'International Regimes, Transactions, and Change: Embedded Liberalism in the Postwar Economic Order', in Krasner (1983a: 423–88).

———. 1995. 'The False Promise of Realism', *International Security* 20, 1: 62–70.

———. 1996. *Winning the Peace: America and World Order in the New Era*. New York: Columbia University Press.

Russett, Bruce. 1993. *Grasping the Democratic Peace: Principles for a Post-Cold War World*. Princeton, NJ: Princeton University Press.

Scharf, Michael. 1998. *ASIL Insight*. July and Aug.

Schnieberg, Marc, and J. Rogers Hollingsworth. 1988. 'Can Transactions Cost Economics Explain Trade Associations?', paper presented at the Swedish Colloquium for Advanced Study of the Social Sciences conference, on 'The Firm as a Nexus of Treaties', Uppsala, 6–8 June.

Sen, Amartya. 1981. *Poverty and Famines: An Essay on Entitlement and Deprivation*. Oxford: Clarendon Press.

———. 1999. 'Global Justice and Beyond', in Kaul et al. (1999a: 116–35).

———. 2000. *Development as Freedom*. New York: Alfred A. Knopf.

Serafini, Margherita. 2000. 'Small Arms: The Emerging Coalition of States for the UN Conference in 2001', Program on Security and Development, Monterey Institute of International Studies, Mar. Available at: http://sand.miis.edu/research/serafini/paper.pdf

Sharpe, William F. 1970. *Portfolio Theory and Capital Markets*. New York: McGraw-Hill.

Shaw, Martin. 1994. 'Civil Society and Global Politics: Beyond a Social Movements Approach', *Millennium: Journal of International Relations* 23, 3: 647–68.

Shawcross, William. 2000. *Deliver Us From Evil*. New York: Simon and Schuster.

Shell, G. Richard. 1996. 'The Trade Stakeholders Model and Participation by Nonstate Parties in the World Trade Organization', *University of Pennsylvania Journal of International Economic Law* 17, 1: 359–82.

Simai, Mihaly. 1995. *The Future of Global Governance: Managing Risk and Change in the International System*. Washington: United States Institute of Peace Press.

Sishi, Enough. 1998. 'Small Arms in Southern Africa: The Job of Rebuilding These Ravaged Societies is Made All the More Difficult', *Peace Magazine* 14, 2 (Mar.–Apr.): 16–18.

Smith, Gordon, and John Hay. 1999. 'Canada and the Crisis in Eastern Zaire', in Chester A. Crocker, Fen Osler Hampson, and Pamela Aall, eds, *Herding Cats: Multiparty Mediation in a Complex World*. Washington: United States Institute of Peace Press, 85–105.

Smith, Jackie, Ron Pagnuco, and George A. Lopez. 1998. 'Globalizing Human Rights: The Work of Transnational Human Rights NGOs in the 1990s', *Human Rights Quarterly* 20: 378–9.

Smith, Michael J. 1999. 'Humanitarian Intervention: An Overview of the Ethical Issues', in Josel H. Rosenthal, ed., *Ethics and International Affairs*. Washington: Carnegie Council on Ethics and International Affairs, 271.

Snidal, Duncan. 1985. 'The Limits of Hegemonic Stability Theory', *International Organization* 39, 4: 579–615.

Solana, Javier. 1999. 'NATO's Success in Kosovo', *Foreign Affairs* 78, 6: 114–20.

Solingen, Ethel. 1994. 'The Domestic Sources of Regional Regimes: The Evolution of Nuclear Ambiguity', *International Studies Quarterly* 38, 2: 305–38.

Sollenberg, Margareta, Peter Wallensteen, and Andrés Jato. 1999. 'Major Armed Conflicts', in *SIPRI Yearbook 1999: Armaments, Disarmament, and International Security*. Oxford: Oxford University Press, 15–33.

Southern African Development Community and the European Union. 1998. *Southern Africa Regional Action Programme on Light Arms and Illicit Weapons Trafficking*, 3–6 May. Available at: http://www.iss.co.za/Pubs/ASR/7.4/regional.html

Steinberg, James B. 1999. 'A Perfect Polemic', *Foreign Affairs* 78, 6: 128–33.

Stern, Nicholas, with Francisco Ferreira. 1997. 'The World Bank as "Intellectual Actor"', in Kapur et al. (1997: 523–611).

Stewart, Frances. 2001. 'Crisis Prevention: Tackling Horizontal Inequalities', in Fen Osler Hampson and David Malone, eds, *From Reaction to Conflict Prevention: Opportunities for the UN in the New Millennium*. Boulder, Colo.: Lynne Rienner. Also published in *Oxford Development Studies* 28, 3 (Oct. 2000).

———— and E.K.V. FitzGerald. 2001. *War and Underdevelopment: The Economic and Social Consequences of Conflict*. Oxford: Oxford University Press.

Stobel, Warren P. 1997. *Late-Breaking Foreign Policy: The News Media's Influence on Peace Operations*. Washington: United States Institute of Peace Press.

Thakur, Ramesh, and William Marley. 1999. 'The Ottawa Convention on Landmines: A Landmark Humanitarian Treaty in Arms Control?', *Global Governance: A Review of Multilateralism and International Organizations* 5, 3: 273–302.

The New Republic Online, 6 June 2000.

Thompson, Dennis F. 1976. *John Stuart Mill and Representative Government*. Princeton, NJ: Princeton University Press.

Tietenberg, Tom. 1984. *Environmental and Natural Resource Economics*. Glenview, Ill.: Scott, Foresman, and Company.

Timmerman, Peter. 1996. 'Breathing Room: Negotiations on Climate Change', in Hampson and Reppy (1996: 221–43).

'Tokyo Guidelines for International Efforts on Anti-Personnel Landmines in the Humanitarian Field' and 'Chairman's Summary, Tokyo Conference on Anti-Personnel Landmines', 6–7 Mar. 1997.

'Too soft by half'. 2000. *National Post*, 28 Feb., A17.

'Top industrial nations plan small-arms curbs'. 1998. *Vancouver Sun*, 6 May, A14.

'Towards a Global Ban on Anti-Personnel Mines: Declaration of the Ottawa Conference'. 1996.

United Nations (UN). 1988. United Nations General Assembly Resolution on General and Complete Disarmament: Section I, 'International Arms Transfers'. UN Document A/RES/43/75, 7 Dec. Available at: http://www.un.org/gopher-data/ga/recs/43/75

———. 1991. United Nations General Assembly Resolution on General and Complete Disarmament: Section H, 'International Arms Transfers'. UN Document A/RES/46/36, 6 Dec. Available at: http://www.un.org/gopher-data/ga/recs/46/36

———. 1995. *The Copenhagen Declaration and Programme of Action*. World Summit for Social Development, 6–12 Mar. New York: Oxford University Press.

———. 1996. United Nations General Assembly Resolution on General and Complete Disarmament: Section B, 'Small Arms'. UN Document A/RES/70/50, 15 Jan. Available at: http://www.un.org/gopher-data/ga/recs/50/res50-70.en

———. 1997a. Report of the Panel of Governmental Experts on Small Arms. UN Document A/52/298, 27 Aug. Available at: http://www.iansa.org/documents/un/un_pub/reports/un30.htm

———. 1997b. United Nations General Assembly Resolution on General and Complete Disarmament: Section J, 'Small Arms'. UN Document A/RES/52/38, 9 Dec. Available at: http://www.un.org/ga/documents/gares52/res5238.htm

———. 1998. Economic and Social Council, Commission on Crime Prevention and Criminal Justice, Seventh Session, 21–30 Apr., Vienna.

———. 1999. Report of the Group of Governmental Experts on Small Arms in Pursuance of General Assembly Resolution 52/38 J. UN Document A/54/258, 19 Aug. Available at: http://www.iansa.org/documents/un/un_pub/reports/rep54258e.pdf

United Nations (DDSMS and UNIDO). 1995. *International Colloquium on Post-Conflict Reconstruction Strategies*. Vienna: UNOV.

United Nations (DESIPA). 1996. *An Inventory of Post-Conflict Peace-Building Activities*. UN Document ST/ESA/246. New York: UN.

United Nations Development Program (UNDP). 1990. *Human Development Report*. New York: Oxford University Press.

———. 1994. *Human Development Report*. New York: Oxford University Press.

———. 1995. *Human Development Report*. New York: Oxford University Press.

———. 1996. *Human Development Report*. New York: Oxford University Press.

———. 1997a. *Human Development Report*, New York: Oxford University Press.

———. 1997b. *Building Bridges Between Relief and Development—A Compendium of the UNDP Record in Crisis Countries.* New York: UNDP.

———. 1998a. *Human Development Report*. New York: Oxford University Press.

———. 1998b. *Overcoming Human Poverty: UNDP Poverty Report 1998.* New York: UN.

———. 1999a. *Human Development Report.* New York: Oxford University Press.

———. 1999b. *Crisis, Opportunity and Change: Building Tomorrow's UNDP,* Transition Team Report to the Administrator. New York: UN, 1 Nov.

———. 2000. *The Way Forward: The Administrator's Business Plans, 2000–2003,* Submitted to the Executive Board. New York: UN, Jan.

United Nations General Assembly. 1993. A/RES/48/75, 81st Plenary Meeting, 16 Dec.

———. 1997. A/RES/51/45, Fifty-first Session, Agenda Item 71, 10 Jan.

United Nations High Commissioner for Refugees (UNHCR). 1994. *The State of the World's Refugees.* New York: Oxford University Press.

United Nations Press Office. 1999. 'Secretary-General Presents His Annual Report to the General Assembly', press release SG/SM/7136/GA/9596. Annex 1. New York: UN, 20 Sept.

US State Department. 1994. *Hidden Killers: The Global Problem with Uncleared Landmines.* Washington: US Department of State.

Van Evera, Stephen. 1994. 'Hypotheses on Nationalism and War', *International Security* 18, 4: 5–39.

Van Ordern, Geoffrey, Thierry Van Der Pyl, Graham Sims, and Alois J. Sieber. 1997. 'Developments in Demining', *UNIDIR Newsletter,* Special Issue no. SI 3/97: 21–43.

Vines, Alex, and Henry Thompson. 1999. *Beyond the Landmine Ban: Eradicating a Lethal Legacy.* Warwickshire: Research Institute for the Study of Conflict and Terrorism, Mar.

Walt, Stephen M. 1987. *The Origins of Alliances.* Ithaca, NY: Cornell University Press.

———. 1998. 'International Relations: One World, Many Theories', *Foreign Policy* no. 110 (Spring): 29–46.

Waltz, Kenneth N. 1979. *Theory of International Politics.* New York: McGraw-Hill.

Wedgwood, Ruth. 1998. 'Fiddling in Rome: America and the International Criminal Court', *Foreign Affairs* 77, 6: 20–4.

Weiss, Thomas G., and Leon Gordenker, eds. 1996. *NGOs, the UN, and Global Governance.* Boulder, Colo.: Lynne Rienner.

Wexler, Lelia. 1996. 'The Proposed Permanent International Criminal Court: An Appraisal', *Cornell International Law Journal* 29: 665–701.

White, Lyman Cromwell. 1951. *International Non-Governmental Organizations: Their Purposes, Methods, and Accomplishments.* New Brunswick, NJ: Rutgers University Press.

Williamson, Oliver E. 1975. *Markets and Hierarchies: Analysis and Antitrust Implications.* New York: Free Press.

———. 1985. *The Economics of Capitalism.* New York: Free Press.

———. 1986. *Economic Organization.* Brighton: Wheatsheaf.

Wolfensohn, James D. 1999. 'Defining New Cooperation in the Humanitarian Agenda, Remarks of the President of The World Bank Group at the Center for Strategic & International Studies', Washington, 2 Nov.

World Bank. 1990. *The World Bank Annual Report 1990*. Washington: World Bank.

———. 1994. *Infrastructure for Development: World Development Report 1994*. New York: Oxford University Press.

———. 1995. *Workers in an Integrated World: World Development Report 1995*. New York: Oxford University Press.

———. 1996. *From Plan to Market: World Development Report 1996*. New York: Oxford University Press.

———. 1997. *The State in a Changing World: World Development Report 1997*. New York: Oxford University Press.

———. 1998a. *Post-Conflict Reconstruction: The Role of the World Bank*. Washington: World Bank.

———. 1998b. *Beyond the Washington Consensus: Institutions Matter*. Washington: World Bank.

———. 1998c. 'World Bank Operational Guidelines for Financing Land Mine Clearance', Annex C to World Bank (1998a: 62–6).

———. 1999. *Knowledge for Development: World Development Report 1998–1999*. New York: Oxford University Press.

———. 2000. *The World Bank Annual Report 1999*. Washington: World Bank.

———. 2001a. *Attacking Poverty: World Development Report 2000–2001*. New York: Oxford University Press.

———. 2001b. *The World Bank Annual Report 2000*. Washington: World Bank.

World Commission on Environment and Development (Bruntland Commission). 1987. *Our Common Future*. New York: Oxford University Press.

Wurst, Jim. 1998. 'Small Weapons of Mass Destruction: A New International Movement is Trying to Stop the Flow of Light Arms', *In These Times* 23 (13 Dec.): 10–13.

Yarborough, Beth V., and Robert M. Yarborough. 1990. 'International Institutions and the New Economic Foundations of Organization', *International Organization* 44, 2: 235–59.

Young, Oran R. 1999. *Governance in World Affairs*. Ithaca, NY: Cornell University Press.

———. 1991. 'Political Leadership and Regime Formation', *International Organization* 45, 3: 281–308.

Zimmern, Alfred. 1969. *The League of Nations and the Rule of Law 1918–1935*. New York: Russell and Russell.

Index

Advisory Council of Jurists, 67
Afghanistan, 101
African Development Bank, 153
Ahtisaari, Marti, 144
Albania, 102, 104, 139, 140
Albright, Madeleine, 74, 123, 134, 140, 144
Alfaro, Ricardo, 67
Algeria, 101
American Friends Service Committee, 25
Amnesty International, 21, 53, 128, 146
Angola, 88, 101, 103, 110, 157
Annan, Kofi, 56, 81, 97, 108, 146
Apartheid Convention, 68
Arab League, 23
Arias Foundation, 113
Aristide, Jean-Bertrand, 21
Arms Control and Disarmament Agency, 105
arms embargoes, 105, 140
Asian Development Bank, 153
Asian economic crisis, 168
Association of Southeast Asian Nations, 121
Atwood, David, 85
Australia, 138; and landmines, 85, 86, 87, 91, 92, 94, 96; and small arms, 101, 119, 120, 122
Austria, 83, 85, 88, 94
Axworthy, Lloyd, 80, 87, 91, 92, 98, 120, 135, 137, 140

Baker plan, 43
Bangladesh, 101
Bank for International Settlements, 42
Baril, Maurice, 131, 136, 137, 138
Bartleman, Jim, 129
Bassiouni, Cherif, 68, 69, 78, 176
Belarus, 144
Belgium: and landmines, 85, 90, 94, 95, 96; and small arms, 99, 101, 112; and Zaire, 129, 135, 136
Better World for All, A, 168–9
Bildt, Carl, 142
biological weapons, 24, 118
Blair, Tony, 71
Bonn International Centre for Conversion, 113
Bos, Adriaan, 70, 72, 78
Bosnia, 1, 4, 80, 131, 139, 177

Boutros-Ghali, Boutros, 26, 128
Brady plan, 43
Brandt Commission, 28–9
Brazil, 105, 114
Bretton Woods, 42
British American Security Information Council, 113, 114, 116
Brundtland, Gro Harlem, 29
Brundtland Commission, 29, 152, 165–6
Bulgaria, 19
Burundi, 101, 127
Bush, George, 82

Cambodia, 1, 8, 22, 80, 101
Cameroon, 136
Campbell, John, 88
Canada: and ICC, 72; and landmines, 81, 85, 86, 87, 91, 94, 95, 96, 97, 180, 184; and small arms, 99, 101, 109, 111, 112, 119, 120; and Zaire, 127, 128, 129–30, 131, 132, 133, 134, 135, 136–8, 148, 182–3
CARE, 25, 128
Catholic Relief Services, 25
Cedras, Raoul, 21
Center for Defense Information, 113
Central African Republic, 101
Centre for European Security and Disarmament, 113
Chad, 101
Chechnya, 101, 106
chemical weapons, 24, 102, 118
Chernomyrdin, Viktor, 144
Chile, 22
China, 10; and ICC, 71, 182; and intervention, 133, 144, 145, 171; and landmines, 81, 84, 90, 93, 171, 182; and small arms, 101, 105
Chirac, Jacques, 129
Chrétien, Jean, 84, 127, 129–30, 132, 138
Chrétien, Raymond, 128, 129
Climate Change Convention, 39
Clinton, Bill, 83, 115, 131; and ICC, 69, 74, 77, 78, 171, 182; and intervention, 129, 130, 132, 143, 144, 180–1; and landmines, 81, 91, 92, 182
Coalition for the International Criminal Court

(CICC), 64, 70, 72, 75, 78, 184
Cold War, 3, 9, 34, 36, 48
Colombia, 101, 104, 108, 112
Commission on Global Governance, 32
Commission on the Responsibility of the Authors of War, 65
Commonwealth, 71
Comoros, 101
Conference of African Experts on Landmines, 89
Conference on Conflict Prevention, Disarmament, and Development in West Africa, 117
Conference on Disarmament (CD), 86, 88, 93
Conference on Sustainable Disarmament for Sustainable Development, 112–13
conflict prevention, 27–8, 33, 35, 36, 152, 155
Congo (Brazzaville), 101
Congo (Kinshasa), 101, 133, 157
Congress of Vienna, 64
Contact Group, 140–1, 144, 148
Cook, Robin, 140
co-optation, 21–2, 33
Co-ordinating Action on Small Arms, 111
Court of the Holy Roman Empire, 64
Crawford, James, 70, 72, 78
Croatia, 139

democracy, 6–7, 8, 170, 171
Denmark, 83, 94, 95, 96, 136
Diana, Princess of Wales, 90, 180
disease, 44, 160, 165
Doctors Without Borders, 25, 128
drug trafficking, 31, 69, 75, 76, 114, 115, 118

East Timor, 1, 4, 101, 138
Economic Community of West African States, 117
economic security, 31, 152, 160
ECOSOC. See UN Economic and Social Council (ECOSOC)
Ecuador, 91
Egypt, 93, 101, 105
El Salvador, 8, 22, 106
environmental security, 14–15, 29, 31, 52, 53, 152, 160, 165
Eritrea, 101
Ethiopia, 101, 116, 133
European Convention on Human Rights, 22
European Court of Justice, 22
European Institute for Research and Information on Peace and Security, 113
European Law Student Association, 71
European Monetary System, 42
European Union (EU), 42, 71, 86–7, 163, 164; and intervention, 136, 139, 140, 142; and small arms, 115–17, 116, 118, 119, 122, 123, 124
Evans, Gareth, 26
ex-FAR, 127, 128, 134

Federation of American Scientists, 113
Finland, 93, 94, 95, 119
Firearms Protocol, 109, 111, 124
Food and Agriculture Organization, 28, 158

Forces Armées Rwandaises, 127, 128, 134
Fowler, Robert, 134
France, 19, 83; and intervention, 129, 132–3, 134, 135, 136, 138, 140; and landmines, 87, 90, 94; and small arms, 101, 105, 116

G-7, 42, 164
G-8, 111–12, 121, 124, 144, 145, 148
GATT/WTO, 39, 42, 43, 56
Geneva Conventions, 24, 67
Geneva Protocol, 66
Genocide Convention, 67
Georgia, 101
Germany, 19, 65, 140; and landmines, 83, 90, 91, 94, 95, 96; and small arms, 101, 112
Global Environment Facility, 159
Gorbachev, Mikhail, 69
governance structures, 33, 35, 158, 171, 174
Greece, 92
Grotius, Hugo, 23
Guatemala, 8, 101, 104
Guinea-Bissau, 101
Gulf War, 69, 77

Hagenbach, Peter von, 64
Hague Conference System, 24, 65
Hague Conventions, 24, 65, 67
Hague Court of Arbitration, The, 65
Haiti, 21, 22, 101, 126, 131, 147, 179
Handicap International, 83
Hashimoto, Ryutaro, 89
Helms, Jesse, 74
Hirohito, Emperor, 66
Hobbes, Thomas, 1–2, 38
Holbrooke, Richard, 74, 140, 143
Honduras, 101
humanitarian intervention, 125–49, 171
Human Rights Watch, 128, 146
human security: defined, 4–5, 16–18, 160, 169; humanitarian/'safety of peoples' approach, 5, 17–18, 23–8, 32–3, 34, 35, 36, 45, 47–8, 62, 151, 156–7, 169, 170–1; rights/rule of law approach, 5, 17, 18–23, 32–4, 35–6, 45, 47–8, 62, 63, 151, 169, 170–1; sustainable human development approach, 5, 18, 28–33, 34–5, 36–7, 40, 42–5, 151, 156–7, 158, 170
Hussein, Saddam, 21

Independent Commission on International Development Issues, 28–9, 165
Independent Territories, 101
India, 71, 81, 84, 90, 93, 144
Institute for Security Studies, 113
Inter-American Development Bank, 153, 157
International Action Network on Small Arms, 105, 123
International Alert, 113
International Bank for Reconstruction and Development, 153
International Campaign to Ban Landmines (ICBL), 80, 82, 83, 85, 88, 91, 94, 97, 119, 184

International Centre for Settlement of Investment Disputes, 153
International Committee of the Red Cross (ICRC), 17, 24, 25, 176, 181; and ICC, 71; and landmines, 81–2, 83, 86, 88, 89, 97, 184; and small arms, 99, 106, 113, 123; and Zaire, 135
International Conference on Firearms Legislation, 120
International Court of Justice, 145
International Criminal Court (ICC), 23, 33, 62–79, 171, 172, 175, 176, 178, 179, 180, 182
International Criminal Tribunal for Rwanda, 23, 70, 77
International Criminal Tribunal for the Former Yugoslavia, 23, 70, 77, 140, 144
international institutions, 13, 158, 161; and ICC, 78; as public goods providers, 5, 40, 41–4, 46–7, 51–2, 53, 55–6, 59, 60, 61, 150–1, 170, 173, 174, 175–6; and small arms, 99
International Law Commission (ILC), 67–8, 69
International Military Tribunal, 66
International Military Tribunal for the Far East, 66
International Monetary Fund (IMF), 42, 154, 168
Internet, 9, 54, 58, 174
Inter-Parliamentary Union, 66
Iran, 93, 101
Iraq, 21, 93, 101, 126, 179, 182
Ireland, 83, 94, 136
Irish Republican Army, 103
Israel, 22, 93, 105
Italy, 66, 94, 129, 136, 140

Japan, 19; and landmines, 89, 91, 92, 94; and small arms, 109, 111, 112, 119; and Zaire, 129, 136

Kabila, Laurent, 128, 134–5, 136, 137
Kanbur, Ravi, 158
Kant, Immanuel, 2, 47, 49
Kashmir, 101
Kellogg-Briand Pact, 24
Kenya, 88, 101, 106
Keynes, John Maynard, 42
Kirsch, Philippe, 74–5, 78, 180
Kosovo, 1, 3, 4, 9, 101, 102, 139–47, 148, 171, 175, 177, 179, 180
Kosovo Liberation Army (KLA), 139, 140, 145
Kouchner, Bernard, 147
Kurdistan, 101
Kyrgystan, 101

Lake, Anthony, 129, 130, 131
landmines campaign, 8, 24, 70, 80–97, 98, 102, 171, 172, 174, 175, 178, 179, 180, 182
Leach, Jim, 69
League of Nations, 19, 24, 46, 47, 51, 65–6, 67
Leahy, Patrick, 82, 92
Lebanon, 101
Lenin, Vladimir, 44
Lesotho, 101
liberalism, 2, 5–6, 38, 41–2, 43, 46–7, 49, 51–2, 171, 172, 173

Liberia, 101
Libya, 69
like-minded states (LMS), 64, 71, 72, 74, 75, 76, 78, 98, 112, 184
Locke, John, 2
Lomé Conventions, 43
London Agreement, 66

McCurry, Mike, 132
Macedonia, 140
Major, John, 129
Malawi, 88, 136
Mali, 110, 112, 116, 122
Mandela, Nelson, 129
Marx, Karl, 44
Mason, Peggy, 110
Médecins Sans Frontières, 25, 128
media, 8–9, 54
Medico International, 82
Mexico, 71, 83, 101, 109, 112, 114, 115, 167–8
Michel, James H., 165
middle powers, 9, 64, 123, 175; as public goods providers, 54, 58–9, 60, 148, 172, 174, 175. See also like-minded states (LMS)
migration, 31, 160
military intervention, 3, 11–12, 33, 48–50, 57–8, 61, 180. See also humanitarian intervention
Mill, John Stuart, 2
Milosevic, Slobodan, 139, 140, 142–3, 144, 145, 148
minority rights, 18, 33, 125
Mobutu Sese Seko, 128, 131, 133
Moher, Mark, 85
Monterey Institute, 113
Moose, George, 138
Mozambique, 8, 22, 80, 88, 93, 101, 104, 122
Muller, Robert (Bobby), 82
Multilateral Investment Guarantee Agency, 153
Museveni, Yoweri, 133
Myanmar, 101

National Rifle Association (NRA), 120, 121
Nepal, 101
Netherlands, 94, 95, 112, 116, 136, 138
neutrality, 36
New Zealand, 71, 85, 120
NGO Committee of Experts, 69
Niger, 101
Nigeria, 71, 101
non-governmental organizations (NGOs), 7, 8, 25, 30, 48, 177, 181; and development, 161, 169; and human rights, 21, 22, 53, 67; and ICC, 64, 69, 70–1, 75, 180; and landmines, 83, 97, 184; as public goods providers, 40, 54–5, 59, 172, 173, 174, 176; and small arms, 99, 112, 113–14, 116, 118, 119–20, 120–1, 122–3, 176; and Zaire, 128, 137
non-intervention, 125, 171
North Atlantic Treaty Organization (NATO), 126, 139, 140, 143–5, 146, 147, 148, 175, 177, 181
Northern Ireland, 101

North Korea, 93, 182
Norway: and landmines, 81, 83, 85, 91, 94, 95, 96, 97, 184; and small arms, 99, 112
Norwegian Institute for International Affairs, 113
nuclear weapons, 15, 24, 34, 39, 46, 73, 76, 118
Nuremberg trials, 3, 66

Ogata, Sadako, 128
oil embargoes, 14, 110
Organization for Economic Co-operation and Development (OECD), 167, 168, 169; Development Assistance Committee (DAC), 150–1, 153, 163–8, 183
Organization for Security and Co-operation in Europe (OSCE), 140, 142, 143
Organization of African Unity (OAU), 89, 121, 135, 136
Organization of American States (OAS), 111, 112, 114–15, 119, 121, 122, 123, 124
Ottawa Convention. See landmines campaign
Oxfam, 25, 113

Pace, William, 70
Pakistan, 90, 93
Palestine Liberation Organization, 103
Palestine (Occupied Territories), 101
Palme Commission, 28–9, 165
Paris Club, 43
Parliamentarians for Global Action, 69
Pax Christi, 113
peacebuilding, 26–7, 33, 35, 36, 155
Peace Society in the United States, 64
Permanent Court of International Justice, 19
Peru, 85, 101
Philippines, 84, 101
Poland, 19, 91
Presidential Decision Directive 25 (PDD-25), 130–1
Project Ploughshares, 113
public goods, 38–40, 45, 50–4, 59–60, 63, 78, 125, 126, 147, 148, 152, 167, 169, 172–6

Ramos, Fidel V., 84
realism, 46, 47, 48–9, 51, 52, 172, 173
Red Cross. See International Committee of the Red Cross (ICRC)
resources, 10, 29, 152
Rhodesia/Zimbabwe, 21
Richardson, Bill, 74
Robinson, A.N.R., 78, 176
Rugova, Ibrahim, 139, 140
Russia: and ICC, 71, 182; and intervention, 19, 133, 140, 142, 144, 145, 147, 148, 171; and landmines, 81, 84, 90, 92, 93, 171, 182; and small arms, 101, 105
Rwanda, 1, 3–4, 101, 106, 127–8, 131, 133, 134, 137, 138; war crimes tribunal, 23, 70, 77

SACEUR, 143
Saferworld, 113, 116
Sahara-Sahel region, 110
sanctions, 21, 33, 139
Sandstrom, Emil, 68

Scharf, Michael, 75
Scheffer, David, 74
Seleby, Jacob, 91
Senegal, 101, 135, 136
Serbia, 126, 143, 180
shaming, 21, 33, 178, 180
Shea, Jamie, 143
Shuttack, Jack, 74
Sierra Leone, 1, 101, 148, 157
Singapore, 74, 76
Slovenia, 139
small arms, 48, 139; control, 5, 98–124, 171, 176; illicit trade, 98, 99, 101, 104–5, 107, 109, 111–12, 115, 116–17, 119, 121–2, 123, 124
Smith, Gordon, 129
socialism, 38, 44
Social Summit, 160, 161–2
Solana, Javier, 140, 143, 146
Somalia, 88, 101, 106, 126, 130, 132, 177, 179, 181
Sommaruga, Cornelio, 82, 98, 176
South Africa, 21, 22, 68, 101; and landmines, 88, 180; and small arms, 101, 104, 106, 112, 120; and Zaire, 129, 133, 136, 138
Southern African Development Community, 89, 117, 118
South Korea, 74, 86, 91, 93
sovereignty, 18, 59, 125, 171
Soviet Union, 8, 10, 68
Spain, 91, 135, 136
Specter, Arlen, 69
Sporting Arms and Ammunition Manufacturers Institute, 120
Sri Lanka, 101
Stigliz, Joe, 158
Sudan, 101, 106
sustainable development, 152, 165. See also under human security
Swaziland, 88
Sweden, 83, 94, 95, 96, 99, 136
Switzerland, 71, 94, 95
Syria, 93

Tajikistan, 101
Talbott, Strobe, 144
Tarnoff, Peter, 129
terrorism, 31, 69, 75, 76, 160
Treaty of Rome, 115
Treaty of Versailles, 65
Trinidad and Tobago, 69
truth commissions, 22, 69
Turkey, 19, 65, 93, 101
Turkmenistan, 90

Uganda, 101, 133, 136, 137
United Kingdom: and ICC, 71, 72; and intervention, 129, 132, 133, 134, 136, 137, 138, 140, 148; and landmines, 87, 90, 94, 95, 96; and small arms, 116, 117, 119, 122
United Nations, 13, 24, 47, 51, 53, 56, 60, 61, 105, 164, 166–7; and development, 168, 169; and ICC, 64, 67, 68, 70–1, 72, 73, 76; and intervention, 135,

139, 148, 177; and landmines, 82–3, 87–8, 89, 94; and small arms, 104, 108–11, 117, 122, 124. *See also* UN Security Council
UN Charter, 19–20, 57, 67, 118, 125, 144, 146, 179; Chapter VII, 21, 127, 129, 130, 132, 133
UN Children's Fund (UNICEF), 25, 158
UN Conference on the Environment and Sustainable Development, 29–30
UN Congress on Crime Prevention and the Treatment of Offenders, 68, 69
UN Convention against Torture and Other Cruel, Inhuman, or Degrading Treatment and Punishment, 20–1
UN Convention against Transnational Organized Crime, 109
UN Convention on Certain Conventional Weapons (CCW), 82, 83–6, 92, 93
UN Convention on the Elimination of All Forms of Discrimination against Women, 20
UN Convention on the Prevention and Punishment of the Crime of Genocide, 20
UN Convention on the Rights of the Child, 21
UN Convention relating to the Status of Refugees, 20, 25
UN Declaration of Human Rights, 3, 19, 20
UN Declaration on the Elimination of All Forms of Intolerance and of Discrimination Based on Religion or Belief, 20
UN Department for Peacekeeping Operations, 94
UN Development Program (UNDP), 25, 116, 150, 152, 158–63, 164, 169, 176; *Human Development Report*, 18, 30–2, 152–3, 159–61, 161–2
UN Diplomatic Conference of Plenipotentiaries on the Establishment of an International Criminal Court, 62, 71
UN Disarmament Commission, 108, 109
UN Economic and Social Council (ECOSOC), 67, 108, 109, 111, 115, 121, 122, 124, 158
UN Environment Program, 159
UN Group of Government Experts, 110–11
UN High Commissioner for Refugees (UNHCR), 25, 127, 138, 143, 177
UN Human Rights Commission, 21, 22, 67, 68, 177
UN International Convention on the Elimination of All Forms of Racial Discrimination, 20
UN International Covenant on Civil and Political Rights, 20, 22
UN International Covenant on Economic, Social, and Cultural Rights, 20
UNMIK, 145, 146
UN Panel of Government Experts on Small Arms,
108, 109, 111, 121, 122
UN Register of Conventional Arms, 113
UN Relief and Rehabilitation Administration, 24
UN Relief and Works Agency, 25
UN Security Council, 17, 23, 146, 174, 176, 179, 183; and Kosovo, 139, 140, 143–4, 145, 148, 175; and landmines, 70, 71, 72, 73, 76; and small arms, 110; and Zaire, 125, 126, 128–9, 130, 133–4, 147
UN War Crimes Commission, 66
United States, 9, 10, 13, 69, 130–1, 184–5; and Bosnia, 131; and Haiti, 131; and ICC, 63, 65, 68, 69, 71, 72–4, 75–6, 77, 171, 175, 182; and Kosovo, 140, 143, 144, 145, 175, 180–1; and landmines, 81, 83, 86, 87, 90, 91, 92, 93, 94–5, 96, 97, 171, 174, 180, 182; as public goods provider, 40, 54, 56, 148, 174–5; and small arms, 101, 104, 105, 106, 109, 111, 119, 120, 121, 122, 123; and Somalia, 130, 132, 181; and Yugoslavia, 132; and Zaire, 127, 129, 130, 131, 132, 133, 134, 135, 136, 137, 138, 181, 182

Védrine, Hubert, 140
Versailles conference, 19

Westphalian system, 3, 18–19, 125, 171
Wilhelm II, Kaiser, 65
Williams, Jody, 82
Wilson, Woodrow, 3, 19, 46
World Bank, 42, 43, 150, 153–8, 159, 161, 163, 164, 167, 168
World Commission on Environment and Development, 29, 152, 165–6
World Conference on Human Rights, 69
World Council of Churches, 113
World Development Movement, 116
World Food Program, 138, 158
World Forum on the Future of Sport Shooting Activities, 120–1
World Health Organization, 25, 158
World Summit on Social Development, 32
World Vision, 25
WTO. *See* GATT/WTO

Yeltsin, Boris, 92, 144
Young, Doug, 135
Yugoslavia, 10, 126, 132, 139, 140, 144, 145, 179; war crimes tribunal, 23, 70, 77, 140, 144

Zaire, 126, 127–38, 147–8, 171, 175, 180, 181, 182–3
Zambia, 88
Zimbabwe, 21, 88, 89